A Pocket Dictionary of the Spoken Arabic of Cairo

A Pocket Dictionary of the Spoken Arabic of Cairo

English–Arabic

New Revised Edition

Virginia Stevens
Maurice Salib

The American University in Cairo Press
Cairo New York

The American University in Cairo Press
113 Sharia Kasr el Aini, Cairo, Egypt
420, Fifth Avenue, New York, NY 10018
www.aucegypt.edu

Second printing 2005

Dar el Kutub no. 16149/03
ISBN 977 424 839 2

Printed in Egypt

Contents

Acknowledgments

The need for a new edition of this Pocket Dictionary, with many additional entries, came about because of the enthusiastic suggestions of users of the first edition who wanted to be able to look up quickly the practical words they needed in their daily life in Cairo. We would like to thank those many people who made suggestions, in particular Kate Coffield, Gretchen Papazis, Paul Sundberg, and Penny Farag.

For help with the entries, we would like to thank Tomader Rifaat, Laila Al-Sawi, Dina El-Hefnawy, Kassem Shafy, Yasmine Salah El-Din, Iman El Abd, Wafaa Wahba, Nihal Talat, Abdel-Aziz F. Sadek, Aziza Mahmoud, Waheed Sami, Sawsan Abdalla, Hoda El-Gamal, Asmaa El-Nabalawi, Sabri Karnouk, Shereen Abou El-Fotouh, Suzanne Salah El-Din, Mona Kamel Hassen, Ahmed Fekry, Yasser El-Sheemy, Samia Abdennour, Fardous Mahmoud, Nagwa Kassabgy, Mona Iskander, and Bahira Ghallab. The final authority on the exact transcription is the definitive Dictionary of Egyptian Arabic by El-Said Badawi and Martin Hinds.

We are grateful too to the people who helped work on the phonetic symbols: Waheed Sami, Tareq Anis, Paul-Hubert Poirier, Rémy Beaumont, and Sharon Casey.

For encouragement and help in face of many difficulties, we would like to thank our editor, Neil Hewison.

Special thanks go to Paul Stevens for his support and invaluable insights both as a linguist and as a meticulous learner of Arabic.

Virginia Stevens would particularly like to thank her parents, Stephen and Veronica Chris, for teaching her that what must be done can be done, and can be done now.

Maurice Salib would like to thank his wife Signe and his daughter Shirley for their help, especially in the area of American English usage, and for their support and inspiration.

Preface

Many newcomers to Egypt start out with brave intentions of learning spoken Egyptian Arabic. They enroll in classes, buy textbooks, and courageously begin to speak. Their efforts, however, may soon be thwarted by the difficulty of reinforcing outside class the words which have been learned in the classroom. The beginner trying to recall a word might ask someone, but the response is likely to be given in Classical Arabic rather than Colloquial, and until now there has been no comprehensive, reliable dictionary to consult. The frustration of not being able to find the word one needs when trying to communicate in Arabic may thus be greater than in other languages such as French or German, whose spoken forms do not differ essentially from the written, and which are well supplied with pocket dictionaries.

This dictionary was compiled with these problems in mind. It is unique for its combination of a variety of features:

- up-to-date colloquial Cairo Arabic equivalents of about 4,600 main entries and over 2,200 subentries;
- a format of singular/plural nouns and perfect/imperfect verbs used most commonly in Arabic language classes;
- basic grammar charts for quick reference to verb endings, negation, numerals, pronominal suffixes, and comparatives;
- a consistent phonetic transcription system.

The basis of this word list was the glossary in *Spoken Arabic of Cairo* by Maurice Salib (AUC Press 1981), a book used in many Colloquial Arabic classes in Cairo. Virginia Stevens has more than doubled that core to encompass the words she found most useful in the actual business of living and talking to people during her years in Egypt. The new edition includes many new entries which users of the first edition have requested, especially food and automobile terms. The final selection, therefore, emerges from the practical experience of foreigners living in Cairo.

The usefulness of Cairo spoken Arabic extends far beyond Cairo itself. Its use on state radio and television means that it has become a standard form understood throughout Egypt, and thanks to Egypt's importance in the Arab television and film industries it is also widely familiar in other Arab countries. The authors hope that their book will encourage foreigners who would like to progress beyond the tourist phrasebook toward real conversation with the people of Egypt and elsewhere in the Arab world.

Key to Symbols

Vowels

ii	: as in 'feet'	uu	: as in 'too'
i	: as in 'big'	u	: as in 'put'
ee	: as in 'ate'	oo	: as in 'boat'
aa	: as in American 'sand'	ɑɑ	: as in 'bar'
a	: like aa but shorter	ɑ	: like ɑ ɑ but shorter
e	: as in 'let'	ᵉ (raised):	transitional vowel

Consonants

Consonants similar to English: b f k m n p s v w y z

d, l, t : pronounced more forward in the mouth than their English counterparts.

g : as 'g' in 'good'

ʃ : as 'sh' in 'ship'

j : as 's' in 'pleasure'

ṭ, ḍ, ṣ, ẓ: 'darker' or 'heavier' than t, d, s, z. They are pronounced with the back of the tongue bunched high in the back of the mouth.

r : a trilled 'r', i.e. it is pronounced by vibrating the tip of the tongue.

h : similar to English, but occurs in positions which are not normal for English 'h'. Special effort is needed in order to pronounce it in these positions.

ʕ : *hamza*–a glottal stop, as between the words 'uh oh'. It is pronounced by momentarily closing the glottis.

q : a 'k' sound pronounced at the extreme back of the mouth. It occurs mainly in words borrowed from literary Arabic, e.g. canal: qɑnaal ʢ : a glottal stop which is an underlying q. This is usually pronounced as a 'g' in Upper Egypt.

x : a friction sound made by raising the back of the tongue toward the roof of the mouth and forcing the breath stream out through the narrow slit thereby made, with a 'scraping' sound similar to the 'ch' in German 'doch' and Scottish 'loch'.

ɣ : basically pronounced like the x, but with voicing. Voicing is produced by vibrating the vocal cords as in humming.

ɦ : friction in the pharynx–the throat cavity situated just behind and below the mouth cavity. This friction is made by tightening that cavity as in swallowing and forcing the outgoing breath stream through it.

ɛ : *ain*–basically produced by the same mechanism as ɦ but with voicing.

Other Symbols

(-ak, etc.) Indicates the addition of any appropriate suffix (see chart of pronominal suffixes).

(adj) Adjective. Adjectives are entered as singular (masculine), plural, e.g. new: gidiid, gudaad.
Note: Singular feminine adjectives are used in agreement with non-human plural nouns. The rules for forming the feminine are listed below under (f).

(adv) Adverb.

(Am) American.

(Br) British.

(Chr) Christian.

(cl) From Classical Arabic

(coll) Collective noun.

(conj) Conjunction.

(Comp) A comparative adjective, which is invariable. Only a few most useful comparative adjectives are listed in the main entries (see chart on formation of comparative adjectives).

(f) Feminine. Feminine nouns, adjectives, and participles are regularly formed by adding –a or –ɑ to the masculine, subject to the following changes:

1. If there is a short i one syllable back, it is dropped, as long as this will not result in a sequence of three consonants: w i ɧ i ʃ > w i ɧ ʃ a.
2. If a long vowel appears before two consonants, it is shortened: ʃ ɑ ɑ ʈ i r > ʃ ɑ t r ɑ
3. If the noun or adjective ends in -i and has the (defective) active-participle pattern CaaCi, the feminine is CaCya: the entry taani, -yiin implies taani, tanya, tanyiin.
4. If the noun or adjective ends in –i but does not have the participial pattern mentioned in rule 3, the feminine adds -yya and shortens any long vowel: maṣri, maṣriyya, maṣriyyiin.

Nouns and adjectives are marked feminine in only two cases:

1. Words whose form is not obviously feminine e.g. leg: rigl (f).
2. Special adjectival forms of colors and physical defects (e.g. deaf: ʕɑtrɑʃ, (f) ʈɑrʃɑ, ʈurʃ).

Singular forms of collective nouns are feminine (e.g. flies: dibbaan, (-a, -aat)—one fly is dibbaana).

Names of towns and countries are regularly feminine in Egyptian Arabic, even when they are not so in Classical Arabic, and are not marked (f).

(gr) Grammatical usage.

(invar) Invariable.

(intr) Intransitive verb; does not take a direct object (e.g. niʃif: to become dry).

(Isl) Islamic.

(m) Masculine. A noun is marked (m) if it is masculine but looks feminine e.g. building: mabna (m).

(n)	Noun. Nouns are entered as singular followed by plural: book: kitaab, kutub. Where several plurals are possible, usually only the most frequently used one is listed.
(part)	Participle, e.g. living (residing): saakin, -iin.
(pl)	Marked for plural -yya, to distinguish it from the identical feminine form: mailman buşţagi, (pl) -yya Plurals formed by change of word pattern are written out completely: book: kitaab, kutub. Plurals formed by adding the plural suffixes -aat, -ɑɑt, -iin, -yya, or –yyiin or –yyiin are indicated by these abbreviations. If the singular has a long vowel, the addition of the suffix shortens it, because the stress position shifts from it to the plural suffix: e.g. written: maktuub, -iin implies maktubiin. If there was a short i one syllable back, it is dropped as long as it will not result in a sequence of three consonants: e.g. smart: ʃaaţir, ʃaţriin; but teacher: mudarris, mudarrisiin. With collective nouns the singular and plural are indicated after the uncountable form: almonds looz (-a, -aat) means that one almond is looza, three almonds is talat luzaat.
(prep)	Preposition.
(pron)	Pronoun.
(s.o.)	Someone.
(s.t.)	Something.
(tr)	Transitive verb; can take a direct object. (e.g. naʃʃif: to dry something, to cause to dry).
(v)	Verb. Verbs are entered as perfect followed by imperfect in 3rd person masculine singular form: write: katab, yiktib, where katab means "he wrote," and laazim yiktib means "it is necessary that he write."
-	(Between two words) means liaison.
/	(Between two words) means alternate forms.

Stress Rules

a. In the spoken Arabic of Cairo, the stress usually falls on the second to last syllable:

sítta (six)	maktába (bookstore, library)
madrása (school)	ʕaanísa (miss)
muxtálif (different, m)	ʕil-qaahíra (Cairo)
máktab (desk, office)	ṭaalíba (female student)

b. However, the stress falls on the last syllable if it contains a long vowel:

gawáab (letter)	maktúub (written, m)
gawabáat (letters)	

or if the word ends in two consonants:

yiɦíbb(to love)	zakírt (I studied)
muhímm (important)	

c. The stress tends to fall on the third to last syllable if the last three syllables have the sequence CvCvCv(C), (where v is a short vowel and C is a consonant):

kánaba (couch)	muxtálifa (different)
kátabit (she wrote)	ʕinkásarit (it (f) was broken)
sáʕal-ak (he asked you)	

Exceptions to rule (c), where rule (a) applies:

Plural nouns having the sequence CuCuCa or CiCiCa:

subúɛa(lions)	ɦiṣína (horses)
kurúta (cards)	

Words where the last two syllables comprise the verbal inflection ending –it (3rd person feminine singular perfect) and a pronoun suffix:

ʃafít-u (she saw him)
saʕalít-ak (she asked you, m)
katabít-u (she wrote it)

Other exceptions:

ʕahú (m), ʕahí (f) (here is)

(because the underlying form is ʕahuwwa and ʕahiyya)

yatára (I wonder)

(because the underlying form is two words: ya + tara).

A

abdomen: baṭn (f), buṭuun.
able: ʕaadir, -iin.
to be able: ʕidir, yiʕdar.
abolish: laɣa, yilɣi.
abort, miscarry: ʕaghaḍ, yighiḍ.
to have a miscarriage: saʕaṭit, tisʕaṭ.
abortion: ʕighaaḍ.
miscarriage: saʕṭ.
about: (*concerning*): ɛan.
about me: ɛalayya; ɛanni.
about you (m.s.): ɛaleek; ɛannak. (f.s.): ɛaleeki; ɛannik.
about (*around*): ɦawaali.
about to (*do*): ɛala waʃk inn- ...; ʕarrab, yiʕarrab (+ imperfect).
above: fooʕ.
abroad (*in a foreign land, out of doors*): barra; fil-xaarig.
abscess: xurraag.
absent (adj): ɣaayib, -iin.
absent (v) *to be absent*: ɣaab, yiɣiib.
academic (adj): diraasi, -yyiin; ʕakadiimi, -yyiin.
accelerator (*gas pedal*): baddaal banziin.
accept: ʕibil, yiʕbal.
(*agree to do something*): riḍi, yirḍa.
accessories, spare parts: ʕaksiswaar, -aat.
accident: ɦadsa, ɦawaadis.
accidentally: muṣaḍafatan, bi-ṣṣudfa.
accompany: waṣṣal, yiwaṣṣal.
accompany musically: ṣaaɦib, yiṣaaɦib.
according to: ɦasab.
account: (*monetary statement*): ɦisaab, -aat.
accountant: muɦaasib, -iin
accounting (*subject*): ɛilm il-muɦasba.
accumulate: ɦawwiʃ, yiɦawwiʃ.
accused (n): muttaham, -iin
accustomed (*to*): mitɛawwid, -iin (ɛala).
to be accustomed: ʕitɛawwid, yitɛawwid.
acidity: ɦumuuḍa.
acquaint: ɛarraf, yiɛarraf bi.
acquaintance (s): maɛrifa, maɛaarif.
across from: ʕuṣaad.
act (v) (*perform in a play*): massil, yimassil.
acting (*performance*): tamsiil.
active: naʃiiṭ, nuʃaṭa / nuʃaaṭ.
activity: naʃaaṭ, -aaṭ / ʕanʃiṭa.
actor: mumassil, -iin.
actress: mumassila, -aat.
adapter (*elect.*): adabtar.
add (*put in additionally*): ɦaṭṭ, yiɦuṭṭ; ḍaaf, yiḍiif; zaad, yiziid; zawwid, yizawwid.
(*calculate sum of*): gamaɛ, yigmaɛ.

addict (n): mudmin, -iin.
drug addict: mudmin muxaddaraat.
addiction: ʕidmaan.
additional, more: ziyaada, kamaan.
another: taani, -yiin.
address (*destination or residence*) (n): ɛinwaan, ɛanawiin.
address (v): kallim, yikallim; xaaṭib, yixaaṭib (cl).
adhesive, sticky (adj): lazzaaʕ.
adjective: ṣifa, -aat.
adjust (*regulate*): ẓabaṭ, yuẓbuṭ.
adjusted: maẓbuuṭ / mazbuuṭ, -iin.
administration: ʕidaara, ʕidaraat.
admirer: muɛgab, -iin.
adopt: ʕitbanna, yitbanna.
adoption: tabanni.
adult: baaliɣ, -iin; kibiir, kubaar.
advance (v) (tr): ʕaddim, yiʕaddim.
(intr): ʕitʕaddim, yitʕaddim.
advanced (adj): mitʕaddim, -iin.
advantage: miiza, mizaat.
to take advantage of, exploit: ʕistaɣall, yistaɣill.
adventure (n): muɣamra, -aat.
adverb: ẓarf, ẓuruuf.
advertisement: ʕiɛlaan, -aat.
advice (n): naṣiiḫa, naṣaayiḫ.
advise (*offer counsel*) (v): naṣaḫ, yinṣaḫ.
aerial, antenna: ʕiryal, -aat.
affect: ʕassar, yiʕassar fi.
affection (*fondness*): ḫinniyya; ḫanaan.
afford *I can't afford it*: ma-ɛandii-ʃ maʕdira.
afraid (*frightened*) (*of*): xaayif, -iin (min).
to be afraid: xaaf, yixaaf.
Africa: ʕafriqya.
African: ʕafriiqi, -yyiin.
afro (*hair style*): kaniiʃ.
after (*following in time or place*): baɛd.
(conj): baɛd^{e}-ma.
afternoon: baɛd-iḍ-ḍuhr.
afterwards: baɛdeen; baɛd^{e} kida.
again: taani; kamaan marra.
against (*in opposition to*): ḍidd.
age (*length or time of life*): sinn; ɛumr, ʕaɛmaar.
How old are you (m)?: ɛand-ak kaam sana; ɛumr-ak kaam?
agenda: ʕajenda; mufakkira, -aat.
aggressive, hostile: ɛudwaani, -yyiin.
dashing, provocative, overbearing: muftari, -yyiin.
fearless, bold: gariiʕ, guraʕa.
agitated (*upset*): haayig, -iin
ago: min.
five years ago: min xamas siniin.
agree (*with*): ittafaʕ, yittifiʕ (maɛa).
agree (*on*), approve: waafiʕ, yiwaafiʕ (ɛala).
agreed: muwaafiʕ, -iin.
agreement: ʕittifaaʕ, -aat.

agricultural: ziraaεi.
agriculture: ziraaεa.
aid (n): εoon; musaεda; maεuuna, -aat.
AIDS: ʕeedz.
aim (*purpose, goal*): ɣaraḍ, ʕaɣraaḍ; hadaf, ʕahdaaf; ʕaṣd.
air: hawa (m).
air conditioner: mukayyif, -aat.
air conditioning: kundiʃan; takyiif (hawa).
air hose: xarṭuum hawa.
Air force, the: silaaɦ iṭ-ṭayaraan.
air filter: filtar hawa.
air pressure: ḍaɣṭ il-hawa.
air shaft, vent: hawwaaya, -aat.
airline: ʃirkit ṭayaraan, ʃarikaat ṭayaraan; xaṭṭ^{e} ṭayaraan, xuṭuuṭ ṭayaraan; xaṭṭ^{e} gawwi, xuṭuuṭ gawwiyya.
airmail: bariid gawwi.
airplane: ṭayyaara, -aat.
airport: maṭaar, -aat.
aisle, corridor: mamarr, -aat.
alarm clock: minabbih, -aat.
alcohol, *liquor*: xamra, xumuur.
rubbing, pure alcohol: sibirtu naʕi; kuɦull^{e} naʕi / naqi.
Alexandria: ʕiskindiriyya.
alfalfa: barsiim ɦigaazi.
algebra: gabr.
Algeria: ʕig-gazaayir.
Algerian: gazayri, -yyiin; gazaaʕiri, -yyiin.
alight, descend: nizil, yinzil.
all: kull (+ def. n. or pron); ʕik-kull; ʕi-gamiiε.
all day: ṭuul in-nahaar.
all day Thursday: il-xamiis ṭuul in-nahaar.
all my life: ṭuul εumri.
all of us: kullina.
all of you: kulluku.
all of them: kulluhum.
allergy: ɦasasiyya.
alley, lane: ɦaara, ɦawaari, zuʕaaʕ.
allotment, share: ɦissa, ɦiṣaṣ.
allow: samaɦ, yismaɦ (li); xalla, yixalli.
allowed: masmuuɦ, -iin.
you are allowed: masmuɦ-l-ak (-ik, -uku).
allspice: buharaat.
almonds: looz (-a, -aat).
almost (*approximately, about*): taʕriiban.
alone: li-waɦd-u (*by himself*), li-waɦd-i (*by myself*), etc. (*with an action*): bi-nafs-i (*by myself, personally*).
alphabet: ʕabgadiyya.
alphabet, letters of: ɦuruuf il-ʕabgadiyya.
alphabetical order: tartiib ʕabgadi.
already: *I already ate*: kalt^{e} xalaaṣ. *I already paid*: dafaεt^{e} xalaaṣ; dafaεt^{e} ʕabl^{e} kida.

also: kamaan; bardu.
although: maεa ʕinn; walaw-inn.
aluminium, aluminum: ʕaluminyum / ʕalamunya.
always: dayman; tamalli.
amateur: haawi, huwaah.
amazing, strange: εagiib, εugaab.
ambassador: safiir, sufara.
ambition: ṭumuuɦ.
ambitious: ṭamuuɦ, -iin.
ambulance: εarabiyyit-il-ʕisεaaf.
amendment: taεdiil, -aat.
America: ʕamriika.
American: ʕamrikaani / ʕamriiki, ʕamrikaniyya / ʕamrikiyya, ʕamrikaan.
American University: ʕig-gamεa-l-amrikiyya.
amiable: ɦabbuub, -iin.
nice: laṭiif, luṭaaf.
charming: ẓariif, ẓuraaf.
amount: mablaɣ, mabaaliɣ.
amphitheater: mudarrag, -aat.
amuse: salla, yisalli.
amuse oneself: ʕitsalla, yitsalla.
amusement park: (madiinit) malaahi (no pl).
amusing: musalli, -yyiin.
analysis: taɦliil, taɦaliil.
analyze: ɦallil, yiɦallil.
anchovy: ʕanʃuuga.
ancient: ʔadiim, ʔudaam.
and: wi.
anemia: faʔrᵉ damm.
anesthetic: bing.
anger: zaεal.
angina: zabɦa; zabɦa ṣadriyya.
angry (*at*): zaεlaan, -iin (min).
very angry (*at*): ɣaḍbaan, -iin (min).
to get angry: ziεil, yizεal, ɣiḍib, yiɣḍab, ʕitɣaaẓ, yitɣaaẓ.
to make angry: ɣaaẓ, yiɣiiẓ.
vexed: mitɣaaẓ, -iin.
animal: ɦayawaan, -aat.
anise, aniseed: yansuun.
anniversary: εiid, ʕaεyaad.
wedding anniversary: εiid gawaaz / zawaag (cl).
announce: ʕaεlan, yiεlin.
announcement: ʕiεlaan, -aat.
announcer: muziiε, -iin.
annoy: daayiʔ, yidaayiʔ
annoyed: middaayiʔ -iin.
to get annoyed: ʕiddayiʔ, yiddayiʔ.
annual: sanawi, -yyiin.
anonymous: maghuul, -iin
another (*additional*): taani, -yiin.
(*different, other than*): ɣeer.
answer (n): radd, ruduud, ʕigaaba, -aat / ʕagwiba.
answer sheet: waraʔit ʕigaaba.
answer (v): gaawib, yigaawib; radd, yirudd (εala).
ant: *see* **ants**
antenna, aerial: ʕiryal, -aat.
anthropology: εilm il-ʕinsaan.
anti- (*e.g. medication against diseases*): ḍidd; muḍaadd li.

antibiotic: muḏaadd ɦayawi.
antiquities:ʕasaar.
ants: naml (-a, -aat).
any: ʕayy; ʕanhi / ʕanhu.
anyone: (ʕayyᵉ) ɦadd.
anyone else: (ʕayyᵉ) ɦaddᵉ taani.
anyway: ɛala-l-ɛumuum; ɛala ʕayyᵉ ɦaal.
anywhere: ʕayyᵉ makaan; ʕayyᵉ ɦitta.
apartment: ʃaʔʔa, ʃuʔaʔ.
apologize (*for*): ʕiɛtazar, yiɛtizir (ɛan).
apology: ʕiɛtizaar.
appear: ẓahar, yiẓhar; baan, yibaan.
it appears; it seems: yiẓhar; baayin.
appearance (*shape, "looks like"*): ʃakl, ʕaʃkaal.
appendicitis: ʕiltihaab iz-zayda-d-dudiyya.
appendix (*anatomy*): ʕil-muṣraan il-ʕaɛwar; ʕiz-zayda-d-dudiyya.
appetite: nifs; ʃahiyya.
appetizers: mazza, -aat; muʃahhiyyaat.
applaud, clap (v): saʔʔaf, yisaʔʔaf.
apples: tuffaaɦ (-a, -aat).
application: ṭalab, -aat.
application for a job: ṭalab ɛamal.
apply (*for*): ṭalab, yuṭlub; ʔaddim, yiʔaddim (fi).
appoint, employ: ɛayyin, yiɛayyin; waẓẓaf, yiwaẓẓaf.
appointment (*date*): maɛaad, mawaɛiid.
appreciate, esteem (v): ʔaddar, yiʔaddar.
approach, draw near: ʔarrab, yiʔarrab (min).
appropriate (adj): munaasib, -iin.
to be appropriate to the occasion: ṣaɦɦ, yiṣaɦɦ.
to be suitable: naasib, yinaasib.
approve: waafiʔ, yiwaafiʔ (ɛala).
approximately (adv): taʔriiban.
around, about (prep): ɦawaali.
apricot juice: ʔamar id-diin.
apricots: miʃmiʃ (-aaya, -aat).
dried apricots: miʃmiʃiyya.
April: ʕabriil. *April fool's joke*: kidbit ʕabriil.
apron: maryala, maraayil.
aquarium: gineenit ʕasmaak.
Arab: ɛarabi, ɛarab.
Arabic: ɛarabi.
Classical: fuṣɦa.
Colloquial: ɛammiyya.
Modern Standard Arabic: ʕil-fuṣɦa-l-muɛaaṣira / muɛaṣra.
archeology: ɛilm il-ʕasaar.
architect: muhandis miɛmaari.
architecture: ʕil-handasa il-miɛmariyya.
area, district: manṭiʔa, manaaṭiʔ; ɦayy, ʕaɦyaaʔ; ɦitta, ɦitat.
argument, discussion: munaʔʃa / munaqʃa, -aat.

arithmetic: ɦisaab.
arm (*limb*): diraaɛ, -aat / ʕidriɛa.
armchair: futeey, -aat.
Armenian: ʕarmanni, ʕarman.
armhole: jiruuh, -aat.
army: geeʃ, guyuuʃ.
army officer: ẓaabiṭ, ẓubbaaṭ (geeʃ).
around the world: ɦawl il-ɛaalam.
around, about, approximately: ɦawaali.
around, surrounding: ɦawaleen.
arrange: waḍḍab, yiwaḍḍab.
organize: naẓẓam, yinaẓẓam; rattib, yirattib.
stack neatly: sattif, yisattif.
arranged, orderly: mitsattif; munaẓẓam; mirattib / murattab, -iin.
arrangement: *preparation, order*: tartiib, -aat.
(*for flowers*): tawḍiib.
arrest (v): ʕabaḍ, yuʕbuḍ ɛala.
arrival: wuṣuul.
arrive: wiṣil, yiwṣal.
arrogance: ɛagrafa / taɛagruf; takabbur; ʕalaaṭa; ɣaṭrasa.
arrogant, conceited, stuck up: mutakabbir / mitkabbar; mutaɛagrif, -iin; ʕaliiṭ, ʕulaṭa; mutaɣaṭris / mitɣaṭras, -iin.
art: fann, funuun.
Faculty of Arts: kulliyyit ʕadaab.
artery (*heart only, not street*): ʃuryaan, ʃarayiin.
artichokes: xarʃuuf (-a, -aat).
article, essay: maqaala / maqaal, -aat.
artificial: ṣinaaɛi, -yyiin.
artificial teeth: sinaan ṣinaɛiyya.
artisan, craftsman: ṣaaniɛ, ṣunnaaɛ; ɦirafi, -yyiin.
artist: fannaan, -iin.
artistic: fanni, -yyiin.
as if, (conj): ɛala ʕinn; ka-ʕinn (+ noun or pron suffix).
as long as: ṭuul ma.
since, because: madaam.
as soon as: taww^{e} ma; ʕawwil ma.
as, like (prep): zayy.
(conj): zayy^{e} ma.
ashamed: maksuuf, -iin.
ashtray: ṭaffaaya, -aat.
ask (*of inquiries*): saʕal, yisʕal.
ask for: ṭalab, yuṭlub.
asleep: naayim, -iin.
aspect: naɦya, nawaaɦi; wugha, -aat; giha, -aat.
asparagus: kiʃkalmaaz.
aspirin: ʕasbiriin (-a, -aat).
assembly: maglis, magaalis.
assistance: musaɛda.
assistant: musaaɛid, -iin.
associate professor (*American system*): ʕustaaz muʃaarik.
assorted, mixed: miʃakkil, -iin.
assortment, mixture: taʃkiila, -aat.
astonished: mistaɣrab, -iin.
to be astonished,

amazed: ʕistaɣrab, yistaɣrab.
astronaut: raaʕid, ruwwaad fadaaʕ.
astronomy: ɛilm il-falak.
Aswan: ʕaswaan.
at (*place*): ɛand; fi.
(*time*): fi (*or a time noun without prep*).
at all: xaalis; ʕabadan.
athlete, athletic: riyaadi, -yyiin.
atlas: ʕatlas, ʕataalis.
atmosphere: gaww.
atomic: zarri.
atomic bomb: qumbila zarriyya, qanaabil zarriyya.
attach (*fasten, join*): ʃabak, yuʃbuk.
attached (adj): maʃbuuk, -iin.
attached (*emotionally*) *to*: mitɛallaʕ bi.
attack (n) (*offensive*): huguum, -aat.
heart attack: galta fil-ʕalb.
heart failure: sakta ʕalbiyya.
attack (v) (tr): hagam, yihgim ɛala; haagim, yihaagim.
(intr): ʕithaggim, yithaggim ɛala.
attempt (n): muɦawla, -aat.
attempt (v): ɦaawil, yiɦaawil.
attend (*be present at*): ɦadar, yiɦdar.
attention: ʕihtimaam; ʕintibaah.
pay attention (m): xalli baalak; xud baalak.
attract: gazab, yigzib.
attraction: gaazibiyya.
attractive: gazzaab, -iin.
aubergines, eggplant: bidingaan / bitingaan (-a, -aat).
audience, spectators: mutafarrigiin; muʃahdiin.
audience, listeners: mustamiɛiin.
public, crowd: gumhuur.
auditor (*of a class*): mustamiɛ, -iin.
(*accounting*): muraagiɛ, -iin.
auditorium: mudarrag, -aat.
August: ʕaɣustus.
aunt (*address form*): tant.
(*maternal aunt*): xaala, -aat.
my aunt: xalt-i.
(*paternal aunt*): ɛamma, -aat.
my aunt: ɛammit-i.
author (*writer*): muʕallif, -iin; kaatib, kuttaab.
authority (*power*): sulta, -aat.
automatic: ʕutumatik (invar).
automobile: ɛarabiyya, -aat.
autumn: ʕil-xariif.
avocado: ʕabukaadu (-haaya, -haat).
available: mitwaffar, -iin.
available, present: mawguud, -iin.
to become available: ʕitwaffar, yitwaffar.
average (n): mutawassit, -iin.

aviation: ţayaraan.
awake: ṣaaɦi, -yiin.
awaken: ṣaɦɦa, yiṣaɦɦi.
away (*far, distant*): biɛiid, buɛaad.
awful: faẓiiɛ, fuẓaaɛ; ʃaniiɛ, ʃunaaɛ; zift.
awning: tanda, tinad.
axle: ʕaks, -aat.

B

B.A. degree: lisans.
B.S. degree: bakaluryuus.
baby: beebi, -haat.
newborn: mawluud, mawluuda, mawaliid.
infant: ṭifl, ṭifla, ʕaṭfaal.
toddler: nuunu.
babysitter: galiis ʕaṭfaal, gulasa ʕaṭfaal.
bachelor: ɛaazib, ɛuzzaab.
back (adj) (*e.g. back door*): warraani, -yiin.
the back tire: ʕil-ɛagala-l-warraniyya.
in the back (*e.g. of a car*): wara.
back (adv): wara.
back (n) (*anatomy*): ḍahr, ḍuhuur.
backgammon: ṭawla.
bacon: beekun.
bad: wiɦiʃ, -iin.
not bad: miʃ baṭṭaal; miʃ wiɦiʃ.
bad, deteriorated: sayyiʕ, -iin (cl).
rotten (*food, etc.*): baayiẓ, -iin
bag, case: ʃanṭa, ʃunaṭ.
bag, sack: kiis, ʕakyaas (tikyaas after nos. 3–10).
money bag: kiis filuus.
baggage (*suitcase*): ʃanṭa, ʃunaṭ.
bake, cook (v): ṭabax, yuṭbux.
bake (*bread, cake, cookies*): xabaz, yixbiz.
baked: fil-furn.
bakery: furn, ʕafraan; maxbaz, maxaabiz.
mechanized bakery: maxbaz ʕaali.
baking powder: bakinbawdar / bikinbawdar / beeking bawdar.
baklava: baʕlaawa.
balance, wheel balance (n): ʕittizaan ɛagala.
balcony: balakoona, -aat.
balcony in a theater: balkoon.
veranda, porch: faranda / varanda, -aat.
terrace: tiraas, -aat.
bald: ʕaṣlaɛ, ṣalɛa, ṣulɛ.
ball: koora, kuwar.
ball-bearings: rummaan bily (-a, -aat).
ball-joint (*auto*): beeḍa, -aat.
ballet: baleeh.
balloon: balluuna, -aat.
bamboo: bambuu.
bananas: mooz (-a, -aat).
bandaid, plaster: bilastar.
bang, knock (v): xabbaṭ, yixabbaṭ.
bangs (*hair on forehead*): franʃa; ʕuṣṣa.
bank (n): bank, bunuuk.
bank book (*for savings*): daftar, dafaatir tawfiir.

bankrupt (adj): mifallis, -iin.
to go bankrupt: fallis, yifallis.
banquet: ɛuzuuma, ɛazaayim.
baptism: maɛmudiyya; tanṣiir.
barbecue (v): ʃawa, yiʃwi.
barbecued: maʃwi, -yyiin.
barber: ɦallaaʕ, -iin.
barely: yadoob / yadoobak (invar).
bargain (n) (*good value*): luʕṭa (no pl).
bargain (v) (*to negotiate*): faaṣil, yifaaṣil.
bargaining: fiṣaal.
bark (*of a dog*) (n): hawhawa.
bark (*of a dog*) (v): hawhaw, yihawhaw.
barley: ʃiɛiir (-a, -aat).
barricade, obstruction (**n**): sadda, -aat.
barrier: maaniɛ, mawaaniɛ; ɦaagiz, ɦawaagiz.
base (*bottom, support, foundation*): qaɛda / qaaɛida, qawaaɛid.
basement: badroon, -aat.
basil, sweet basil: riɦaan.
basis: ʕasaas, ʕusus.
basket: sabat, ʕisbita / sibita; salla, silal.
basketball: baskitbool; kurt-is-salla.
bass (*fish*): ʕaruṣ (-a).
bat (n) (*animal*): wiṭwaaṭ, waṭawiiṭ; xuffaaʃ, xafafiiʃ.
(*baseball, etc.*): maḍrab, maḍaarib.
bath, bathroom: ɦammaam, -aat.
(*toilet*): tiwalitt; doorit mayya.
bathe: ʕistaɦamma, yistaɦamma.
bathing suit: mayooh, -haat.
bikini: bikiini.
one piece bathing suit: mayooh hitta waɦda.
two piece bathing suit: mayooh hittiteen.
bathrobe: roob, ʕarwaab.
bathroom: *see* **bath**
bathtub: banyu, -haat.
batter (*for cooking*): ɛagiina.
battery (*for car*): baṭṭariyya, -aat.
(*for flashlight, radio, etc*): ɦagar (-a, ɦigaara).
bay leaves: waraʕ (-a, -aat) lawra.
be: kaan, yikuun.
I have been here three years: baʕaa-li hina talat siniin.
beach: bilaaj, -aat.
beachrobe: burnus, baraanis.
beans: *seeds, grains* (coll): ɦabb, ɦubuub.
fava, broad beans: fuul.
coffee beans, unground: bunnᵉ ɦabb, ɦubuub.
coffee beans, ground: bunnᵉ matɦuun.
cooked broad beans: fuul midammis.
dish of mashed dried broad beans: biṣaara / buṣaara.
fried bean patties: falaafil; ṭaɛmiyya.

green beans: faṣulya xaḍra.
white beans: faṣulya beeḍa.
bear (n): (m) dibb, dibab. (f) dibba, -aat.
bear, tolerate (v): ʕistaɦmil, yistaɦmil.
beard: daʕn (f), duʕuun; liɦya, liɦa.
beat (v): *hit*: ḍarab, yiḍrab.
beat, defeat: hazam, yihzim; ɣalab, yiɣlib.
surpass, beat in a race: sabaʕ, yisbaʕ
beautiful: gamiil, gumaal; hilw, -iin.
because: ɛaʃaan; liʕinn; ʕaṣl.
become: baʕa, yibʕa.
bed: siriir, saraayir.
bedbugs: baʕʕ (-a, -aat).
bedroom: ʕooḍit noom, ʕuwaḍ noom.
beef: laɦma kanduuz.
beer: biira.
bees: naɦl (-a, -aat).
beet (*root*): bangar (-aaya, -aat).
before (prep): ʕabl.
before this: ʕablᵉ kida.
like before: zayy il-ʕawwil.
before (conj): ʕablᵉ ma.
beg: (*ask for alms*): ʃaɦat, yiʃɦat.
beg, entreat, plead with: ʕitragga, yitragga.
I beg you: ʕarguuk (-ki, -ku).
beggar: ʃaɦɦaat, -iin.
begin: ʕibtada, yibtidi, badaʕ, yibdaʕ (cl).
beginner: mubtadiʕ, -iin.
beginning: bidaaya.
at the beginning: fil-ʕawwil.
the beginning of the month: ʕawwil iʃ-ʃahr.
behavior: taṣarruf, -aat, suluuk.
behind: wara.
beige: beej.
believable: maɛʕuul, -iin.
believe: saddaʕ, yisaddaʕ; ṣaddaʕ, yiṣaddaʕ (cl).
have faith (*in*): ʕaamin, yiʕaamin (bi).
bell: garas, ʕagraas.
belly, pot belly, paunch: kirʃ, kuruuʃ.
stomach: baṭn (f), buṭuun.
belly dance: raʕṣᵉ baladi (raʕṣa, -aat).
belly dancer: raʕʕaaṣa baladi, raʕʕaṣaat baladi.
belly dancing: raʕṣᵉ baladi.
belonging to: bitaaɛ, (f) bitaaɛit, bituuɛ.
below: taɦt.
belt: ɦizaam, ʕaɦzima / ɦizima.
conveyer belt: seer, suyuur.
fan belt: seer marwaɦa.
safety belt: ɦizaam ʕamaan, ʕaɦzimit ʕamaan.
benefit (n) (*advantage*): fayda, fawaayid.
benefit (v) (intr): ʕistafaad, yistafiid (min).
(tr): faad, yifiid; nafaɛ, yinfaɛ.
beside, next to: gamb.
besides, other than: ɣeer.
best: ʕaɦsan.

bet (n): rahaan, -aat.
bet (v): raahin, yiraahin.
better (*than*): ʕaɦsan (min).
between: been ... wi ....
Bible, the: ʕik-kitaab il-muqaddas.
gospel: ʕingiil, ʕanagiil.
bicarbonate: bikarbunaat.
bicycle: ɛagala, -aat; biskilitta, -aat.
big: kibiir kubaar.
bigger (comp): ʕakbar (invar).
bilharzia: bilharsiya.
bill (*monetary statement*): ɦisaab, -aat; fatuura, fawatiir; boon, -aat.
bind: (*a book*): gallid, yigallid.
tie: rabaṭ, yurbuṭ.
binding (n) (*in a book*): tagliid.
biology: ɛilm il-ʕaɦyaaʕ.
bird: ṭeer, ṭuyuur; (*sparrow*): ɛaṣfuur (-a), ɛaṣafiir.
birth (*to give birth to*): wildit, tiwlid; gaabit beebi, tigiib beebi.
birth certificate: ʃihaadit milaad.
birth control: taɦdiid in-nasl.
birthday festival of the Prophet or a holy man: muulid, mawaalid.
birthday party: ɦaflit ɛiid milaad.
biscuits (*Am.: cookies*): baskoot (-a, -aat).
bite (n): *insect bite* (*s*): ʕarṣ (-a, -aat).
bite, mouthful, morsel (*of food*): luʕma, luʕam.
have a bite (*of food*): kal, yaakul luʕma.
bite (v): ɛaḍḍ, yiɛuḍḍ.
bite, sting (v): ʕaraṣ, yuʕruṣ.
black: ʕiswid, (f) sooda, suud.
blackboard: taxta, tuxat; sabbuura, -aat.
blade (*of razor*): muus ɦilaaʕa, ʕamwaas ɦilaaʕa.
blame (v): laam, yiluum (s.o. ɛala s.t.).
is blaming s.o. (part): laayim, -iin.
I'm not to blame; it's not my fault: miʃ zamb-i.
what fault is it of mine (*don't blame me*): ʕana zamb-i ʕeeh.
blanket: baṭṭaniyya, baṭaṭiin.
bleach (n) (*whitening*): bayaaḍ (-a, -aat); kuloor.
bleach (v) (*whiten*): bayyaḍ, yibayyaḍ.
bleed: nazaf, yinzif.
blender (*appliance*): xallaaṭ, -aaṭ.
bless: baarik, yibaarik.
God bless you: ʕallaah yibaarik fiik (fiiki, fiikum).
blessing (*divine favor*): baraka, -aat.
divine gift, grace: niɛma, niɛam.
blind: ʕaɛma, (f) ɛamya, ɛumy / ɛumyaan.
blister: ɦurreeʕa, ɦarariiʕ.
block, dam (n): sadd, suduud.
block, dam (v): sadd, yisidd.

blocked, blocked up: masduud, -iin.
the pipe is blocked up: ʕil-masuura masduuda.
to be blocked up: ʕitsadd / ʕissadd, yitsadd.
blond (e): ʕaʃʕar, (f) ʃaʕra, ʃuʕr.
blond hair: ʃaɛr^e ʕaʂfar.
blood: damm.
blood pressure: ḍaɣṭ id-damm.
he has high blood pressure: ḍaɣṭu ɛaali; ɛandu-ḍ-ḍaɣṭ (*chronically*).
blouse: biluuza, -aat.
blow (*n*) (*hard stroke*): ḍarba, -aat; xabṭa, -aat.
a blow dry: seʃwaar, -aat.
blow (v) (*e.g. the wind*): habb, yihibb.
blow the (*car*) *horn*: ḍarab kalaks, yiḍrab kalaks.
blow out (*a candle, flame*): ṭafa, yiṭfi.
blow up (*e.g. a balloon, a tire*): nafax, yunfux.
blow up (*explode*) (tr): faggar, yifaggar; farʕaɛ, yifarʕaɛ.
(intr): ʕinfagar, yinfigir; ʕitfarʕaɛ, yitfirʕiɛ.
blue: ʕazraʕ, (f) zarʕa, zurʕ.
pale blue: labani (invar).
navy blue: kuɦli (invar).
board (v) (*e.g. a train*): rikib, yirkab.
board, *plank* (n): looɦ, ʕalwaaɦ.
board, council: maglis, magaalis.
boarding house: *see* **hotel**
boardwalk, corniche: kurneeʃ / kurniiʃ.
boasting, bragging (n): faxr; ʕiftixaar.
boat: markib (m and f), maraakib.
small boat: markiba, -aat.
boatsman: marakbi, (pl) -yya.
bobby pins, hair pins: binas (binsa, binsaat).
body (*frame of man, animal, or car*): gism, ʕagsaam.
corpse: gussa, gusas.
body work, metal work (*on a car*): samkara.
metal worker: samkari, -yya.
boil (v) (tr & intr) (*e.g. water*): ɣala, yiɣli.
(tr) *cook in boiling water*: salaʕ, yisluʕ.
to boil over (intr) (*e.g. milk*): faar, yifuur.
(tr): fawwar, yifawwar.
boiled (food): masluuʕ.
boiled water: mayya maɣliyya.
bolt (n) (*for a door*): tirbaas, tarabiis.
(*rivet*): birʃaam (-a, -aat).
bolt (v) (*to lock with a bolt*): tarbis, yitarbis.
bolted: mitarbis, -iin.
(*to rivet*): barʃim, yibarʃim.
bomb (n): qumbila, qanaabil.
bon voyage: riɦla saɛiida.

bones: ɛaḍm (-a, -aat); ɛiḍaam.
spinal column:
silsilit iḍ-ḍahr, (salaasiil).
fish bones: ʃook (-a, -aat).
bonnet (*Am.*: *hood of a car*):
kabbuut.
bonus, reward: mukafʕa, -aat.
book (n) (*volume*): kitaab, kutub.
book (v) (*reserve*): ɦagaz, yiɦgiz.
bookcase, shelf: raff, rufuuf, ʕurfuf.
bookend: sinaadit kitaab,
sinadaat kitaab.
booking (*reservation*): ɦagz.
bookstore: maktaba, -aat.
boot (*Am.*: *trunk of a car*):
ʃanṭa, ʃunaṭ.
boots, *a pair of*: buut.
border, limit: ɦadd, ɦuduud.
bored: *to become bored*: mall,
yimill.
boring, tedious: mumill, -iin.
born: mawluud, -iin. *to be born*
(v): ʕitwalad, yitwilid.
borrow: ʕistalaf, yistilif.
borrow (*book from library*):
ʕistaɛaar, yistaɛiir.
boss (n): rayyis, ruyasa; raʕiis,
ruʕasa.
both: l-itneen. *both of you*:
ʕintu l-itneen.
both of them: humma l-itneen.
both of us: ʕiɦna l-itneen.
bother (v): daayiʕ, yidaayiʕ;
taɛab, yitɛib.
bottle (n): ʕizaaza, ʕazaayiz.
gas bottle:
ʕanbuuba, ʕanabiib.

bottom (n): ʕaɛr, ʕuɛuur.
bottom, lower (adj): taɦtaani, -yyiin.
bound (*e.g. book*): mitgallid, -iin.
bouquet: bukeeh, -aat.
bow (v): ʕinɦana, yinɦini.
bowl (n) (*receptacle*):
sulṭaniyya, salaṭiin.
soup bowl: ṣaɦn ʃurba.
box (n): ɛilba, ɛilab.
cardboard box: kartoona,
karatiin; ɛilba, ɛilab kartoon.
large box, chest:
sanduuʕ, sanadiiʕ.
boy: walad, wilaad / ʕawlaad.
bra: suntiyaan, -aat.
bracelet: ʕaswira, ʕasaawir;
ɣiweeʃa, ɣawaayiʃ.
braid (n): ḍifiira, ḍafaayir.
brain (n): muxx, ʕamxaax.
brake (n): farmala, faraamil.
brake pads: tiil faraamil
brake (v): farmil, yifarmil.
branch (n): farɛ, furuuɛ.
brand, type (n): marka, -aat;
nooɛ, ʕanwaaɛ.
brass (*metal*): naɦaas ʕaṣfar.
brave, courageous: ʃugaaɛ,
ʃugɛaan.
bread: ɛeeʃ.
bread sticks (*long, thin,*
salted): batunsaleeh.
brown pita bread: ɛeeʃ baladi.
dried bread slices, rusks,
breadsticks: buʕsumaaṭ.
flakey breakfast bread:
fiṭiir (-a, faṭaayir).
French bread: ɛeeʃ fiinu.

hard (dry) bread: ɛeeʃ naaʃif; mifaʕʕaɛ; miladdin.
hot dog bun (petit pain): bitibaa.
roll: ɛeeʃ kayzar.
sandwich bread / toast: ɛeeʃ tust.
sandwich French bread, rolls: ɛeeʃ sandawitʃaat.
soft bread: ɛeeʃ ṭari.
white pita bread: ɛeeʃ ʃaami.

break (n) (*rest*): ʕistiraaḥa, -aat; fusḥa, fusaḥ.
(*fracture*): kasra, -aat.

break (v) (tr): kasar, yiksar.
break into small pieces (tr): kassar, yikassar.
(intr): ʕitkassar, yitkassar.

breakfast: fiṭaar; fuṭuur; (cl) ʕifṭaar.
breakfast after a fast (during Ramadan): ʕifṭaar.
to eat breakfast: fiṭir, yifṭar.

breast, chest: sidr / ṣadr, ṣuduur / ʕiṣdaar.

breathe: ʕitnaffis, yitnaffis.
smell, sniff: ʃamm, yiʃimm.

breeze (n): nisiim; hawa; nismit hawa.

bribe (n): raʃwa, raʃaawi.

bribe (v): raʃa, yirʃi.

bricks: ṭuub (-a, -aat).

bride: ɛaruusa, ɛaraayis.

bridegroom: ɛariis, ɛirsaan.

bridge (n): kubri, kabaari.
26 July Bridge: kubri ʕabu-l-ɛila.

briefcase: ʃanṭa, ʃunaṭ.

bright, intelligent: nabiih, nubaha; zaki, ʕazkiya.
bright (light): saaṭiɛ.

bring: gaab, yigiib. (imperative): haat, -i, -u.
bring back: raggaɛ, yiraggaɛ.
bring down: nazzil, yinazzil.
bring out / up: ṭallaɛ, yiṭallaɛ.
deliver, take to someone or some place: wadda, yiwaddi.

Britain: biriṭaanya.

British: biriṭaani, -iyyiin.

broadcasting: ʕizaaɛa.

broccoli: brakli.

broil: see **grill**.

broke, penniless: mifallis, -iin.
to go broke: fallis, yifallis.

broken: maksuur, -iin.
broken, damaged: baayiẓ, -iin, xasraan, -iin.
broken, out of order: xasraan, -iin; ɛaṭlaan, -iin.
broken, to pieces: mikassar, -iin; midaʃdiʃ, -iin.

broker: simsaar, samasra.

broom: maʕaʃʃa, -aat; maknasa, makaanis.

broth: maraʕa.

brother: ʕaxx, ʕixwaat. *brother of*: ʕaxu…
The Muslim Brotherhood: ʕil-ʕixwaan (il-muslimiin).

brown (adj): bunni (invar).
brown-skinned, brown-haired: ʕasmar, (f) samra, sumr.
honey-color, used in reference to eyes: ɛasali.

brown (v) (*e.g. meat*): ɦammar, yiɦammar.
brunet: ʕasmar, (f) samra, sumr.
brush (n): furʃa, furaʃ.
brush (v): farraʃ, yifarraʃ.
(*hair*): sarraɦ, yisarraɦ.
(*teeth*): ɣasal is-sinaan, yiɣsil is-sinaan.
bucket: gardal, garaadil.
buckle (n): tuuka, tuwak.
buckle (v) (*fasten*): rabaṭ, yurbuṭ.
budget: mizaniyya, -aat.
buffalos: gamuus (-a, gawamiis).
buffet (*furniture, buffet meal, canteen*): bufeeh, -aat.
bug, insect: ɦaʃara, -aat.
bedbugs: baʕʕ (-a, -aat).
build (v): bana, yibni.
building (n): ɛimaara, -aat; mabna (m), mabaani.
bulb: lamba, -aat; lanḍa, lumaḍ.
bulb in toilet tank: ɛawwaama.
bulgar (*wheat*): burɣul.
bull (*animal*): toor, tiraan.
bulletin board: looɦit ʕiɛlanaat, luɦat ʕiɛlanaat.
bullets: ruṣaaṣ (-a, -aat).
bump, knock, shock (n): ṣadma, -aat.
bump in road: maṭabb, -aat.
bump, knock, shock (v): ṣadam, yiṣdim.
bumper: ʕikṣidaam, -aat.
bun (*hair style*): ʃinyoon.
bunch, cluster (n) (*fruit*): zubaaṭa, -aat.
buoy, float: ɛawwaama, -aat.
burial: dafn (-a, -aat).
burial site, place: madfan, madaafin; ʕabr, ʕubuur.
burn (v) (tr): ɦaraʕ, yiɦraʕ (intr): ʕitɦaraʕ, yitɦiriʕ.
something is burning: haaga bititɦiriʕ.
scorch: lasaɛ, yilsaɛ.
burner (*on a stove*): ɛeen, ɛuyuun.
burnt out (adj) (*e.g. bulb*): maɦruuʕ, -iin.
bury: dafan, yidfin.
bus (*large public bus, includes standing*): ʕutubiis, -aat.
(*small public bus, sitting only*): minibaṣṣ.
(*small private van*): mikrubaṣṣ.
(*Peugeot station wagon 'bus'*): sirviis.
bus terminal: ʕaaxir il-xaṭṭ; mawʕif, mawaaʕif.
business: ʃuɣl, ʕaʃɣaal.
it's none of my business: da miʃ ʃuɣl-i.; ma-lii-ʃ daɛwa
what business is it of yours?: (to m) w-inta maa-lak; (to f) w-inti maa-lik.
business administration: ʕidaarit ʕaɛmaal.
businessman: raagil ʕaɛmaal / ragul ʕaɛmaal, rigaal ʕaɛmaal.
busy: maʃɣuul, -iin.
but: laakin; bass.
butagas bottle: ʕanbuubit butagaaz, ʕanabiib butagaaz.
butagas seller: bitaaɛ il-butagaaz.

butane gas: butagaaz.
butcher (*dealer in meat*): gazzaar, -iin.
butter (n): zibda.
clarified butter, ghee: samna.
butterflies, moths: faraaʃ (-a, -aat).
button (n) (*push button, clothes button*): zuraar, zaraayir.
button (v): zarrar, yizarrar.
button hole: ɛirwa, ɛaraawi.
buy: ʕiʃtara, yiʃtiri.
by, near: ɛand, gamb.
by God's name: w-allaahi.
by means of: bi.
by myself: bi-nafs-i.
by the way: ɛala fikra.

C

CD: sidii, sidihaat.
cab, taxi: taks / taksi, taksaat / taksiyyaat.
cabbage: kurumb.
Cabinet (*council of ministers*): wizaara, -aat; maglis il-wuzara.
(*wardrobe*): dulaab, dawaliib.
cable: kabl, -aat.
battery cable: kabl baṭṭariyya.
brake cable: tiij faraamil.
cactus: ṣabbaar (-a, -aat).
cafe: ʕahwa, ʕahaawi.
(*open-air type café with a view*): kazinu, -haat.
cafeteria: kafitirya, -aat.
caftan: ʕufṭaan, ʕafaṭiin.
cage: ʕafaṣ, ʕaʕfaaṣ.
Cairene: maṣraawi, -yyiin; qaahiri, -yyiin.
Cairo: maṣr; ʕil-qaahira.
Old Cairo: maṣr ilʕadiima.
cake: gatoo, -haat; keek.
a cake: turta; keeka.
calculations: ɦisaab, ɦisabaat.
calculator: ʕaala ɦasba, ʕalaat ɦasba.
calendar: natiiga, nataayig.
caliph: xaliifa (m), xulafa.
call (n) (*telephone*): mukalma, -aat.
call (v) (*shout someone's name*): nadah, yindah; naada, yinaadi.
call s.o. by telephone: kallim, yikallim bit-tilifoon; ḍarab, yiḍrab tilifoon li ...; ʕittaṣal, yittiṣil bi ...
calorie: suεr, -aat.
camel: gamal, gimaal.
camera: kamira, -aat.
camp (n): muεaskar, -aat; muxayyam, -aat.
camp (v): εaskar, yiεaskar; xayyim, yixayyim.
can (n) (*Br.*: *tin*): εilba, εilab.
(*large can*): ṣafiiɦa, ṣafaayiɦ
canned goods: muεallabaat.
can, be able (v): ʕidir, yiʕdar; mumkin (invar).
permitted: masmuuɦ.
Canada: kanada.
Canadian: kanadi, -iyyiin.
canal: qanaal (no pl) / qanaah, qanawaat.
Suez Canal: qanaal is-siwees.
irrigation canal: tirεa, tiraε.
cancel: laɣa, yilɣi.
cancel an appointment: kansil, yikansil maεaad.
to be canceled: ʕitlaɣa, yitliɣi.
cancer: saraṭaan.
(*euphemisms for cancer*) *malignant tumor*: waram xabiis.
the bad disease: ʕil-maraḍ il-wiɦiʃ.
candles: ʃamε (-a, -aat).
candlestick: ʃamεidaan, -aat.

candy (*Br.*: *sweets*): bunboon (-a, -aat).
candy favors at a party: milabbis (-a, -aat.)
cane (n): xɑrɑzɑɑn (-ɑ, -ɑɑt).
(*stick*): ɛaṣɑɑya, -ɑɑt.
cannon: madfaɛ, madaafiɛ.
cantaloupe: kantalubb (-a, -aat).
cap (n) (*screw cap for tank*): ṭɑbbɑ, -ɑɑt.
(*headgear*): ṭɑʕiyyɑ; ṭɑwɑɑʕi.
capital (*city*): ɛɑɑṣima, ɛɑwɑɑṣim.
(*money*): rɑsmaal / rɑʕsᵉ maal (cl).
capital punishment: ʕiɛdaam
car (*any wheeled vehicle*): ɛɑrɑbiyya, -aat / -ɑɑt.
caraway: kɑrɑwya.
carburetor: karbirateer, -aat.
card: kart, kuruut / kuruta.
identity card: biṭɑɑʕɑ, -ɑɑt (ʃɑxṣiyyɑ).
deck of playing cards: kutʃiina.
cardamom: ɦabbahaan.
cardboard: kɑrtoon.
care (n): ʕihtimaam (bi).
care, concern: ɛinaaya.
when someone is sick: riɛaaya.
intensive care: ɛinaaya murakkaza.
care (v): care, be concerned: ʕistaɛna, yistaɛna.
care for, look after: rɑɛɑ, yirɛɑ.
take care!: xalli baal-ak; xud baal-ak (min).
careful: be careful: xalli baalak; xud baalak (min).
careful: ɦaasib!, ɦasbi, ɦasbu; ʕiwɛa!, (f) ʕiwɛi!, ʕiwɛu!
careless: muhmil, -iin.
caretaker (*Am.*: *janitor*): fɑrrɑɑʃ, -iin.
carnation: ʕurunfil (-a, -aat).
carpenter: nɑggɑɑr, -iin.
carpet (n): siggaada, sagagiid.
fitted carpet (*moquette*): mukitt.
corridor runner: maʃʃaaya, -aat.
carriage: *horse drawn cab*: ɦɑnṭuur, ɦɑnɑṭiir.
train car: ɛɑrɑbiyya, -aat / -ɑɑt.
carrots: gɑzɑr (-ɑ, -ɑɑt).
carry: ʃaal, yiʃiil. *carrying* (part): ʃaayil, -iin.
carry s.t. down: nazzil, yinazzil.
carry s.t. up: ṭɑllɑɛ, yiṭɑllɑɛ.
cart (*with donkey*): ɛɑrɑbiyya kɑrru.
case (n) (*sheath, as for a mobile*): giraab, girabaat.
condition: ɦaal, ʕaɦwaal.
a case: ɦaala, -aat.
in this case: fil-ɦaala di.
cash (n): naʕd; kaaʃ.
cash payment: naʕdiyya, -aat.
in cash: naʕdi; bin-naʕd; kaaʃ.
cash (v), *receive payment*: ʕɑbɑḍ, yiʕbɑḍ.
cash a check: ṣɑrɑf ʃiik, yiṣrif ʃiik.

cash, money (n): filuus (pl).
cash register: xazna.
cashier: ṣarraaf, -iin.
cashier's desk/office: xazna, xizan.
casino, gambling hall: ṣaalit ʕumaar, ṣalaat ʕumaar.
cassette, tape: ʃiriiṭ, ʃaraayiṭ / ʕaʃriṭa; kasitt, -aat.
cassette recorder: kasitt, -aat; gihaaz tasgiil, ʕaghiza.
cast, plaster of Paris: gibs.
cat: ʕuṭṭa (m. ʕuṭṭ), ʕuṭaṭ.
catapult: (*Am.: slingshot*) nibla, nibal.
cataract (Nile), waterfall: ʃallaal, -aat.
catastrophe: muṣiiba, maṣaayib; karsa, kawaaris.
catch (*capture, grasp*): misik, yimsik.
catch hold of: laʕaf, yulʕuf.
catch up with: liɦiʕ / laɦaʕ, yilɦaʕ.
catch (*e.g. a train*): liɦiʕ, yilɦaʕ.
catch a disease, be infected by s.o.: ʕitɛada, yitɛidi min.
category, grade: fiyya, -aat.
type: ṣanf, ʕaṣnaaf; nooɛ, ʕanwaaɛ.
cauliflower: ʕarnabiiṭ (-a, -aat).
cause (v): sabbib, yisabbib.
cause, reason (n): sabab, ʕasbaab.
cave (n): kahf, kuhuuf; maɣaara, -aat.
cavities (*caries*): taswiis; tasawwus.
cavity (*decayed molar*): ḍirs^{e} misawwis, ʕaḍraas misawwisa.
ceiling (*of a room*): saʕf, ʕasʕuf.
celebrate: ʕiɦtafal, yiɦtifil (bi).
celebration: ʕiɦtifaal, -aat.
celery: karafs.
celery salt: budrit karafs.
celery seed: bizr^{e} karafs.
cellar: maxzan, maxaazin; badroom, -aat.
cemetery: ʕaraafa, -aat; madfan, madaafin.
graveyard (*graves*): maʕaabir / maqaabir (cl).
censorship: riʕaaba/riqaaba, -aat.
center (*of town*): wiṣṭ (il-balad).
center (*for activities*): markaz, maraakiz.
centimeter: santi; santimitr, -aat.
century: qarn, quruun.
ceremony: ɦafla, ɦafalaat.
certain, *sure*: mutaʕakkid, -iin.
certain, confirmed: muʕakkad, -iin.
certain, specific: muɛayyan, -iin.
certainly, surely: ʕakiid.
certificate: ʃahaada, -aat.
chain (n): silsila, salaasil.
tow chain: ganziir, ganaziir.
bicycle chain: ganziir ɛagala.
chain smoke: ʃirib, yiʃrab sigaara min sigaara.
chair: kursi, karaasi.
chairman: raʕiis, ruʕasa.

chaise-longue: ʃizlung / ʃazlung.
chalk (n): ṭabaʃiir.
piece of chalk:
ṭabaʃiira; ḥittit ṭabaʃiir.
champagne: ʃambanya.
champion, hero: baṭal, ʕabtaal.
championship: buṭuula, -aaṭ.
chance, opportunity: furṣa, furaṣ.
by chance: biṣ-ṣudfa.
chandelier: nagafa, -aat.
change (n) (*a change)*: taɣyiir, -aat.
change (*money*): fakka;
change for a pound:
fakkit gineeh
give me the change:
ʕiddiini-l-baaʕi
keep the change: xalli-l-baaʕi.
I can't make change:
maɛayiiʃ fakka; maykammilʃ.
change (v) (tr): ɣayyar, yiɣayyar.
(intr): ʕitɣayyar. yitɣayyar.
change into small cash:
fakk, yifukk.
transfer: ḥawwil, yiḥawwil.
changeable, inconsistent:
mutaqallib, -iin.
channel (on tv): qanaah,
qanawaat.
chaos: fawḍa.
chapter: faṣl, fuṣuul.
characteristic, quality: ṣifa, -aat;
ʕawṣaaf (pl).
charge (*elect.*) (v): ʃaḥan, yiʃḥan.
charge the battery:
mala, yimla-l-baṭṭariyya.
charge, entrust, s.o.
to do s.t.: kallif, yikallif.
charming: ẓariif, ẓuraaf; damm-u
(-aha. etc.) xafiif.
chart (n), *table schedule*:
gadwal, gadaawil
picture: ṣuura, ṣuwar.
explanatory description:
ʕiḍaaḥ, -aat; bayaan, -aat.
chase, pursue: ṭaarid, yiṭaarid.
chase away (*e.g. flies*): haʃʃ,
yihiʃʃ; ṭarad, yuṭrud.
chat (n): ḥadiis, ʕaḥadiis;
dardaʃa.
chat (v): dardiʃ, yidardiʃ.
chatter: raɣa, yirɣi.
chatterbox: raɣɣaay, -iin;
kalamangi, -yya.
chauffeur: sawwaaʕ, -iin.
cheap: rixiiṣ, ruxaaṣ.
become cheap: rixiṣ, yirxaṣ.
it costs almost nothing:
bi-balaaʃ.
cheat (v): ɣaʃʃ, yiɣiʃʃ.
crib notes for cheating:
birʃaam (-a, -aat).
check (v), *examine carefully*:
ʕallib, yiʕallib.
check, inspect:
tammim, yitammim (ɛala).
check the oil (see
the oil): ʃaaf, yiʃuuf iz-zeet.
check the mail (see
the mail): ʃaaf, yiʃuuf il-
busṭa.
examine, inspect:
kaʃaf, yikʃif (ɛala).
check book: daftar ʃikaat,
dafaatir ʃikaat.

check, cheque (n) (*bank slip*): ʃiik / ʃeek, -aat.
(*Br.*: *bill, amount due*): ɦisaab, -aat.
checks, squares: karooh, -aat.
checkup (*medical*): kaʃf (ṭibbi), kuʃufaat.
cheek: xadd, xuduud.
cheers! (*with drink*): fi siɦɦit-ak (-ik, -ku)!
cheese: gibna, giban.
Edam cheese: falamank.
Gouda cheese: gibna guuda.
Romano cheese: gibna ruumi.
white cheese: gibna beeḍa.
cottage cheese: gibna ʕariiʃ.
chemistry: kimya.
cheque (*bank slip*): ʃiik / ʃeek. -aat.
cherries: kireez (-a, -aat).
chess: ʃaṭarang.
chest, breast: sidr / ṣadr, ṣuduur / ʕiṣdaar.
chestnuts: ʕabu farwa.
chewing gum: libaan.
chic, elegant: ʃiik (invar).
chick peas: ɦummuṣ (-a, -aat).
chicken, hen: farxa, -aat / firaax.
chicken meat to eat: firaax.
chick: katkuut, katakiit.
chicken pox: gudeeri.
chicory: ʃikurya.
chief: raʕiis, ruʕasa; rayyis.
chignon: ʃinyoon.
child: ɛayyil, ɛiyaal.
infant: ṭifl, ʕaṭfaal.
childhood: ṭufuula.
children: wilaad / ʕawlaad.
children, kids: ɛiyaal.
children, infants: ʕaṭfaal.
chin: daʕn, duʕuun.
China: ʕiṣ-ṣiin.
china dinnerware: ṣiini.
Chinese: ṣiini, -yyiin.
chips (*Am.*: *French fries*): baṭaaṭis miɦammara.
chlorine: kuloor.
chocolate: ʃukulaaṭa.
chocolate candy: ʃukulaaṭa.
cholera: kureera / kuleera / kulira.
choose, select: ʕixtaar, yixtaar; naʕʕa, yinaʕʕi.
pick out: naʕaḍ, yunʕuḍ.
chop (v): xarraṭ, yixarraṭ.
Christian: masiiɦi / misiiɦi, -yyiin.
Coptic Christian: ʕibṭi, ʕaʕbaaṭ.
Christmas: ɛiid il-milaad; ʕik-kirismas.
chrome: kuroom.
chronological order: tartiib zamani.
church: kiniisa, kanaayis.
cigarette: sigaara, sagaayir.
at the cigarette store: ɛand^{e} btaaɛ is-sagaayir.
cigarette butt: ɛuʕb^{e} sigaara, ɛiʕaab/ʕaɛʕaab sagaayir.
cilantro, coriander: kuzbara / kusbara.
cinema: sinima, -aat; siima, siyam.
cinnamon: ʕirfa.
circle: dayra, dawaayir.
circle of people: ɦalaʕa, -aat.

circumstance: ẓarf, ẓuruuf.
circus: sirk, -aat.
citadel: ʕalɛa.
city: madiina, mudun; balad, bilaad.
civil engineering: handasa madaniyya.
civilian (n, adj): madani, -yyiin.
civilization: ɧaḍaara, -aat; madaniyya, -aat.
civilized (*materially*): mitmaddin, -iin.
(*morally respectable*): muhazzab, -iin.
clap, applaud (v): saʕʕaf, yisaʕʕaf.
class (*in school*): faṣl, fuṣuul; dars, duruus.
class period: ɧiṣṣa, ɧiṣaṣ.
class, grade, rank: daraga, -aat.
social class: ṭabaʕa, -aat.
the upper class: ʕiṭ-ṭabaʕa-l-ɛulya.
the middle class: ʕiṭ-ṭabaʕa-l-mutawassiṭa.
the poor class: ʕiṭ-ṭabaʕa-l-faʕiira.
high class, refined (adj): raaʕi, raʕyiin.
social high class: ʕiṭ-ṭabaʕa-r-raʕya.
(*on a train*): *1st class*: daraga ʕuula.
2nd class: daraga tanya.
3rd class: daraga talta.
(*on a plane*): 1st class: daraga ʕuula.
business class: daragit rigaal il-ʕaɛmaal.
economy class: daraga siyaɧiyya.
Classical Arabic: ʕil-luɣa-l-ɛarabiyya-l-fuṣɧa; ʕil-fuṣɧa.
classmate: zimiil, zumala / zamaayil.
classroom: faṣl, fuṣuul.
claw (n) (*of a cat*): ḍufr, ḍawaafir.
clean (adj): niḍiif, nuḍaaf.
clean (v): naḍḍaf, yinaḍḍaf.
to become clean: niḍif, yinḍaf.
cleaning: tanḍiif.
dry cleaning: tanḍiif gaaff.
clear, obvious: waaḍiɧ, -iin.
the weather is clear: ig-gawwᵉ raayiʕ / ṣaafi.
clerk: kaatib, kuttaab / kataba.
clever: ʃaaṭir. -iin; naaṣiɧ, - iin.
climb (v): ṭiliɛ, yiṭlaɛ.
clinic: ɛiyaada, -aat.
clip, paper clip: kilibs, -aat.
clock: saaɛa, -aat.
alarm clock: minabbih, -aat.
close (v): ʕafal, yiʕfil.
close eyes: ɣammaḍ, yiɣammaḍ.
close, near: ʕurayyib, -iin.
closed: maʕfuul, -iin.
(*referring to store hours*): ʕaafil, -iin.
closer than: ʕaʕrab min.
closest: ʕaʕrab (+ indef. noun).
closet, wardrobe: dulaab, dawaliib.

cloth: ʕumaaʃ, -aat / ʕaʕmiʃa.
clothes: huduum; malaabis.
clothesline: ɦablᵉ ɣasiil, ɦibaal ɣasiil.
small rack for drying: manʃar, manaaʃir.
clothespins: maʃbak ɣasiil, maʃaabik ɣasiil.
clot (*blood*): galṭa, -aat.
clouds: saɦaab (-a, suɦub); ɣeem (-a, ɣuyuum).
cloudy: miɣayyima.
to be cloudy: ɣayyimit, tiɣayyim.
clove: ʕurunfil (-a, -aat).
clove of garlic: faṣṣᵉ toom, fuṣuuṣ toom.
clover: barsiim.
club (*social or sports*): naadi, nawaadi.
clue (*to hint to*) (v): lammaɦ, yilammaɦ (li); *hinting*: talmiiɦ.
clutch (n) (*on a car*): dibriyaaj.
clutch cable: tiij dibriyaaj.
clutch pedal: baddaal dibriyaaj.
coal, charcoal: faɦm (faɦmaaya / faɦma, -aat).
coast: saaɦil, sawaaɦil.
coat: balṭu, balaaṭi.
sport coat, jacket: jaakit, -aat / jawaakit; swiitar, -aat.
suit coat: jakitta, -aat.
cocaine: kukayiin.
cockroach: ṣurṣaar, ṣaraṣiir.
cocoa: kakaaw.
coconut: gooz hind.
coeducational school: madrasa muxtalaṭa, madaaris muxtalaṭa.
coffee: ʕahwa.
coffee with milk: ʕahwa bil-laban.
French coffee: ʕahwa faransaawi.
instant coffee: niskafee.
Turkish coffee: ʕahwa turki.
with no sugar: ʕahwa saada.
with a little sugar: ʕahwa ɛa-r-riiɦa.
with some sugar: ʕahwa mazbuuṭ / maẓbuuṭ.
with lots of sugar: ʕahwa ziyaada.
raw coffee: bunn.
beans: bunnᵉ ɦabb.
coarse-ground: maṭɦuun faransaawi; magruuʃ.
fine-ground: maṭɦuun turki; naaɛim.
roasted, unground: miɦammaṣ; miʃ maṭɦuun; ɦabbaat.
coffee pot (*for Turkish*): kanaka, -aat / kanak.
coffeeshop (*café*): ʕahwa, ʕahaawi.
(*where food is served*): kafitirya, -aat.
coil (n) (*electric*): bubinaaj, bubiina.
coin (n), *currency*: ɛumla.
silver coins: faḍḍa.

metal currency:
εumla maεdaniyya.
coincidence: ṣuḍfa, ṣuḍaf.
by coincidence:
biṣ-ṣuḍfa; ṣuḍfa.
colcassia, taro roots: ʕulʕaas (-a, -aat).
cold (adj): *I'm* (m) *cold*: ʕana bardaan;
she's cold: hiyya bardaana.
to get / feel cold:
birid, yibrad; siʕiε, yisʕaε.
it (*the weather*) *is cold*:
ʕid-dinya bard.
cold carbonated drink:
ɦaaga saʕεa.
ice cold: saaʕiε, -iin; mitallig, -iin.
ice cold water: mayya saʕεa.
ice cold beer: biira saʕεa.
cold (n) (*illness*): bard.
colic: mayaṣ.
collar: koola, -aat; yaaʕa. -aat.
colleague: zimiil, zumala / zamaayil.
collect (v): gamaε, yigmaε; lamm, yilimm.
collection: magmuuεa. -aat.
collector: gaamiε, -iin; muɦaṣṣil, -iin.
college (*school, part of a university*): kulliyya, -aat.
collide: ʕitṣaaḍim, yitṣaaḍim (bi, maεa).
collision: taṣaaḍum, -aat.
Colloquial Arabic: (ʕil-luya) il-εammiyya.
colon (*large intestine*): qawloon.
colonel: εaqiid.
color: loon, ʕalwaan.
in color: bil-ʕalwaan; milawwin, -iin.
color blindness: εama ʕalwaan.
colored: milawwin, -iin.
colt: muhr, muhuur.
column, pillar: εamuud, εawamiid / ʕaεmida.
comb (n): miʃt, ʕamʃaaṭ.
comb (v): sarraɦ, yisarraɦ.
come: ga, yiigi; (imperative): taεaala, -i (f), -u (pl).
come back: rigiε, yirgaε.
come before: sabaʕ, yisbaʕ.
come in: daxal, yudxul; xaʃʃ, yixuʃʃ.
come out: xarag, yuxrug.
come up / out: ṭiliε, yiṭlaε.
coming (part): gayy, -iin.
he's coming soon:
zaman-u gayy.
the coming, the next:
ʕilli gayy / ʕig-gayy.
comedy: kumidya, -aat.
comfort (n): raaɦa.
comforts, luxuries:
kamaliyyaat.
comfortable (*e.g. a chair*): muriiɦ, -iin.
feeling comfortable:
mistirayyaɦ, -iin; mirtaaɦ -iin.
comma: faṣla, -aat.
comment (n): taεliiʕ, -aat; taεliiq, -aat (cl).
comment (v) (on): εallaʕ, yiεallaʕ (εala).

commerce (n): tigaara.
commercial (adj): tugaari, -yyiin.
commercial, advertisement (n): ʕiεlaan, -aat.
committee: lagna, ligaan.
common, wide-spread: muntaʃir, -iin.
shared: muʃtarak, -iin.
commotion: dawʃa.
communicate intelligently with: ʕitfaahim, yitfaahim maεa.
communications: muwaṣlaat.
communism (n): ʕiʃ-ʃuyuεiyya.
communist: ʃiyuuεi -yyiin.
company: *firm, business*: ʃirka / ʃarika, ʃarikaat.
guests: ḍuyuuf; maεaziim.
compared to: bil-muqarna bi.
comparison: muqarna, muqaranaat.
compensate, make up for: εawwaḍ, yiεawwaḍ.
compete with: naafis, yinaafis; ʕitnaafis, yitnaafis maεa.
competition: munafsa.
complain: ʕiʃtaka, yiʃtiki.
complaint: ʃakwa, ʃakaawi.
complete (adj): kaamil, -iin.
complete (v): kammil, ykammil.
complete, finish: xallaṣ, yixallaṣ.
complex (n) (*as in Oedipus*): εuʢda, εuʢad.
complex, complicated (adj): miεaʢʢad, -iin.
component, element: εunṣur, εanaaṣir.
compose: ʕallif, yiʕallif.
composer: muʕallif, -iin.
composition: *school subject*: ʕinʃa / ʕinʃaaʕ.
essay: ʕinʃa taɦriiri; maqaala, -aat.
compulsory: ʕigbaari; ʕilzaami.
computer: εaʢl^e ʕiliktirooni; kumbiyuutar.
conceited: maɣruur, -iin; mutakabbir / mitkabbar.
concentrate (v): rakkiz, yirakkiz (εala).
concentration: tarkiiz.
concept: mafhuum, mafahiim; fikra, ʕafkaar.
concern (v): hamm, yihimm.
to be concerned with: ʕihtamm, yihtamm bi.
as far as I'm concerned: bin-nisbaa-li.
concern, case (n): daεwa, daεaawi.
it's no concern of mine: ma-lii-ʃ daεwa.
concert: ɦafla musiqiyya, ɦaflaat musiqiyya.
conclude (tr): tammim, yitammin; ʕanha, yinhi.
condenser: kundinsar, -aat.
condition: *state*: ɦaal, ʕaɦwaal.
a particular situation, case: ɦaala, -aat.
stipulation: ʃarṭ, ʃuruuṭ.
condolences (*on a death*): taεziyya, -att / taεaazi.
paying of condolences (n): εaza.

to pay condolences (v): ɛazza, yiɛazzi.
place where condolences are offered: maɛza, maɛaazi.
condom: waaqi zakari.
conductor, ticket man: kumsaari, (pl) -yya.
conference, convention, meeting: muʕtamar, -aat.
confidence: siqa.
I (m) *have confidence in you* (m): ʕana waasiq fiik; ɛand-i siqa fiik.
confirm, verify: ʕakkid, yiʕakkid.
confuse: laxbaṭ, yilaxbaṭ; bargil, yibargil.
confused: mitlaxbaṭ, -inn.
to get confused: ʕitlaxbaṭ, yitlaxbaṭ.
confusion: laxbaṭa, laxabiiṭ; bargil, yibargil.
congested, crowded: zaɧma (invar); muzdaɧim, -iin..
congratulate: hanna, yihanni; baarik, yibaarik li.
congratulations!: mabruuk!
conjugate (*e.g. a verb*): ṣarraf, yiṣarraf.
connection: ɛilaaʕa, -aat; ṣila, -aat.
in connection with: bin-nisba li.
connections: *communication, transportation, business*: ʕittiṣalaat.
(*improper*) *connections, influence*: wasṭa, wasaayiṭ; koosa.
to use connections and bribes: kawwis, yikawwis.
conscience: ḍamiir, ḍamaayir.
consider, believe: ʕiɛtabar, yiɛtibir.
considerate, good-hearted (adj): ṭayyib, -iin.
consonant: ɧarf^{e} saakin, ɧuruuf sakna / sawaakin.
constipation: ʕimsaak.
consul: ʕunṣul, ʕanaaṣil.
consulate: ʕunṣuliyya, -aat.
contact (n): ʕittiṣaal, -aat.
(*improper*) *contacts, influence*: wasṭa, wasaayiṭ; koosa.
ignition contact: kuntakt / kuntaak.
contact (v): ʕittaṣal, yittiṣil bi.
contagious: muɛdi.
contagious disease: maraḍ muɛdi.
contents (*table of*): muɧtawayaat.
contest (n): musabʕa, -aat.
continue: ʕistamarr, yistamirr+fi.
complete, finish: kammil, yikammil (+def. n);
fiḍil, yifḍal (+adj or imp. v)
continuously: bi-stimraar.
contract (n): ɛaʕd, ɛuʕuud.
contract for wedding: katb ik-kitaab.
contrary: ɛaks.
on the contrary: bil-ɛaks.
act contrary to: xaalif, yixaalif.

control (v): saytٟar, yisaytٟar
(εala).

convenient: munaasib, -iin.
*to be convenient
for*: naasib, yinassib.

convention center: qaaεit
muʃtamaraat.

conversation: ĥadiis, ʕaĥadiis.
*conversation exercise in
classroom*: muĥadsa, -aat.

cook (n): tٟabbaax, -iin.

cook (v): tٟabax, yutٟbux.

cooked (adj): matٟbuux.

cooked, not raw: mistiwi, -yyiin.

cooker (*Am.: stove*): butagaaz,
-aat.

cookies (*Br.: biscuits*): baskoot
(-a, -aat).

cooking (n) *act of cooking*: tٟabx;
tٟabiix.
a cooked meal: tٟabxa, -aat.

cool: baarid, -iin.
cool (*weather*): tٟaraawa (invar).

cool off: birid, yibrad.

coolness (*weather*): tٟaraawa
(invar).

cooperate: ʕitεaawin, yitεaawin
(maεa).

cooperation: taεaawun.

copper: naĥaas ʕaĥmar.

Copt, Coptic: ʕibtٟi, ʕaʕbaatٟ.

copy, photocopy (n): sٟuura,
sٟuwar; nusxa, nusax.

copy, photocopy (v): sٟawwar,
yisٟawwar.

copying, photocopying (n):
tٟasٟwiir.

coral: murgaan / margaan.
(*coral*) *reef*: ʃieba, ʃieab.

cord, wire: silk, ʕaslaak.

corduroy: ʕatٟiifa midٟallaεa.

core, central part: sٟulb; ʕalb.

coriander: kuzbara / kusbara.

coriander seeds: bizr[e] kuzbara.

cork (n): fill (-a, -aat).

corkscrew: fattaaĥjit fill,
fattaĥaat fill.

corn (*Br.: maize*): dura; (*Am.:
wheat*): ʕamĥ.
corn cob: kuuz dura,
kizaan dura.

corner (*of street*): nasٟya,
nawaasٟi.
(*of room*): rukn, ʕarkaan.

cornstarch, starch: niʃa.

correct (adj): mazbuutٟ, -iin;
sٟaĥĥ (invar).
you're right: εandak
(-ik, -uku) ĥaʕʕ.

correct (v): sٟaĥĥaĥ, yisٟaĥĥaĥ,
sٟallaĥ, yisٟallaĥ.

correspond with (*write to*):
raasil, yiraasil;
ʕitraasil, yitraasil maεa.

corrupt (adj): faasid;
fasdaan, -iin.

corrupt (v) (tr): fasad, yifsid.
*to become corrupt
(intr)*: fisid, yifsad.

corruption: fasaad (no pl).

cost (n): taklifa, takaliif.

cost (v) (s.o.): kallif, yikallif.
*How much does it
cost?*: bi-kaam?

cotton: ʕuʈn.
a piece of cotton:
ɦittit ʕuʈn; ʕuʈna, -aat.
cotton wool, absorbant cotton: ʕuʈn ʈibbi.
sewing cotton (thread):
xeeʈ, xuyuuʈ / xiʈaan.
couch, sofa: kanaba, kanab / -aat.
cough (n): kuɦɦa; suεaal.
cough (v): kaɦɦ, yikuɦɦ.
could (*from "can"*): ʕidir, yiʕdar.
could you ...?:
mumkin ...?; tiʕdar ...?
council: maglis, magaalis.
count, enumerate: εadd, yiεidd.
counter (*in a store*): kawntar.
(*in a kitchen*): dulaab, dawaliib.
counterfeit, false: falʂu (invar);
mizayyif / muzayyaf;
mizawwar.
country: balad, bilaad.
(*countryside*): riif, ʕaryaaf.
courage: ʃagaaεa.
take courage: ʃiddᵉ ɦeelak.
courageous, brave: ʃugaaε,
ʃugεaan.
courgettes, zucchini: koosa /
kuusa (kusaaya, -aat).
course (**class**): kurs, -aat;
maadda, mawaadd.
course of a river, etc.:
magra, magaari.
of course: ʈabεan.
court (*e.g. a tennis court*):
malεab, malaaεib.
court of law:
maɦkama, maɦaakim.

courtyard: ɦooʃ, ʕiɦwaaʃ /
ɦiʃaan; ʂaɦn, ʂuɦuun.
couscous: kuskusi.
cousin: *son / daughter of paternal uncle / aunt*:
ʕibn / bintᵉ εamm / εamma.
son / daugher of maternal uncle / aunt:
ʕibn / bintᵉ xaal / xaala.
cousins: (m) wilaad /
(f) banaat εamm / xaal etc.
cover (n) (lid, top): ɣaʈa, ɣuʈyaan.
wrapper, casing:
ɣilaaf / ɣulaaf, -aat / ɣilifa /
ʕaɣlifa / ʕiɣlifa.
cover (v) (tr): ɣaʈʈa, yiɣaʈʈi.
coward: gabaan, gubana.
cowardice: gubn.
cowboy: raaεi baʕar, ruεaat
baʕar.
cows: baʕar (-a, -aat).
crabs: kaburya (kaburaaya, -aat);
ʕabu galambu.
cramp (n) (*contraction*):
taqalluʂ, -aat.
stomach cramps e.g., during period: maɣaʂ.
muscle cramp: taqalluʂ
εaɖali.
crankcase: εilbit karank;
karteer.
crankshaft: εamuud karank.
crash, collide (v): ʕitʂaadim,
yitʂaadim (bi, maεa).
crash, collision (n): taʂaadum,
-aat.
crazy: magnuun, maganiin.

cream (n): ʕiʃṭa.
sour cream: ʕiʃṭa fallaaɦi; ʕiʃṭa miziz.
whipping cream: kireem ʃantii.
full cream: kaamil id-dasam.
half cream: niṣf id-dasam; nuṣṣ^e dasam.
creche, nativity stable: maɣaara.
credit (*delayed payment*): ʃukuk.
on credit: bid-deen; ʃukuk.
crescent: hilaal.
cress, rocket, arugula: gargiir.
crewcut: ɦalʕa-ngiliizi.
crime: gariima, garaayim; ginaaya, -aat.
crisis: ʕazma, ʕazamaat.
crisps (*Am.: potato chips*): ʃibs.
crocodile: timsaaɦ, tamasiiɦ.
croissant: kurwasaan.
crop (n): maɦṣuul, maɦaṣiil.
cross (n): ṣaliib, ṣulbaan.
cross (v): ɛadda, yiɛaddi.
a crossing: taɛdiyya.
cross off: ʃaṭab, yuʃtub.
crossroads, intersection: taʕaaṭuɛ, -aat.
crosswalk, pedestrian crossing: ɛubuur muʃaah.
crow (n): ɣuraab, ɣirbaan.
crowded, crowdedness: zaɦma (invar).
crumb: fatfuuta, fatafiit.
cry, weep (v): ɛayyaṭ, yiɛayyaṭ.
cry, make a trilling sound: zaɣrat, yizaɣrat.
cubes of meat: kabaab ɦalla.
cucumbers: xiyaar (-a, -aat).
cuff, fold, hem (n): ṭanya, -aat.
(*on trousers, Br.: turn-up*): ṭanya, -aat.
(*on shirt*): ʕaswira, ʕaṣaawir.
cuff, fold, hem (v): tana,˙yitni.
cuff links: zaraayir, ʕamiiṣ.
culture (*arts, etc.*): saqaafa, -aat.
cultured: musaqqaf, -iin.
cumin: kammuun.
cup: fingaan / fingaal, fanagiin / fanagiil.
cupboard, closet: dulaab, dawaliib.
curfew: ɦaẓr it-tagawwul.
lifting the curfew: rafɛ^e ɦaẓr it-tagawwul.
curiosity (*love of knowledge*): ɦubb il-istiṭlaaɛ; fuḍuul.
curious: fuḍuuli, -yyiin; ɛand-u (-aha, etc.) fuḍuul; ɛand-u (-aha, etc.) ɦubb istiṭlaaɛ.
curl (v) (tr): laff, yiliff.
curler (*for hair*): bigudii; rulooh, -aat.
curly: mimawwig; ʕundulee.
coarse textured hair: ʃaɛr^e xiʃin; ʃaɛr^e zayy^e liif.
current (*elect.*): tayyaar, -aat.
curriculum (*list of courses*): manhag, manaahig.
curry: kaari.
curtain: sitaara, sataayir.
cushion: *pillow on bed*: maxadda, -aat.
large pillow to sit on on floor or sofa: ʃalta, ʃilat.

pillow to lean against on sofa: xudadiyya, -aat.
custom, habit: ɛaada, -aat.
custom, tradition: taqliid, taqaliid / taʕaliid.
customer: zibuun, zabaayin.
customs (*e.g. at airport*): gumruk, gamaarik.
cut, (v) *cut off*: ʕaṭaɛ, yiʕṭaɛ.
cut off, severed (part): maʕṭuuɛ.
cut up (*into pieces*): ʕaṭṭaɛ, yiʕaṭṭaɛ.
cut with scissors: ʕaṣṣ, yiʕuṣṣ.
cut, wound (*e.g. one's finger*): garaḥ, yigraḥ.
cut, wounded (part): magruuḥ, -iin.
cut, hair cut (n): (*men*): ḥilaaʕa. (*men or women*): ʕaṣṣa.
cute (*charming*): ẓariif, ẓuraaf; (*sweet*): ʕammuur, ʕamamiir.
cutlery: sirviis.
cutter (*paper cutter*): sikkiinit waraʕ, sakakiin waraʕ.
cylinder: silindar / ʃilindar, -aat.
Cyprus: ʕubruṣ.

D

Dad (**father**): baaba.
dam: sadd, suduud. *The High Dam*: ʕis-sadd il-ɛaali.
damage (v): bawwaẓ, yibawwaẓ.
damaged: baayiẓ, -iin; xasraan, -iin.
to get damaged: baaẓ, yibuuẓ; xisir, yixsar.
Damascus: dimiʃq.
dance (n): raʕṣa, -aat.
dance (v): raʕaṣ, yurʕuṣ.
dancer (f): raʕʕaaṣa, -aat.
belly dancer: raʕʕaaṣa baladi.
dancing: raʕṣ.
dandruff: ʕiʃr.
danger: xaṭar, ʕaxṭaar.
dangerous: xaṭiir, -iin.
daring, bold, audacious: garii ʕ, -iin.
dark (*color*): ɣaamiʕ, -iin.
dark skinned: ʕasmar, (f) samra, sumr.
dark meat (*thigh, leg*): wirk.
dark, darkness (*absence of light*): ḍalma.
it is dark: ʕid-dinya ḍalma.
date (*e.g. of a letter*): tariix, tawariix.
date, appointment: maɛaad, mawaɛiid.
dates (*fruit*): balaɦ (-a, -aat).
daughter: bint, banaat.
dawn: fagr.
day: yoom, ʕayyaam (tiyyaam after nos. 3–10).
these days, nowadays: ʕil-ʕayyaam di.
daydreaming (part): sarɦaan, -iin.
daylight saving time, summer time: tawqiit / tawʕiit ṣeefi.
daytime: nahaar.
dead (n, adj): mayyit, -iin.
passed away: mitwaffi, -yiin.
deadline: maɛaad nihaaʕi, mawaɛiid nihaʕiyya; ʕaaxir maɛaad.
deaf: ʕaṭraʃ, (f) ṭarʃa, ṭurʃ.
deal (n) *make a deal*: ʕittafaʕ, yittifiʕ (maɛa *s.o.* ɛala *s.t.*).
dean: ɛamiid, ɛumada.
dear (*term of endearment*): ɛaziiz, ɛuzaaz.
expensive: ɣaali, -yiin.
death: moot; wafaa.
debt: deen, diyuun.
in debt, indebted: madyuun, -iin.
deceitful: xaddaaɛ, -iin.
deceitful, swindler: ʕawanṭagi, (pl), -yya.
deceive: xadaɛ, yixdaɛ; xamm, yixumm; diɦik, yidɦak ɛala; waham, yiwhim.
December: disimbir.
decide: qarrar, yiqarrar.
decision: qaraar, -aat.
deck of cards: kutʃiina.
decorate: zayyin, yizayyin.
decoration: ziina, zinaat.

deep water (*in swimming pool, sea*): ɣariiʕ.
defeat (n): haziima, hazaayim.
defeat (v): hazam, yihzim.
(*in a game*): ɣalab, yiɣlib.
defendant, accused: muttaham, -iin.
defense: difaaɛ.
defense of a thesis: munaqʃit risaala.
deficit: ɛagz.
definition: taɛriif, taɛariif.
defraud (*e.g., prices*): ʕitlaaɛib, yitlaaɛib bi.
defrost: sayyaɦ, yisayyaɦ.
degree (*diploma*): dibloom, -aat; ʃahaada, -aat.
(*temperature*): daraga, -aat.
delay (v): ʕaxxar, yiʕaxxar.
delay, interrupt work, study, etc.: ɛaṭṭal, yiɛaṭṭal.
delicate, fragile: raʕiiʕ, ruʕaaʕ.
delicious: laziiz, luzaaz.
deliver, hand over: sallim, yisallim.
transport: wadda, yiwaddi; waṣṣal, yiwaṣṣal.
transmit: ballaɣ, yiballaɣ.
delivery: tawṣiil.
home delivery: tawṣiil manazil.
Delta (*The Nile Delta*): ʕid-dilta; ʕil-wagh il-baɦari.
demand (v): ṭalab, yuṭlub; ṭaalib, yiṭaalib bi.
demon: ɛafriit, ɛafariit.
demonstration (*political, etc.*): muẓahra, -aat.
(*explanation*): ʃarɦ, ʃuruuɦ; tawḍiiɦ.
den, study, office: ʕooḍit maktab.
dentist: duktoor ʕasnaan, dakatrit ʕasnaan.
dentistry, college of: kulliyyit ṭibb il-ʕasnaan.
deny: nafa, yinfi; nakar, yinkir.
depart, leave: miʃi, yimʃi.
department: ʕism / qism, ʕaʕsaam / ʕaqsaam.
governmental administration: maṣlaɦa, maṣaaliɦ; ʕidaara, -aat.
depend on: ʕiɛtamad, yiɛtimid ɛala; ʕittakal, yittikil ɛala.
it depends (*on*): ɦasab; yitwaʕʕaf (ɛala).
dependable, reliable: ṣulb, yuɛtamad ɛaleeh.
deposit (n), *down payment*: ɛarbuun, ɛarabiin.
(*on a bottle*): rahn, ruhunaat.
advance payment: muʕaddam.
deposit (v) (*money, in a bank*): ɦaṭṭ, yiɦuṭṭ; wadaɛ, yiwdaɛ (filuus).
depressed, sad: muktaʕib, -iin.
depression, low spirits: ʕiktiʕaab.
dermatologist: duktoor ʕamraaḍ gildiyya.
descend: nizil, yinzil.
describe: waṣaf, yiwṣif.
description: waṣf, ʕawṣaaf.
desert (adj): ṣaɦraawi.
desert (n): ṣaɦra, ṣaɦaara.

desert (v) (tr): hagar, yuhgur.
deserted: mahguur.
design, interior design: dikoor, -aat.
interior designer: muhandis dikoor.
desk: maktab, makaatib.
despite, in spite of: *against the wishes of*: ɣaṣbin ɛan.
in spite of (*the circumstances*): bir-raɣm^e min.
dessert: ɦilw.
destroy: dammar, yidammar; xarrab, yixarrab.
demolish: hadd, yihidd.
detail: tafṣiil (-a, -aat / tafaṣiil).
in detail: bit-tafṣiil.
detain, block: ɦagaz, yiɦgiz.
develop (*film*): ɦammaḍ, yiɦammaḍ.
development, *progress* (tr): taṭwiir.
(intr): taṭawwur, -aat.
(*of film*): taɦmiiḍ.
devil, devilish: ʃiṭaan, ʃayaṭiin.
diabetes: maraḍ is-sukkar.
dial (*a number*): ḍarab, yiḍrab (nimra).
dialect: lahga, -aat.
Colloquial Arabic: (ʕil-luɣa) il-ɛammiyya.
dialogue: ɦiwaar.
diamond: ʕalmaaẓ.
diaper (*Br.*: *nappy*): kafuula, kawafiil;
bambas (*Pampers*).
diarrhea: ʕishaal.
diary (*memoirs*): muzakkaraat.
(*appointment book*): ʕajenda.
dictate: malla, yimalli.
dictation: ʕimla.
dictator: diktatoor; ɦaakim mustabidd, ɦukkaam mustabiddiin.
dictionary: qamuus, qawamiis.
die: maat, yimuut
I nearly died: kunt^e hamuut.
pass away: ʕitwaffa, yitwaffa.
diesel: diizil.
diet: rijiim.
be on a diet: ɛaamil (ɛamla) rijiim.
differ (*from*): ʕixtalaf, yixtilif (ɛan).
difference: ʕixtilaaf, -aat; farʕ, furuuʕ.
different (*from*): muxtalif, -iin (ɛan).
a little different: muxtalif ʃiwayya.
other than: ɣeer.
difficult: ṣaɛb, -iin.
difficulty: ṣuɛuuba, -aat.
with difficulty: bi-ṣuɛuuba.
dig: ɦafar, yuɦfur; faɦar, yifɦar; faɦat, yifɦat.
digest (v): haḍam, yihḍim.
digging: ɦafr.
dill: ʃabat.
dimple: ɣammaaza, -aat.
dine: ʕitɛaʃʃa, yitɛaʃʃa.
dining room: ʕooḍit sufra.

dinner: εaʃa.
to eat dinner:
ʕitεaʃʃa, yitεaʃʃa.
diploma: dibloom, -aat;
ʃahaada, -aat.
diplomat, diplomatic:
diblumaasi, -yyiin.
diplomatically, tactfully: bis-siyaasa.
direct: mubaaʃir, -iin.
direct communication:
ʕittiṣaal mubaaʃir.
direction: ʕittigaah, -aat.
one-way street:
ʃaariε ittigaah waaɦid.
director: mudiir, -iin.
directory: daliil (no pl).
dirt, *dust, earth*: turaab, ʕatriba.
filth: wasax, ʕawsaax;
qazaara, ʕaqzaar (cl).
dirty: wisix, -iin; miʃ niḍiif, miʃ nuḍaaf.
obscene: ʕabiiɦ.
disadvantage: εeeb, εuyuub;
εaaʕiq; ḍarar .
disagree (*with*): ʕixtalaf, yixtilif (maεa).
disagreement: xilaaf, -aat;
ʕixtilaaf, -aat.
disappoint (tr) (*my hopes*):
xayyib, yixayyib (ʕamaal-i).
(intr) *be disappointed*:
ʕitxayyib, yitxayyib.
discount: taxfiiḍ, -aat; xaṣm, xuṣumaat.
discover: ʕiktaʃaf, yiktiʃif.
discrimination, racial: tafriʕa εunṣuriyya; tamyiiz εunṣuri.
sexual discrimination:
tafriʕa ginsiyya.
discuss: naaʕiʃ, yinaaʕiʃ.
discuss (s.t. with s.o.):
ʕitnaaʕiʃ, yitnaaʕiʃ (fi ... maεa).
disease: maraḍ, ʕamraaḍ.
chronic disease:
maraḍ muzmin.
disgusted: ʕarfaan, -iin.
disgusting: muʕrif, -iin.
dish: plate: ṭabaʕ, ʕaṭbaaʕ / ʕiṭbaaʕ (tiṭbaaʕ after nos. 3–10); ṣaɦn, ṣuɦuun.
meal: ʕakla, -aat;
wagba, -aat (*one of the daily three meals*).
(*to wash*) *the dishes*:
(ɣasal, yiɣsil) ʕil-mawaεiin.
dish drainer: maṭbaʕiyya, -aat.
dish washer: ɣassaalit, ɣassalaat mawaεiin / ṣuɦuun.
disk: disk, -aat.
disobey: xaalif, yixaalif.
disorganization: fawḍa.
disposition: mazaag, ʕamziga;
keef.
dispute: xilaaf, -aat.
dissertation: risaaḷa, rasaayil.
distance: masaafa, -aat; buεd.
at a distance of:
εala buεd.
distant: biεiid, buεaad.
distilled water: mayya mʕaṭṭara.
distress, upset (n): zaεal.

distress, upset (v): zaεεal, yizaεεal.
distressed: zaεlaan, -iin; middaayiʕ, -iin.
distributor: ʕasbirateer, -aat.
distributor cap: ɣaṭa ʕasbirateer.
distributor rotor: ʃakuuʃ, ʃawakiiʃ.
district: *region, area*: manṭiʕa, manaaṭiʕ.
suburb: ḍaaɦiya, ḍawaaɦi.
disturb: daayiʕ, yidaayiʕ; ʕazεag, yizεig.
be disturbed: ʕinzaεag, yinziεig; ʕiddaayiʕ, yiddaayiʕ.
disturbance: dawʃa; ʕizεaag.
dive (n): ɣaṭsa, -aat.
dive (v): ɣiṭis / ɣuṭus, yiɣṭas.
diving (n): ɣaṭs.
diving center: markaz ɣaṭs.
diving mask: naḍḍaarit ɣaṭs.
diver: ɣaṭṭaas, -iin.
divide: ʕasam, yiʕsim.
division (*part in hair*): farʕ.
division, department: qism, ʕaqsaam.
divorce (n): ṭalaaʕ.
divorce (v) (*man*): ṭallaʕ, yiṭallaʕ.
to be divorced (*woman*): ʕiṭṭallaʕit, tiṭṭallaʕ.
divorced (part): miṭṭallaʕa, -iin.
dizziness: dooxa.
dizzy: daayix, -iin.
to become dizzy: daax, yiduux.
to make dizzy: dawwax, yidawwax.
do: εamal, yiεmil.
doctor: duktoor, dakatra.
doctorate: dukturaa.
dog: kalb, kilaab.
doily: mafraʃ danteel ṣuɣayyar.
doll (*girl doll*): εaruusa, εaraayis.
dollar: dolaar, -aat.
donkey: ɦumaar, ɦimiir.
don't (*order to cease s.t. or cancel previous request*): balaaʃ.
door: baab, ʕabwaab / bibaan.
door bell: garas baab.
doorkeeper, doorman: bawwaab, -iin.
doorknob: ʕukra, ʕukar.
dormitory, hostel: beet, buyuut ṭalaba.
for female students: beet, buyuut ṭalibaat.
double (adj): muzdawag.
double image (*on television*): xayaal, -aat; ṣurteen.
double (n) (*room in hotel*): ʕooḍa waɦda li-ʃaxṣeen.
doubt (n): ʃakk, ʃukuuk.
no doubt: min ɣeer ʃakk.
there is no doubt: mafiiʃ ʃakk.
doubt (v): ʃakk, yiʃukk.
I doubt it: ʕaʃukk^e f-kida.
down, downstairs: taɦt.
downtown: wisṭ il-balad.
to go downtown: nizil il-balad, yinzil il-balad.

dozen: dasta, disat.
draft, rough copy: muswadda, -aat.
dragoman: turgumaan, taragma.
drain (n): ballaaεa, -aat.
drain (v) (*through a strainer*): ṣaffa, yiṣaffi.
drainer (*for dishes*): maṭbaʕiyya.
drama: diraama.
draw near: ʕarrab, yiʕarrab (min).
drawer: durg, ʕadraag.
drawing pin (*Am.*: *thumb tack*): dabbuus, dababiis rasm.
dream (n): ɦilm, ʕaɦlaam
dream (v): ɦilim, yiɦlam.
dress (n): fustaan, fasatiin.
dress (v) (intr): libis, yilbis. (tr): labbis, yilabbis.
dressed (part): laabis, -iin.
dressing room, changing room: ʕooḍit, ʕuwaḍ libs.
dressmaker: *woman*: xayyaaṭa, -aat.
man: (*does dresses only*): xayyaaṭ, -iin.
(*does coats too*) tarzi, (pl) -yya (ɦariimi).
dried: naaʃif, -iin.
dried fruit: mugaffaf, -iin.
drill (n) (*tool*): ʃanyuur, ʃanayiir.
drink (n): maʃruub, -aat.
drink (v): ʃirib, yiʃrab.
I (m) *have just had a drink*: ʕana lissa ʃaarib.
drinking fountain: ɦanafiyya, -aat.
drip (n): nuʕṭa, nuʕaṭ.
drip (v): naʕʕaṭ, yinaʕʕaṭ.
drive: saaʕ, yisuuʕ.
drive s.o. crazy: gannin, yigannin.
driver: sawwaaʕ, -iin.
hey driver!: ya ʕusṭa.
driver's license: ruxṣit siwaaʕa.
drop (n): *drop, fall*: saʕṭa, -aat; waʕεa, -aat.
drop of water: nuʕṭit mayya.
drop (v) (*intr into a hole, etc.*): saʕaṭ, yisʕaṭ.
(tr): waʕʕaε, yiwaʕʕaε.
fall down: wiʕiε, yuʕaε.
drown (intr): ɣiriʕ, yiɣraʕ.
drowsy, sleepy: naεsaan, -iin.
drug (v): xaddar, yixaddar.
drugs (*pharmaceutical*): dawa, ʕadwiya.
(*illegal*): muxaddaraat.
drum (n) (*cylinder*): ṭambuur, ṭanabiir.
brake drum: ṭambuurit farmala.
drum (*musical instrument*): ṭabl, ṭubuul.
drunk (adj): sakraan, -iin / sakaara.
to get drunk (v): sikir, yiskar.
dry (adj): naaʃif, -iin.
dry (v) (tr): naʃʃif, yinaʃʃif.
(intr) *to get dry*: niʃif, yinʃaf.
dry-cleaners: tanturleeh.
dry-cleaning: tanḍiif gaaff.
steam cleaning: tanḍiif buxaar.
dryer (n) (*clothes*): mugaffif.
(*hair*): siʃwaar, -aat.

ducks: baṭṭ (-a / -aaya, -aat).
dumb: *mute, unable to speak*: ʕaxras, xarsa, xurs. *stupid*: ɣabi, ʕaɣbiya.
during: fi xilaal; fi waʔt; ʕasnaaʔ.
dust (n): turaab; ɛufaar.
dust (v): naffaḍ, yinaffaḍ.
dust rag, dusting cloth: fuuṭa, fuwaṭ ṣafra; fuuṭit, fuwaṭ turaab.
dustbin, trash can: ṣafiiḥit, ṣafaayiḥ zibaala.
dustpan: garuuf, gawariif.
duty: waagib, -aat.
dwell, reside: sikin, yuskun.
dye (v): sabaɣ, yusbuɣ. *dyeing establishment*: masbaɣa, masaabiɣ.
dye (n): sabɣa, -aat.

E

e-mail: ʕimeel, -aat.
each: kull (+ indef n).
each one: kullᵉ waaɦid.
each other: baɛḍ.
ear: widn (f), widaan.
early: badri.
earn: kisib, yiksab.
earphone: sammaaɛa, -aat.
earrings (*a pair*): ɦalaʕ, ɦilʕaan / ɦulʕaan.
one earring: fardit ɦalaʕ.
clip-on earrings: ɦalaʕ kilibs.
earthquake: zilzaal, zalaazil; hazza, -aat.
ease: suhuula.
easier (comp): ʕashal (invar).
east: ʃarʕ.
the Middle East: ʕiʃ-ʃarq il-ʕawsaṭ.
Easter: ɛiid il-fiṣɦ; ɛiid il-ʕiyaama; ʕil-ɛiid ik-kibiir.
eastern: ʃarʕi, -yyiin.
Middle Eastern: ʃarʕi, -yyiin.
easy: sahl, -iin.
easily, with ease: bi-suhuula.
eat: ʕakal / kal, yaakul.
eat junk food: ramram, yiramram.
eat breakfast: fiṭir, yifṭar.
eat dinner, supper: ʕitɛaʃʃa, yitɛaʃʃa.
eat lunch: ʕitɣadda, yitɣadda.
economic, economical: ʕiqtiṣaadi, -yyiin.
economics, economy: ʕiqtiṣaad.
economize: ʕiqtaṣad, yiqtiṣid.
edge, border (n): ɦaffa, -aat.
tip; extremity: ṭarf / ṭaraf, ṭuruuf / ʕaṭraaf.
edition, printing (*e.g. first edition*): ṭabɛa, -aat.
editor: muɦarrir, -iin.
educated: mutaɛallim, -iin.
education: taɛliim.
college of education: kulliyyit tarbiya.
Ministry of Education: wizaarit it-tarbiya.
educational: taɛliimi; tarbawi.
effort: maghuud, -aat.
eggplant, aubergines: bidingaan / bitingaan (-a, -aat).
eggs: beeḍ (-a, -aat).
egoistic: ʕanaani, -yyiin.
Egypt: maṣr.
Lower (northern) Egypt: ʕil-wagh il-baɦari.
Upper (southern) Egypt: ʕiṣ-ṣiɛiid; ʕil-wagh il-ʕibli.
Egyptian: maṣri, -yyin.
Upper (southern) Egyptian: ṣiɛiidi, ṣaɛayda.
eight: tamanya; taman (before pl. n.).
eighteen: tamantaaʃar.
eighty: tamaniin.
either ... or: ya ... ya; ʕimma ... ʕaw; ya ʕimma ... ya ʕimma / ʕaw.

elastic (n): ʕastik.
piece of plastic (pl): ʕasaatik.
elbow: kuuɛ, kiɛaan.
election: ʕintixaab, -aat.
electric, electrical: kahrabaaʕi; bik-kahraba.
electric switch: muftaaɦ nuur, mafatiiɦ nuur.
push button: zuraar, zaraayir.
electrical outlet: bariiza.
electrician: kahrabaaʕi, -yya.
electricity: kahraba.
elegant, neat: ʃiik (invar); ʕaniiq, -iin.
element, component: ɛunṣur, ɛanaaṣir.
elementary school: madrasa-btidaʕiyya.
elephant: fiil, ʕafyaal.
elevator: ʕasanseer, -aat.
eleven: ɦidaaʃar.
eloquent: faṣiiɦ, fuṣaɦa.
embarrass: kasaf, yiksif; ʕaɦrag, yiɦrig.
embarrassed (adj): maksuuf, -iin; muɦrag, -iin.
to be embarrassed: ʕitkasaf, yitkisif.
embarrassment: *being embarrassed*: kusuuf.
embarrassing someone: ʕiɦraag.
embassy: sifaara, -aat.
embroidered: miṭarraz.
embroidery: burudri; taṭriiz.
emerald: zumurrud (-a, -aat).
emergency: ṭaariʕ, ṭawaariʕ.
state of emergency: ṭawaariʕ.
emperor: ʕimbiraṭoor.
employ: ɛayyin, yiɛayyin; waẓẓaf, yiwaẓẓaf.
employed, appointed: mitɛayyin, -iin.
employee: muwaẓẓaf, -iin; mustaxdam, -iin.
employment: tawẓiif.
empty (adj): faaḍi, -yiin.
empty (v) (tr): faḍḍa, yifaḍḍi.
(*intr*) *to become empty*: fiḍi, yifḍa.
encourage: ʃaggaɛ, yiʃaggaɛ.
encyclopedia: dayrit maɛaarif: mawsuuɛa.
end (n): nihaaya, -aat.
end of: ʕaaxir, ʕawaaxir; nihaayit.
at the end: fil-ʕaaxir.
end, edge (*top, bottom*): ṭarf, ṭuruuf / ʕaṭraaf.
end (v) (tr): ʕanha, yinhi; xallaṣ, yixallaṣ.
(intr): ʕintaha, yintihi; xiliṣ, yixlaṣ.
energetic: naʃiiṭ, nuʃaṭa / nuʃaaṭ.
energizer, vitalizer: miʕawwi / muqawwi, -yaat.
engage, get engaged to (v) (*man*): xaṭab, yuxṭub;
(*woman*): ʕitxaṭabit, titxiṭib li.
engaged (*man*): xaaṭib, -iin.
(*woman*): maxṭuuba, maxṭubiin.
engaged to each other: maxṭubiin li baɛḍ.

engagement: xuṭuuba, -aat.
engagement gift: ʃabka, -aat.
engagement ring: dibla, dibal.
engagement party: ɦaflit xuṭuuba.
engine, motor: mutoor, mawatiir / -aat.
engineer: muhandis, -iin.
engineering: handasa.
England: ʕingiltira.
English: ʕingiliizi, ʕingiliiz.
English Channel: ʕil-manʃ.
enjoy: ʕitmattaɛ, yitmattaɛ bi.
enjoy oneself: ʕinbasaṭ, yhinbisiṭ.
enjoyable: mumtiɛ, -iin; laziiz, luzaaz.
enlarge: kabbar, yikabbar.
enough: kifaaya (invar).
to be enough: kaffa, yikaffi; ʕaḍḍa, yiʕaḍḍi.
enroll (in): ʕiltaɦaʢ, yiltiɦiʢ (bi); daxal, yudxul.
enter: daxal, yudxul; xaʃʃ, yixuʃʃ.
entertaining: musalli, -yiin.
enthusiastic: mitɦammis, -iin.
entrance: (*act of entering*): duxuul.
(*door*): madxal, madaaxil; baab, ʕabwaab / bibaan.
entreat, beg: ʕitragga, yitragga; ʕitɦaayil, yitɦaayil ɛala.
entry, entering: duxuul.
enumerate: ɛaddid, yiɛaddid.
envelope: ẓarf, ʕuẓruf.
envious: ɦasuud, ɦussaad.
envy (n): ɦasad.
envy (v): ɦasad, yiɦsid.
Epiphany: ʕil-ɣiṭaas.
episode (*e.g. on TV*): ɦalaʢa, -aat.
episode, story: ɦikaaya, -aat.
equal (adj): mutasaawi, -yyiin.
equal (v): ɛaadil, yiɛaadil; ʕitsaawa, yitsaawa (maɛa).
equal to: ʢadd.
I'm not your equal (*I can't meet your standard*): ʕana miʃ ʢadd-ak.
equality: musawaah.
erase: masaɦ, yimsaɦ.
eraser; (*rubber eraser*): ʕastiika, ʕasatiik; gooma.
(*blackboard*): massaaɦa, -aat; baʃawra, -aat.
errand: miʃwaar, maʃawiir.
business, official errand: maʕmuriyya, -aat.
I have an errand to do: waraaya miʃwaar.
error: ɣalṭa, -aat.
escalator: sillim mutaɦarrik, salaalim mutaɦarrika.
escort (*e.g. someone home*) (v): waṣṣal, yiwaṣṣal.
especially: xuṣuuṣan.
essay, article: maqaala, -aat.
essential: ḍaruuri, -yyiin.
estimate (n) (*an approximate cost*): muʢaysa, -aat.
estimate, appraise (v): ʢaddar, yiʢaddar.
etc.: ʕilaxx … ʕilaxx.
ethics: ɛilm il-ʕaxlaaʢ.
Europe: ʕuruppa / ʕurubba.

evaluation, assessment: tɑqyiim.
even (adv): ɦatta.
even though: walaw; walaw-inn.
evening: misa.
good evening: masaaʕ il-xeer.
evening activity, party: sɑhrɑ, -ɑɑt.
evening dress: fustaan sɑhrɑ.
event, incident: ɦadas, ʕaɦdaas.
every: kull (+ indef. n).
every day: kull^{e} yoom.
every Sunday: kull^{e} yoom ɦadd.
every other day: yoom ʕaywa wi yoom laʕ; yoom wi yoom.
everyone, everybody: ʕik-kull; ʕig-gamiiɛ.
each one: kull^{e} waaɦid.
everything: kull^{e} ɦaaga.
everything is fine: kullu tamaam.
evil (adj): bɑṭṭɑɑl, -iin; wiɦiʃ, -iin; ʃirriir, ʕɑʃrɑɑr.
evil (n): ʃɑrr, ʃuruur.
exact: mɑẓbuuṭ, -iin.
exactly: biẓ-ẓɑbṭ.
exaggerate: hawwil, yihawwil; baaliɣ, yibaaliɣ.
exaggeration: mubalɣa; tahwiil.
examination: ʕimtiɦaan, -aat.
medical examination: kaʃf.
examine, to be examined: ʕimtaɦan, yimtiɦin.
examine medically: kaʃaf, yikʃif ɛala.
example: masal, ʕamsila.
for example: masalan.

exasperate: ɣɑɑẓ, yiɣiiẓ.
to become exasperated: ʕitɣɑɑẓ, yitɣɑɑẓ.
excel: ʕitfɑwwɑq, yitfɑwwɑq; ʕimtaaz, yimtaaz (ɛala).
excellency (*as polite address*): ɦɑḍrit-ɑk (-ik); siyadt-ak (-ik).
excellent: mumtaaz, -iin.
outstanding (*e.g., a student*): mutɑfɑwwiq, -iin.
except: ʕilla; maɛada.
exception: ʕistisnaaʕ, -aat.
exceptional: ʕistisnaaʕi, -yyiin.
exchange (v) (tr): ɣɑyyɑr, yiɣɑyyɑr.
(intr) (*be exchanged*): ʕitɣɑyyɑr, yitɣɑyyɑr.
interchange: ʕitbaadil, yitbaadil (maɛa).
excited, emotional: munfaɛil, -iin; haayig, -iin.
excursion: riɦla, -aat.
excuse (n): ɛuzr, ʕɑɛzɑɑr.
excuse, pretext: ɦigga, ɦigag.
excuse (v) *to offer excuses*: ʕitɦaggig, yitɦaggig. (bi).
to excuse oneself, to depart: ʕistaʕzin, yistaʕzin.
excuse me! (*apology*): maɛliʃʃ; la muʕaxza; ʕaasif, -iin; mutaʕassif, -iin.
(*get out of my way; excuse me for leaving*): ɛan ʕiznak, (-ik).
(*if you permit; calling attention*): law samaɦt (-i).

execute, *put to death*: ʕaɛdam, yiɛdim.
carry out, implement: naffiz, yinaffiz.
execution (*death sentence*): ʕiɛdaam.
(*implementation*): tanfiiz.
exempt (v): ɛafa, yiɛfi.
exempted: maɛfi, -yyiin; muɛaafa, muɛafiin.
exemption: ʕiɛfa; ʕiɛfaaʕ, -aat.
exercise (n): tamriin, tamariin.
physical exercise: riyaaḍa.
exercise (v): liɛib, yilɛab riyaada.
exhaust pipe: ʃakmaan, -aat.
exhausted: murhaq, -iin; taɛbaan, -iin; halkaan, -iin.
exhibition: maɛraḍ, maɛaariḍ.
existence: wuguud.
existing: mawguud, -iin.
expecting, pregnant: ɦaamil, ɦawaamil.
expel: rafad, yirfid; ṭarad, yuṭrud.
to be expelled: ʕitrafad, yitrifid; ʕiṭṭarad, yiṭṭirid.
expense: maṣruuf, maṣariif.
expensive: ɣaali, -yiin.
to become expensive: ɣili, yiɣla.
experience (n): xibra, -aat.
experiment (n): tagriba, tagaarib.
expert (adj): ɦirafi, -iin / -yya; ɦarriif, ɦarriifa.
expert (n): xabiir, xubara.
expire: ʕintaha, yintihi.
explain: ʃaraɦ, yiʃraɦ.
(*to cause to understand*): fahhim, yifahhim.
(*to cause to know*): ɛarraf, yiɛarraf.
explode: farʕaɛ, yifarʕaɛ; ʕinfagar, yinfigir.
exploit (v): ʕistaɣall, yistaɣill.
explosion: ʕinfigaar, -aat; farʕaɛa, -aat / faraʕiiɛ.
export (n): taṣdiir.
import and export: ʕistiraad wi taṣdiir.
export (v): ṣaddar, yiṣaddar.
express (adj): sariiɛ.
express letter: gawaab mistaɛgil.
express (v): ɛabbar, yiɛabbar (ɛan).
expression, phrase: ɛibaara, -aat; taɛbiir, -aat.
extension (*on phone*): daxli / daaxili (cl).
transfer me to ...: ɦawwil-ni ɛala ...
extension cord: waṣla, -aat (kahraba); silk^{e} / kabl^{e} tawṣiila.
with multi-plugs: muʃtarak (bis-silk); silk^{e} / kabl^{e} muʃtarak.
multi-socket plug: muʃtarak.
exterminate: (ʕa)baad, yibiid.
external, outside: xaarigi.
extinguish: ṭafa, yiṭfi.

extra: ziyaada.
extraordinary: ɣeer ɛaadi, -yyiin; fooʕ il-ɛaada.
extremely: xaaliṣ; giddan; fi muntaha (+ def. abstract n).
extremism: taṭarruf.
extremist: mutaṭarrif, -iin.
eye: ɛeen (f), ɛineen (dual), ɛuyuun.
his (her, etc.) eyes: ɛineeh (-ha etc.).
my eyes: ɛinayya.
eyeglasses: naḍḍaara, -aat.
sunglasses: naḍḍaarit ʃams.
eyeglass case: giraab, giriba / girabaat naḍḍaara.

F

fabric, cloth: ʕumaaʃ, -aat / ʕaʕmiʃa.
face (n): wiʃʃ, wuʃuuʃ / wuguuh.
face, confront (v): waagih, yiwaagih.
facing, opposite: ʕuṣaad; fi wiʃʃ.
fact: ɦaʕiiʕa, ɦaʕaayiʕ.
factory: maṣnaɛ, maṣaaniɛ.
faculty: (*college*): kulliyya, -aat.
(*teaching staff*): hayʕit tadriis; mudarrisiin; ʕasatza.
Faculty of Arts: kulliyyit ʕadaab.
fad, craze: taʕliiɛa, taʕaliiɛ; ɛulleema.
fail: fiʃil, yifʃal.
fail in an exam: siʕiṭ, yisʕaṭ.
failure: faʃal.
(*in an exam*): suʕuuṭ.
a total failure (*ref. to a person*): xaayib, -iin; faaʃil, -iin.
fair (adj) (*just*): ɛaadil, -iin.
(*hair or skin*): ʕaʃʕar, (f) ʃaʕra, ʃuʕr.
fair (n) (*exhibition*): maɛraḍ, maɛaariḍ.
fairy tale, legend: ʕusṭuura, ʕasaṭiir.
fake, imitation (adj): taqliid / taʕliid (invar).
counterfeit, false: muzayyaf, -iin.
fall (v): wiʕiɛ, yuʕaɛ.
fall into (*e.g. a hole*): siʕiṭ, yisʕaṭ.
fall, autumn (n): ʕil-xariif; faṣl il-xariif.
family: ɛeela, -aat / ɛaaʕilaat (cl).
parents: ʕahl.
famous: maʃhuur, -iin.
well-known: maɛruuf, -iin.
fan (n):
admirer: muɛgab, -iin.
enthusiast, devotee: ɣaawi.
ventilator: marwaɦa, maraawiɦ.
fan belt: seer marwaɦa.
fantastic, wonderful: haayil, -iin; mahuul, iin.
far: biɛiid, buɛaad.
fare (n): ʕugra.
farewell: wadaaɛ.
bid farewell, say goodbye to, see off: waddaɛ, yiwaddaɛ.
farm (*country estate*): ɛizba, ɛizab.
(*commercial*): mazraɛa, mazaariɛ.
farmer: muzaariɛ, -iin.
farther (comp): ʕabɛad (invar).
fashion: mooḍa, -aat.
fast (adv) (*quickly*): bi-surɛa.
fast (*quick*): sariiɛ, -iin.
(*ref. to watch / clock*): miʕaddima.
fast (v) (*abstain from food*): ṣaam, yiṣuum.
fasten, tie (v): rabaṭ, yurbuṭ.

fasting (n): ṣiyaam; ṣoom.
fasting (part): ṣaayim, -iin.
fat (adj): tixiin, tuxaan; simiin, sumaan.
to become fat: tixin, yitxan.
big like a wall: zayy il-ɦeeṭa.
fatter: ʕatxan.
fat (n): dihn, duhuun.
fat for cooking: samn / samna.
fate (n, pl): ʕil-maʕadiir; (n, s): ʕadar, qadar.
an act of fate / God: qaḍaaʕ wi-qadar.
father: ʕabb, ʕabbahaat; waalid (*formal*).
father of ...: ʕabu ...
dad: baaba
your dad: babaa-k (-ki, etc.).
father-in-law: ɦama.
my father-in-law: ɦamaaya.
faucet (*Br.*: *tap*): ɦanafiyya, -aat.
fava beans: fuul.
favor (n): gimiil, gamaayil.
do me the favor: ʕiɛmil maɛruuf; min faḍlak.
(*candy given to wedding guests*): milabbis.
favorable, preferable: mufaḍḍal, -iin.
favorite: ʕaɦabb; mufaḍḍal.
e.g. my favorite meal: ʕaɦabb^e ʕakla ɛand-l; ʕil-ʕakla-l-mufaḍḍala ɛandi.
fear (n): xoof.
fear, be afraid of (v): xaaf, yixaaf (min).
fearing (part): xaayif, -iin.
feast, holiday: ɛiid, ʕaɛyaad.
some Islamic feasts:
feast at end of Ramadan, Ramadan Bairam, Lesser Bairam: ɛiid il-fiṭr; ʕil-ɛiid iṣ-ṣuɣayyar.
feast of the sacrifice, Qurban Bairam, Greater Bairam: ɛiid il-ʕaḍɦa; ʕil-ɛiid ik-kibiir.
night of Muhammad's night journey and ascent to heaven: lelt-il-ʕisraaʕ wi-l-miɛraag.
night the Quran was revealed: lelt-il-ʕadr.
eve of a feast: yoom il-waʕfa.
feathers: riiʃ, (-a, -aat)
feather duster (*for cleaning*): riiʃa, riyaʃ (it-tanḍiif).
February: fibraayir.
fed up (part): zahʕaan, -iin; ʕarfaan, -iin.
to become fed up (*of*): zihiʕ, yizhaʕ (min).
feddan (*1.038 acres*): faddaan, fadadiin.
fee: rasm, rusuum.
feed (v): ʕakkil, yiʕakkil; wakkil, yiwakkil.
feel (v) (tr): gass, yigiss. (*e.g.* in-nabḍ, *the pulse*).
(intr): ɦass, yiɦiss (bi); ʃaɛar, yuʃɛur (bi).

I don't feel like eating: nifs-i masduuda; ma-lii-ʃ nifs aakul.
feeling: ʃuεuur, maʃaaεir; ʕiɦsaas, ʕaɦasiis.
female (adj) (*plants or animals*): nitaaya, nity.
(*human*): ʕunsa, ʕinaas.
feminine (gr): muʕannas.
fence: suur, ʕaswaar.
fender (*Br.*: *bumper*): rafraf, rafaarif.
fennel: ʃamar.
fenugreek: ɦilba.
ferry: miεaddiyya, -aat / maεaadi.
fertilizer: samaad, ʕasmida.
festival: mahragaan, -aat (*e.g. film festival*: mahragaan il-ʕaflaam).
celebration: ʕiɦtifaal, -aat.
religious, for birth of holy man: muulid / mawlid, mawaalid.
fever: (*infectious disease*): ɦumma, ɦummiyaat.
yellow fever: ɦumma ṣafra.
high temperature: ɦaraara; suxuniyya.
few, fewer, less: ʃiwayya; ʕaʕall.
fiancé(e): xaṭiib, xuṭṭaab (m): xaṭiiba, -aat (f).
ficticious: wahmi.
field (n): ɣeeṭ, -aan.
playing field: malεab, malaaεib.
field of specialization: taxaṣṣuṣ, -aat; magaal, -aat.
racing field: ʕarḍ is-sabaʕ.
oil field: ɦaql bitrool, ɦuquul bitrool.
fifteen: xamastaaʃar.
fifth: xaamis.
fifty: xamsiin.
fight (n): xinaaʕa, -aat.
fight (v) (*with*): ʕitxaaniʕ, yitxaaniʕ (maεa).
(*in a war*): ɦaarib, yiɦaarib; ʕitɦaarib, yitɦaarib (maεa).
figs: tiin (-a, -aat).
file (n) (*tool*): mabrad, mabaarid.
file, folder for papers: duseeh, -aat; malaff, -aat.
file (v) (*cut away*): barad, yubrud.
arrange in order: waḍḍab bit-tartiib, yiwaḍḍab bit-tartiib.
file cabinet: ʃaanun (no pl.).
cupboard: dulaab, dawaliib.
drawer: durg, ʕadraag.
filet (*of meat*): filittu.
fill: mala, yimla.
(*a tooth*): ɦaʃa, yiɦʃi.
fill it up!: fawwil-ha; ʕimlaa-ha.
filled: malyaan.
film (*camera, movie*): film, ʕaflaam.

filter (n): filtar, falaatir.
air filter: filtar hawa.
fuel filter: filtar banziin.
oil filter: filtar zeet.
final: nihaaʕI, -yyiin.
finally: ʕaxiiran.
finance (v): mawwil, yimawwil.
financing: tamwiil.
find (v): laʔa, yilaaʔi; liʔi, yilʔa.
fine (adj): kwayyis, -iin.
fine, splendid: ɛaal (invar); haayil, -iin.
fine, OK (*positive response*): ʈayyib.
fine, soft: naaɛim, -iin.
fine arts: funuun gamiila.
fine (n) (*penalty*): ɣaraama, -aat; muxalfa, -aat.
finger: ʂubaaɛ, ʂawaabiɛ.
fingernail: ɖufr, ɖawaafir.
fingernail clipper: ʔaʂʂaafit, ʔaʂʂafaat ɖawaafir.
finish (v) (tr): xallaʂ, yixallaʂ; ʕanha, yinhi.
(intr): xiliʂ, yixlaʂ.
finished: (*having run out*): xaaliʂ, -iin.
it's finished (*exclamation*): xalaaʂ.
we've run out of it: xiliʂ (m), xilʂit (f).
fire (n): naar (f), niraan.
destructive fire (*as in an accident*): ɦariiʔa, ɦaraayiʔ.
fire brigade; fireman; fire station: maʈaafi (pl).
fire truck: ɛarabiyyit maʈaafi.
fire, expel (v): rafad, yirfid; ʈarad, yuʈrud.
to be fired: ʕitrafad, yitrifid.
fire-extinguisher: ʈaffaayit ɦariiʔ, ʈaffayaat ɦariiʔ.
fire-hydrant: ɦanafiyyit ɦariiʔ, ɦanafiyyaat ɦariiʔ.
firecrackers: bumb (-a, -aat).
fireplace: daffaaya, -aat; daffayit ɦeeʈa.
fireworks, rockets: sawariix / ʂawariix.
first: (m) ʕawwil, (f) ʕuula, (pl) ʕawaaʕil.
at first: fil-ʕawwil.
firstly: ʕawwalan.
first aid: ʕisɛafaat ʕawwaliyya.
fiscal stamp: waraʔit damɣa, waraʔaat damɣa.
fish: samak (-a, -aat).
fit: *it fits*: maʐbuuʈ (-a), -iin.
fitting (*at the tailor's*): biroova, -aat.
five: xamsa; xamas (before pl. n.).
five piasters: ʃilin, -aat.
fix: (*e.g. an appointment*): ɦaddid, yiɦaddid.
repair: ʂallaɦ, yiʂallaɦ.
stabilize: sabbit, yisabbit.
flag, banner: ɛalam, ʕaɛlaam; bundeera, banadiir.
flamboyant trees, flame trees: bwinsiʕaana.
flame: naar (f), niraan: ʃuɛla, -aat.
flannel: kastuur.

flash (*on camera*): filaaʃ, -aat.
flashlight (*Br.: torch*): baṭṭariyya, -aat.
flat (adj): musaṭṭaɦ, -iin.
flat (*Am.: apartment*): ʃaʕʕa, ʃuʕaʕ.
flat tire: εagala nayma (*lit: sleeping wheel*).
flattery, buttering up: masɦ[e] guux.
flea: barɣuut, baraɣiit.
flea market: suuʕ il-εaṣr.
flexibility: muruuna.
flexible: marin, -iin.
flies: dibbaan (-a, -aat).
flight attendant: (m) muḍiif, -iin, (f) muḍiifa, -aat.
flirt with: εaakis, yiεaakis.
float, buoy (n): εawwaama, -aat.
flood (n): fayaḍaan, -aat.
flood (v) (tr): ɣarraʕ, yiɣarraʕ.
(intr) *flood, overflow*: faaḍ, yifiiḍ.
to be flooded, submerged: ʕitɣarraʕ, yitɣarraʕ; ɣiriʕ, yiɣraʕ.
flooded (*car engine*): ʃarʕaana.
floor (n): ʕarḍ (f).
flight in a building: door, ʕadwaar (tidwaar after nos. 3–10).
florist: bayyaaε zuhuur.
flour: diʕiiʕ.
flower pot, plant pot: ʕaṣriyya, -aat / ʕaṣaari (zarε).
flower-bed: ɦooḍ, ʕiɦwaaḍ.
flowers: ward (-a, -aat); zuhuur.
flu: ʕanfilwanza.
fluorescent light: lamba naylun; niyoon.
fly (n): *see* **flies**
fly (v) (intr): ṭaar, yiṭiir.
travel by air: saafir, yisaafir biṭ-ṭayyaara.
fly swatter: maḍrab, maḍaarib dibbaan.
flying, aviation: ṭayaraan.
flyover (*Am.: overpass*): kubri, kabaari.
fog: ʃabbuura; ḍabaab.
fold (n): ṭanya, tanyaat.
fold (v): ṭawa, yiṭwi; ṭabbaʕ, yiṭabbaʕ.
bend, hem: tana, yitni.
folder, file: duseeh, -aat.
folk (adj) (*e.g. folk art*): ʃaεbi, -yyiin.
folk song: ʕuɣniya ʃaεbiyya, ʕaɣaani ʃaεbiyya.
folklore: fulkiloor; ʕil-fann iʃ-ʃaεbi.
follow: *go after*: tabaε, yitbaε.
chase after: ṭaarid, yiṭaarid.
catch up with: liɦiʕ, yilɦaʕ.
pursue, continue, follow up: taabiε, yitaabiε.
understand: fihim, yifham.
food: ʕakl.
fool (v): diɦik, yidɦak εala; xamm, yixumm.
foolish, stupid: ɣabi, ʕaɣbiya.
foolish, crazy: εabiiṭ, εubṭ; magnuun, maganiin.
imbecile: ʕahbal, (f) habla, hubl.

foot: (*part of body*): rigl (f), -een (dual), ruguul.
(as measurement) ʕadam, ʕaʕdaam.
on foot: ɛala / bi-riglee (+ -ha, *etc.*).
football (*soccer*): koora; kurt-il-ʕadam / il-qadam.
footstool: puff; buffa.
for: ɛaʃaan, li.
for (*a period of*) …: li-muddit …
for (*in favor of*): maɛa.
for example: masalan.
for 20 piasters: bi-ɛaʃriin ʕirʃ.
I work for Amaco: baʃṭaɣal fi ʕamaku.
thank you for: ʕaʃkurak ɛala.
forbid: manaɛ, yimnaɛ.
forbidden: mamnuuɛ.
force: *by force*: bil-ɛafya; bil-ʕiwwa.
with great difficulty, by force: biz-zuur.
forced, obliged: muṭṭarr, -iin.
forehead: gibiin; ʕuura.
foreigner: ʕagnabi, ʕagaanib.
(*Westerner*): (m) xawaaga, (f) xawagaaya, -aat.
forest, jungle: ɣaaba, -aat.
forever, continuously: ɛala ṭuul.
all your life: ṭuul ɛumr-ak (-ik, -ku).
forget: nisi, yinsa.
(part): naasi, -yiin. *I have forgotten*: ʕana naasi.
fork (n): ʃooka, ʃuwak.
fork in the road: muftaraʕ ṭuruʕ.
form (n): furma, furam; ʃakl, ʕaʃkaal.
blank form: (*to be filled out*): ʕistimaara, -aat.
fort: ʕalɛa; ɦiṣn, ɦuṣuun.
fortunate: maɦẓuuẓ, -iin.
fortunately: li-ɦusn il-ɦaẓẓ.
forty: ʕarbiɛiin.
forward, *at or toward the front*: ʕuddaam.
fountain: fasʕiyya, -aat; nafuura, -aat.
drinking fountain: ɦanafiyya, -aat.
four: ʕarbaɛa; ʕarbaɛ (before pl. n.).
fourteen: ʕarbaɛtaaʃar.
fourth: raabiɛ.
one-fourth: rubɛ, ʕirbaɛ.
three-fourths: talat tirbaɛ.
fragile: biyitkisir bi-surɛa (*it breaks quickly*); haʃʃ; kasuur.
frame, picture: birwaaz, barawiiz.
France: faransa.
frank: ṣariiɦ, -iin.
frankly: bi-ṣaraaɦa.
fraudulence: talaaɛub; ʕiɦtiyaal.
free (*enjoying freedom*): ɦurr, -iin / ʕaɦraar.
(*free of charge*): maggaani (adj); magaanan; min ɣeer filuus; bi-balaaʃ (adv).
(*not busy*): faaḍi, -yiin.

become free (*not busy*): fiḍi, yifḍa.
free trade zone: manṭiʕa ɦurra, manaaṭiʕ ɦurra.
freedom: ɦurriyya, -aat.
freeze (v): gammid, yigammid.
freezer: friizar, -aat.
French: faransaawi, -yyiin.
French fried potatoes (*Br.*: *chips*): baṭaaṭis miɦammara.
frequently: kitiir; saɛaat kitiira.
fresh (*food*): ṭaaẓa (invar).
invigorated, refreshed: minaɛniʃ / mitnaɛniʃ, -iin.
presumptuous, impudent: waqiɦ, -iin (cl).
freshman (*first year*): sana ʕuula.
Friday: yoom ig-gumɛa.
Good Friday: ʕig-gumɛa-l-ɦaziina / -l-ɛaẓiima.
fried: maʕli, -yyiin; miɦammar, -iin.
friend: (m) ṣadiiq, (f) ṣadiiqa, (pl) ʕaṣdiqaaʕ (cl).
friend, boyfriend: ṣaaɦib, ʕaṣɦaab / ṣuɦaab.
friend, girlfriend: ṣaɦba, ʕaṣɦaab.
friendly (*person*): laṭiif, luṭaaf.
friendship: ṣadaaʕa / ṣadaaqa (cl), -aat; ṣuɦubbiyya.
frighten (v) (tr): xawwif, yixawwif.
frightened, apprehensive (*of*) (adj): mitxawwif (min).
terrified: marɛuub, -iin.
frightened, *to be frightened* (v) (intr): ʕitxawwif, yitxawwif.
frightening: muxiif, -iin; murɛib, -iin.
fringe (*Am.*: *bangs*): franʃa; ʕuṣṣa.
frizzy (*hair*): kaniiʃ; ʕakrat.
frog: ḍufdaɛa, ḍafaadiɛ.
from: min; mi- (*abbreviated form before article*).
from where?: mineen / min feen?
from now on: min hina-w raayiɦ; min dilwaʕti w-raayiɦ.
front (adj): ʕuddamaani, -yyiin.
in front of: ʕuddaam.
frosting (*hair style, Br.*: *highlighting*): meʃaat; meʃ.
frozen: migammid.
fruit: fakha, fawaakih.
fruitseller: fakahaani, -yya.
fry: ʕala, yiʕli.
fry until golden brown: ɦammar, yiʃammar.
frying pan: ṭaasit taɦmiir.
fuel gauge: ʕambeer il-banziin.
fuel line: *the fuel line is blocked*: ʕil-banziin masduud.
fuel pump: turumbit banziin.
full: malyaan, -iin.
full, complete: kaamil, -iin.
full (*after eating*): ʃabɛaan, -iin.
full stop (*punctuation, Am.*: *period*): nuʕṭa, nuʕaṭ.
fumigate: raʃʃ, yiruʃʃ; baxxar, yibaxxar.

fumigation: raʃʃ; tabxiir.
fun (adj): musalli, -yyiin;
mumtiɛ, -iin; ẓariif, ẓuraaf.
fun (n): mutɛa, mutaɛ
(*enjoyment*); ʕinbisaaṭ;
farfaʃa.
to have fun: ʕinbasaṭ, yinbisiṭ;
farfiʃ, yifarfiʃ.
rejoice: hayyaṣ, yihayyaṣ.
functioning, working: ʃaɣɣaal, -iin.
fundamentalism: ʕuṣuliyya.
fundamentalist: ʕuṣuuli.
funeral, funeral procession:
ganaaza, -aat.
funeral service (*Chr*):
ginnaaz, gananiiz.
funnel: ʕumɛ, ʕiʕmaaɛ.
funny: *merry*: fakiih, -iin /
fukaha.
causing laughter, comic:
muḍḥik, -iin.
funny, strange: ɣariib, ɣuraab.
fur: farw (farwa, faraawi).
furnish (*e.g. an apartment*):
faraʃ, yifriʃ.
furnished: mafruuʃ, -iin.
furniture: farʃ.
furnishings: ɛafʃ;
mubilya.
fuse: fiyuuz, -aat.
fuse box: tablooh, -aat.
future: mustaʕbal.

G

gain (v): kisib, yiksab.
to gain weight: tixin, yitxan.
gale: ɛaaṣifa, ɛawaaṣif.
gall bladder: maraara.
gambling: ʕumaar.
game: liɛba, ʕalɛaab.
garage: *mechanic's shop*: warʃa, wiraʃ.
at the mechanic's: ɛand il-mikaniiki.
fuel station: maɦaṭṭit banziin; banziina.
parking garage: garaaj / garaaʃ, -aat.
garage attendant: saayis, suyyaas / siyyaas.
garage sale, flea market: suuʕ il-ɛaṣr.
garbage: zibaala.
garbage can: ṣafiiɦit zibaala.
garbage chute: masuurit zibaala.
garbage collector: zabbaal, -iin.
garbage truck: ɛarabiyyit zibaala.
garden: gineena, ganaayin.
gardener: ganayni, (pl), -yya.
gargle (intr): ɣarɣar, yiɣarɣar.
gargling: ɣarɣara.
garlic: toom. *clove of garlic*: faṣṣ^{e} toom, fuṣuuṣ toom.
gas bottle, butane bottle: ʕanbuubit, ʕanabiib butagaaz.
gas station: maɦaṭṭit banziin; banziina, -aat.
gas tank: tank^{e} banziin, tankaat banziin.
gasket, seal: juwaan, -aat.
gasoline: banziin.
gate: bawwaaba, -aat.
gauge (n): ʕambeer.
fuel gauge: ʕambeer banziin.
temperature gauge: ʕambeer ɦaraara.
gear (n): tirs, tiruus.
gearbox: sanduuʕ tiruus.
gearshift: fitees.
gecko: burṣ, ʕabraaṣ.
general: ɛumuumi, -yyiin; ɛaamm.
generalize: ɛammim, yiɛammim.
generally: ɛumuuman; ɛala-l-ɛumuum.
generation: giil, ʕagyaal.
generator, dynamo: dinamu, -haat / -waat.
generous: kariim, kurama.
genius: ɛabqari, ɛabaqra.
gentle: laṭiif, luṭaaf.
geography: guɣrafya.
geometry: ɛilm il-handasa.
German: ʕalmaani, ʕalmaan.
Germany: ʕalmanya.
gesundheit (*when s.o. sneezes*): yarɦamu-kumu-llaah (cl).
get, bring: gaab, yigiib; (imperative): haat, -i, -u.
get gas: xad, yaaxud banziin.

get in, enter: daxal, yudxul; xaʃʃ, yixuʃʃ.
get in, on (*e.g. a bus, taxi*): rikib, yirkab.
get off, out (*e.g. a bus, taxi*): nizil, yinzil.
getting off (part): naazil, -iin.
get up, rise: ʕaam, yiʕuum; (*wake up*): ṣiḥi, yiṣḥa.
get in touch with: ʕittaṣal, yittiṣil bi.

get well (*see also* **health**): rabb-i-na yiddii-k iṣ-ṣiḥḥa, salamt-ak.

ghee: samna / samn.

giant: ɛimlaaq, ɛamaaliqa / ɛamalqa.

gift: hidiyya, hadaaya.

ginger: ganzabiil / zangabiil.

girl: bint, banaat.

give: ʕidda, yiddi.
give a research paper: ʕaddim, yiʕaddim baḥs.
give a ride: rakkib, yirakkib.
can you (m) *give me a ride*: mumkin tiwaṣṣal-ni; mumkin tirakkib-ni maɛaak.
give birth: wildit, tiwlid.

glad: mabsuuṭ, -iin; saɛiid, suɛada.
glad to have met you: furṣa saɛiida; taʃarrafna.

glass (*material*): ʕizaaz.
drinking glass: kubbaaya, -aat.
wine glass: kaas, -aat.

glasses, eyeglasses: naḍḍaara, -aat.

globalization: ɛawlama.

globe (*the earth*): ʕik-kura-l-ʕarḍiyya.
(*lamp bulb*): kilubb, -aat.

glory: ɛizz.

glossy, shining: lammiiɛ. (invar).

gloves (*pair*): guwanti, -yyaat.

glue (n) *adhesive*: laaṣiʕ; lazzaaʕ.
glue for wood: ɣira.
gum, resin: ṣamɣ / samɣ.

glue (v) (tr): lazaʕ, yilzaʕ; laṣaʕ, yilṣaʕ.
glue wood: ɣarra, yiɣarri.
stick with gum: sammaɣ / ṣammaɣ, yiṣammaɣ.

go: raaḥ, yiruuḥ.
going (*part*): raayiḥ, -iin.
going, leaving, moving (part): maaʃi, -yiin.
go away, leave: miʃi, yimʃi.
go away!: ʕimʃi!
go back, return: rigiɛ, yirgaɛ.
go by, pass: faat, yifuut; ɛadda, yiɛaddi; marr, yimurr (ɛala).
go down: nizil, yinzil
go downtown: nizil, yinzil il-balad.
go home: rawwaḥ, yirawwaḥ.
going home (part): mirawwaḥ, -iin.
go in, enter: daxal, yudxul; xaʃʃ, yixuʃʃ.
go out: xarag, yuxrug.

go out (*for entertainment*): ʕitfassaɦ, yitfassaɦ.
go out / up: ṭiliɛ, yiṭlaɛ.
let's go! (imperative): yalla biina!
goal (n): *point scored*: hadaf, ʕahdaaf; gool / goon, ʕigwaan / giwaan.
net (*e.g. in soccer*): gool / goon, ʕigwaan / giwaan.
goalkeeper: gool / goon; gool kiibar.
goat: miɛza, -aat / miɛiiz.
God: ʕallaah.
by God!: w-allaahi; w-alla.
our Lord: rabb-i-na.
O God: ya rabb.
God willing: ʕin ʃaaʕ allaah; ʕin ʃa-lla.
gold: dahab.
golden (*color*): dahabi (invar).
good: kwayyis, -iin.
good, fine: ɛaal (invar).
good, skillful (*at one's profession*): ʃaaṭir, -iin.
good, strong: ʕawi (*e.g. good friends*: ʕaṣɦaab ʕawi).
a good-for-nothing: zayy^{e} ʕillit-u (-ha, etc.); xaayib, -iin.
Good Friday: ʕig-gumɛa-l-ɛaẓiima / -l-ɦaziina.
good luck!: ɦaẓẓ^{e} saɛiid; ʕallaa-ywaffaʕ-ak.
have courage!: ʃidd^{e} ɦeel-ak.
good afternoon, good evening (*starts around 3 pm*): masaaʕ il-xeer (*response*: masaaʕ in-nuur).
good morning: ṣabaaɦ il-xeer (*response*: ṣabaaɦ in-nuur).
good night: tiṣbaɦ (-i, -u) ɛala xeer (*response*: w-inta (-i, -u) min ʕahlu).
goodbye: maɛa-s-salaama (*response*: ʕallaah ysallim-ak, -ik); bayy-bayy; salaam.
said by person leaving: saɛiida; ʕis-salaamu ɛaleeku(m) (*response*: wa ɛaleeku(m) is-salaam).
good looking, handsome: wagiih, wugaha; ʃakl-u ɦilw / kwayyis.
good-natured, kind:ṭayyib, -iin.; laṭiif, luṭaaf.
goodness, well-being: xeer.
goose: wizz (-a, -aat).
gossip (n): namiima.
gossip (v): namm, yinimm.
gossip about (*s.o.*): gaab, yigiib fi siirit (*s.o.*).
government: ɦukuuma, -aat.
governmental: ɦukuumi, -yyiin.
governor: muɦaafiẓ, -iin.
governorate: muɦafẓa, -aat.
gown (*e.g. graduation, bathrobe*): roob, ʕarwaab.
grab, catch (v): misik, yimsik.

grade, rank: daraga, -aat; rutba, rutab.
grade, class (*in school*): faṣl, fuṣuul; sana (e.g. sana ʕuula).
grade one: daraga ʕuula.
grade for course: daraga, -aat.
grade point average: magmuuɛ, magamiiɛ; mutawassiṭ.
category, type: fiyya, -aat.

graduate (v): ʕitxarrag, yitxarrag.

graduate of (n); xirriig, -iin.
graduate student: ṭaalib dirasaat ɛulya.

graduate studies (*higher studies*): dirasaat ɛulya.

graduation: taxarrug.
graduation ceremony: ɦaflit taxarrug.

grain, seed: ɦabba / ɦabbaaya, -aat / ɦubaat.
grains, seeds (coll): ɦabb, ɦubuub.

grammar (*rules*): qawaaɛid.
(*syntax*): naɦw.
grammar class: ɦiṣṣit naɦw; ɦiṣṣit qawaaɛid.

grandchild: ɦafiid, ʕaɦfaad.

granddaughter:
(*daughter of son*): bint-ibn, banaat-ibn.
(*daughter of daughter*): bint^{e} bint, banaat bint.

grandfather: gidd, guduud.
(*endearment, usu. by child*): giddu / giddi.

grandmother: gidda, -aat.
(*endearment*): sittu / teeta / neena.

grandson: (*son of son*): ʕibn-ibn, ʕawlaad-ibn.
(*son of daughter*): ʕibn^{e} bint, ʕawlaad bint.

grant (n): minɦa, minaɦ.

grape: *see* **grapes**

grape leaves: waraʕ ɛinab.

grapefruit: giriffiruut / giribfiruut.

grapes: ɛinab (-a, -aat).
seedless grapes: ɛinab banaati; ɛinab min ɣeer bizr.

grass: (*for lawn*): nigiil.
grass seeds: buzuur nigiil
hashish: ɦaʃiiʃ.

grated: mabʃuur, -iin.

grateful: mamnuun, -iin.

grave (n): maʕbara, maʕaabir / maqaabir.
tomb: ʕabr, ʕubuur.

graveyard (*graves*): maqaabir; madaafin.

gray: rumaadi; ruṣaaṣi.

grease, lubricant (n): ʃaɦm, ʃuɦuum.

grease, lubricate (v): ʃaɦɦam, yiʃaɦɦam.

greasy, oily: miʃaɦɦam.

great: ɛaẓiim, ɛuẓaam.
superb: haayil, -iin.

Greece: ʕil-yunaan.

greedy: ṭammaaɛ, -iin.
Greek: yunaani, -yyiin; giriigi, giriig.
green: ʕaxḍar, (f) xaḍra, xuḍr.
greengrocer: xuḍari, -yya.
greet: sallim, yisallim ɛala.
say hello to your (m) *brother for me*: sallim-li ɛala-xuu-k.
say hello to him: sallim-li ɛaleeh.
greeting card: kart^e muɛayda, kuruut muɛayda.
grill (n): ʃawwaaya, -aat.
car grill: ʃabaka, -aat.
grill (v) (*to cook with direct heat, broil*): ʃawa, yiʃwi.
grilled: maʃwi, -yyiin.
grind (v): *mince* (*e.g. meat*): faram, yufrum.
pulverize, crush (*e.g. coffee*): ṭaɦan, yiṭɦan.
gristle, cartilage: ɣaḍruuf, ɣaḍariif.
grocer: baʕʕaal, -iin.
groom: *bridegroom*: ɛariis, ɛirsaan.
groom for animals: saayis, suyyaas / siyyaas.
ground (adj) *minced* (*e.g. meat*): mafruum, -iin.
pulverized (*e.g. coffee*): maṭɦuun, -iin.
ground (n): ʕarḍ (f).
grounding (*electrical, Br.: earth*): ʕarḍi; ʕirs.
group: magmuuɛa, -aat; gamaaɛa, -aat.
grouper, sea bass: waʕaar (-a, -aat).
grow (tr) (*cultivate*): zaraɛ, yizraɛ.
(*e.g. a beard*): rabba, yirabbi.
to make grow bigger: kabbar, yikabbar.
grow old (*grow up*): kibir, yikbar.
become an old man/woman: ɛaggiz, yiɛaggiz.
guarantee (n): ḍamaan, -aat.
guarantee (v): ḍaman, yiḍman.
guard (n) (*security*): ɦaaris (ʕamn), ɦurraas (ʕamn).
guard (v): ɦaras, yuɦrus.
guava: gawaafa (-aaya, -aat).
guess (v): ɦazzar, yiɦazzar; xammin, yixammin.
guest: (*visitor*): ḍeef, ḍuyuuf; naas.
invited guest (*e.g. at wedding*): maɛzuum, -iin / maɛaziim.
guide (n): murʃid, -iin.
guide book: daliil.
tourist guide: murʃid, -iin; turgumaan, taragma.
guilty: muznib, -iin.
gulf: xaliig, xilgaan.
gum (**chewing gum**): libaan.
gun (n): *pistol*: musaddas, -aat.
rifle: bunduʕiyya, banaadiʕ.
gynecologist: duktoor ʕamraaḍ nisa.

H

habit: ɛaada, -aat.
hair: ʃaɛr (-a, -aat).
hair pins, bobby pins: binas (binsa, binsaat).
haircut: (*men*) ɦilaaʕa; (*men or women*) ʕaṣṣa.
to have a haircut:
ɦalaʕ, yiɦlaʕ ʃaɛr-u;
ʕaṣṣ, yiʕuṣṣ ʃaɛru (-aha, etc.).
hairdresser: kwafeer, -aat.
hairdryer: seʃwaar.
hairspray: spree.
hairstyle: tasriiɦa, -aat.
half: nuṣṣ, ʕanṣaaṣ.
hall, vestibule: ṣaala, -aat; qaaɛa, -aat.
long narrow hall, corridor: ṭurʕa, -aat; kuridoor.
hammer: ʃakuuʃ, ʃawakiiʃ.
hand: ʕiid (f), -een (dual), ʕayaadi.
your hands: ʕidee-k.
my hands: ʕidayya.
hand-grenade: ʕunbila, ʕanaabil yadawiyya.
handbag, purse: ʃanṭa, ʃunaṭ; ʃanṭit yadd.
handicrafts: ʕaʃɣaal yadawiyya.
hand-made: maɛmuul bil-ʕiid / bil-yadd.
handkerchief: mandiil, manadiil.
handle: ʕiid (f) / yadd (f), ʕayaadi.
brush handle: ʕiid furʃa.
knob of a door:
ʕukrit baab, ʕukar baab.
handlebar: gaduun, -aat.
handsome, elegant, well-dressed: wagiih, wugaha;
ʃakl-u (-ak, etc.) -kwayyis / ɦilw / ʃiik; ɦileewa.
handwriting: xaṭṭ, xuṭuuṭ.
handyman, janitor: farraaʃ, -iin.
hang (v): *e.g. put on a wall*:
ɛallaʕ, yiɛallaʕ.
execute: ʃanaʕ, yiʃnuʕ.
hang on (*just a moment; don't hang up*): xallii-k (-ki) maɛaaya.
hanger: ʃammaaɛa, -aat.
happen: ɦaṣal, yiɦṣal; gara, yigra.
what happened?: ɦaṣal ʕeeh?
what happened to you; what's wrong?:
garaa-l-ak ʕeeh?
happiness: saɛaada; (*joy*) faraɦ.
happy: mabsuuṭ, -iin; saɛiid, suɛada.
make s.o. happy:
basaṭ, yibsiṭ; farraɦ, yifarraɦ;
hanna, yihanni.
happy to have seen you (*again*): furṣa saɛiida.
(*response*: *I'm the more happy*): ʕana ʕasɛad (invar).

Happy Holiday,
Happy New Year (*greeting for any annual occasion*): kull^e sana wi-nta (-i, -u) ṭayyib (-a, -iin).

harbor: miina, mawaani.

hard: difficult: ṣaεb, -iin.
solid: gaamid, -iin; ʃidiid, ʃudaad.
hard-headed, stubborn: raas-u (-ak, etc.) naʃfa; dimaaɣu naʃfa.

hard working (*person*): mugtahid, -iin.

harder (comp): ʕaṣεab (invar).

harm, damage: ḍarar, ʕaḍraar.

harvest (v): ɦaṣad, yuɦṣud.

hashish: ɦaʃiiʃ.

hassle, pester (v): εaakis, yiεaakis; daayiʕ, yidaayiʕ.

hat: burneeṭa, baraniiṭ.

have: (*poss.*): εandak (-ik, etc.); maεaak (-ki etc.); liik (-ki, etc.)
have, let (*s.o. do s.t.*): xalla, yixalli.
have a tailor make clothes: faṣṣal, yifaṣṣal.
have to, must: laazim.

hazelnuts: bunduʕ, (-a, -aat).

he: huwwa.

head: raas (f), ruus.
head, president, chief: raʕiis, ruʕasa.; rayyis.

headache: ṣudaaε.
trouble, fuss: wagaε dimaaɣ.

headdress (*Arab*): ɣuṭra, ɣuṭar (*held in place by ring called* εuʕaal, -aat).

headlight: fanuus εarabiyya, fawaniis εarabiyya; kaʃʃaaf, -aat.

headman of a village: εumda (m), εumad.
headman of a neighborhood: ʃeex il-ɦaara.

heal, cure (v) (tr): εaalig, yiεaalig.

health: ṣiɦɦa.
health to you (m) (*get well soon*): salamt-ak; la baʕs^e εaleek.

hear: simiε, yismaε.

heart: ʕalb, ʕuluub.
heart attack, coronary thrombosis, clot: galṭa fil-ʕalb.

heat (n): ɦaraara; suxuniyya.

heat (v) (tr): saxxan, yisaxxan.
to become hot (intr): sixin, yisxan.

heat wave: moogit ɦarr; mooga ɦarra.

heater: room heater: daffaaya, -aat.
water heater: saxxaan, -aat.

heaven, paradise: ʕig-ganna.

heavy: tiʕiil, tuʕaal.

Hebrew: εibri.

heel (n): kaεb, kuεuub.

hell: gahannam / guhannam (f); ʕin-naar.

hello: (*on telephone*): ʕaloo.
hi: ʕahlan.
(*when entering a store, office, etc*): ʕis-salaamu ɛaleekum
(*response*: wa ɛaleekum is-salaam).
hello, welcome:
ʕahlan wa sahlan
(*response*: ʕahlan biik (-ki, -ku)).
say hello to ...: *see* **greet**.
(*see also* **good morning** *and* **good afternoon**).
help (n): musaɛda, -aat.
help (v): saaɛid, yisaaɛid; ɛaawin, yiɛaawin.
God help you (m):
rabb-i-na-ykuun fi-ɛoon-ak;
ʕallaah yisahhil-l-ak.
rescue: liɦiʕ / laɦaʕ, yilɦaʕ.
help me!: ʕilɦaʕuu-ni!
hem, fold, cuff (n): tanya, -aat.
hem, fold, cuff (v): tana, yitni.
hemorrhoids: bawasiir.
hepatitis: ʕiṣ-ṣafra.
her: *see pronominal suffix chart*.
herbalist: ɛaṭṭaar, -iin.
herbs: ɛuʃb (coll), (pl) ʕaɛʃaab.
herbs and spices: ɛiṭaara.
here: hina.
here is / are (demonstrative): ʕaadi.
here he / it (m) *is*: ʕahu.
here she / it (f) *is*: ʕahi.
here they are: ʕahumm(a).
(*on telephone*) e.g.
here is Ali: ɛali maɛaak (-ki).
hero, champion: baṭal, ʕabṭaal.
hers: (m) bitaɛ-ha, (f) bitaɛit-ha, (pl) bituɛ-ha.
hi, hello: ʕahlan.
hibiscus: karkadeeh.
hide (tr): xabba, yixabbi.
(intr): ʕistaxabba, yistaxabba.
hierarchy, sequency: tasalsul; niẓaam ṭabaʕaat.
high: ɛaali, -yiin.
the High Dam: ʕis-sadd il-ɛaali.
high school:
madrasa sanawiyya.
highlighting (*Am.*: *hair frosting*): meʃaat; meʃ.
hijack (v): ʕixtaṭaf, yaxtaṭif; xaṭaf, yixṭaf.
hijacked: muxtaṭaf, -iin; maxṭuuf, -iin.
hijacker: muxtaṭif, -iin.
hijacking (n): ʕixtiṭaaf.
hill: tall, tilaal.
him: *see pronominal suffix chart*.
hinge: mifaṣṣala, -aat.
hint (v): lammaɦ, yilammaɦ.
hinting (part): talmiiɦ.
hippopotamus: sayyid ʕiʃṭa; faras, ʕafraas in-nahr.
hire, rent: ʕaggar, yiʕaggar; kara, yikri.
his (adj): *see pronominal suffix chart*.
his (pron, as hers): (m) bitaaɛ-u, (f) bitaɛt-u, (pl) bituuɛ-u.
historian: muʕarrix, -iin.
history: tariix.

hit (v): xabaṭ, yixbaṭ;
beat: ḍarab, yiḍrab;
run into: ṣadam, yuṣdum.
hoard, save: ɦawwiʃ, yiɦawwiʃ.
hobby: ɣiyya, -aat; hiwaaya, -aat.
hold, catch: misik, yimsik.
holding (part): maasik, -iin.
pull tight: ʃadd, yiʃidd.
hole: xurm, ʕaxraam / xuruum.
button hole: ɛirwa, ɛaraawi.
pit, ditch: goora, -aat;
ɦufra, ɦufar.
hole punch: xarraama, -aat.
holiday (*religious or national occason*): ɛiid, ʕaɛyaad.
(*time off from work or school*): ʕagaaza, -aat.
Holy Saturday: sabt in-nuur.
Holy Thursday: xamiis il-ɛahd.
home: beet, buyuut.
home economics (*school subject*): tadbiir manzili.
homework: waagib, -aat.
honest: ʃariif, ʃurafa; ʕamiin, ʕumana.
honey: ɛasal.
bee honey: ɛasal naɦl.
molasses: ɛasal ʕiswid.
honey color (*brown, usually for eyes*): ɛasali.
honeymoon: ʃahr il-ɛasal.
honor (n): ʃaraf.
honor (v) (*e.g. by one's presence*): ʃarraf, yiʃarraf.
(*treat with high regard*): karram, yikarram;
ʕakram, yikrim.
honored (*to know you, etc.*): taʃarrafna.
hood of a car (*Br.*: *bonnet*): kabbuut.
hook (n) (*for hanging*): ɛallaaʕa, -aat.
window hook: ʃankal, ʃanaakil.
hope (n): ʕamal, ʕamaal.
hope (v): raga, yargu (cl);
ʕitmanna, yitmanna.
I hope: ʕargu;
ʕinʃalla (*God willing*).
hopefully: ʕinʃalla; ʕin ʃaaʕ allaah.
hopeless case (*total failure*): xaayib, -iin; faaʃil, -iin.
horn (*on car*): kalaks, -aat.
hornet: dabbuur ʕaɦmar, dababiir ɦamra/ɦumr.
horrible: faẓiiɛ, fuẓaaɛ; ʃaniiɛ, ʃunaaɛ.
hors d'oeuvres (*appetizers*): muʃahhiyaat.
hors d'oeuvres served with drinks: mazza, -aat.
horse: faras, ʕafraas.
(*mare*): farasa, -aat.
(*stallion*): ɦuṣaan, ɦiṣina.
horses (coll): xeel.
horse riding: rukuub xeel.
to go horse riding: rikib, yirkab xeel.
horse-drawn carriage: ɦanṭuur, ɦanaṭiir.
horse-drawn cart: ɛarabiyya karru, -aat karru.
horseradish: figl^{e} baladi.

hose: xarṭuum, xaraṭiim.
hospital: mustaʃfa, -yaat.
hostage: rahiina, rahaayin.
hostel, students' dormitory:
beet, buyuut ṭalaba.
for female students:
beet, buyuut ṭalibaat.
hostess (*e.g. on airplane*):
muḍiifa, -aat.
hot: suxn, -iin.
I'm hot: ʕana ɦarraan.
hot weather: ɦarr.
peppery: ɦarraaʕ, -iin;
ɦaami, -yiin.
hot plate: saxxaan kahraba,
saxxanaat kahraba.
hotel: ʕuteel, ʕutilaat; lukanda,
-aat; funduʕ, fanaadiʕ.
boarding house:
pansyoon / bansiyoon, -aat.
hour: saaεa, -aat.
hours (*that a store is open*):
mawaεiid.
what are your hours?:
ʕeeh mawaεiid il-εamal?
hourly (*by the hour*): bis-saaεa.
house: beet, buyuut.
housing unit: maskan,
masaakin.
how: ʕizzaay / ʕizzayy.
how big, far, long, etc.:
ʕaddᵉ ʕee.
how come (*in surprise or protest*): ʕiʃmiεna.
how many, much: kaam.
how much (*ref. to price*):
bi-kaam.

hubcap: ṭaasa, -aat.
huge: ḍaxm, ḍuxaam.
human being: (m and generic)
ʕinsaan, (f) ʕinsaana;
(m) bani-ʕaadam,
(f) bani-ʕadma,
(pl) bani-ʕadmiin.
human, humane (adj): ʕinsaani.
humanity: ʕinsaniyya.
humble, modest: mutawaaḍiε,
-iin.
humidity: ruṭuuba.
hundred: miyya (miit before n).
two hundred: miteen.
3 (*etc.*) *hundred*: tultumiyya
(rubεumiyya, xumsumiyya,
suttumiyya, subεumiyya,
tumnumiyya, tusεumiyya).
Hungary: ʕil-magar.
hungry: gaεaan, -iin.
to get hungry: gaaε, yiguuε.
Hurghada: ʕil-ɣardaʕa.
hurricane, tornado, cyclone:
ʕiεṣaar, ʕaεaṣiir.
gale: εaaṣifa, εawaaṣif.
hurry (n) *in a hurry*: mistaεgil,
-iin.
hurry (v): ʕistaεgil, yistaεgil.
(*hurry when walking*):
madd, yimidd (rigl-u etc.).
hurt (*physically*): wagaε,
yiwagaε.
my leg hurts: rigli-btiwgaε-ni.
hurt (*s.o.'s feelings*):
garaɦ, yigraɦ (ʃuεuur-u etc.).
husband: gooz / zoog,
ʕazwaag.

hydraulic fluid: zeet baakim.
hydraulic system: baakim.
hypochondriac: mariiɖ bil-wahm.
hypocrisy: nifaaq.
hypocrite: munaafiq, -iin.

I

I (1st pers pron): ʕana.
ice (n): talg.
ice bucket: ʃambanyee; gardal talg, garaadil talg.
ice cream: jilaati; ʕayis kriim.
ice pick: kassaarit talg, kassaraat talg.
ice skate (v): ʕitzaɦlaʕ ɛala g-galiid, yitzaɦlaʕ ɛala g-galiid.
idea: fikra, ʕafkaar.
identity card (*government*): biṭaaʕa, -aat ʃaxṣiyya.
school I.D.: karnee, -haat.
idiot: ɛabiiṭ, ɛubṭ; ʕahbal, (f) habla, hubl.
if: ʕiza; law; ʕin.
if God wills: ʕin ʃaaʕ allaah.
if it were not for (*the fact that*): lawla / loola (ʕinn).
ignite, light: wallaɛ, yiwallaɛ.
ignition, starter: marʃ, -aat; kuntakt / kuntaak.
ignition key: muftaaɦ ik-kuntakt.
ignorance: gahl.
ignorant: gaahil, -iin / gahala.
ill: ɛayyaan, -iin.
to get ill: ɛiyi, yiɛya.
illegal: ɣeer qanuuni.
forbidden by religion: ɦaraam (invar).
illiteracy: ʕummiyya.
illiterate: ʕummi, -yyiin.
illusion: wahm, ʕawhaam.
imagine: ʕitṣawwar, yitṣawwar; ʕitxayyil, yitxayyil.
imitate: ʕallid, yiʕallid.
imitation: taʕliid.
immediately: ɦaalan; bi-surɛa; ʕawaam; ɛala ṭuul.
immunity (*against*): manaaɛa (ḍidd).
impertinence: ʕadaara; waqaaɦa (cl); bagaaɦa.
impertinent, impudent: waqiɦ (cl); bigiɦ, -iin.
impolite: ʕaliil ʕadab; ʕulalaat ʕadab.
import (v): ʕistawrid, yistawrid.
import and export (n): ʕistiraad wi taṣdiir.
importance: ʕahammiyya.
important: muhimm, -iin.
imported: mustawrad, -iin; min barra.
impose: faraḍ, yifriḍ.
impossible: miʃ mumkin; miʃ maɛʕuul; mustaɦiil.
impress, please: ɛagab, yiɛgib.
impressive, *excellent*: mumtaaz, -iin.
wonderful: haayil, -iin.
imprison: sagan, yisgin; ɦabas, hiɦbis.
improve (tr): ɦassin, yiɦassin.
(intr): ʕitɦassin, yitɦassin.
improvement (*making better*): taɦsiin, -aat.

(becoming better): taɦassun.
in: fi; guwwa.
in order to: εaʃaan; εalaʃaan.
incense (n): buxuur.
inch: buuṣa, -aat.
incident, event: ɦadas, ʕaɦdaas.
income: daxl, duxuul; ʕiraad, -aat.
income tax: dariibit daxl.
inconsistent, changeable: mutaqallib, -iin.
increase (v) (tr): zawwid, yizawwid; kattar, yikattar.
(intr): zaad, yiziid; kitir, yiktar.
indeed: fiεlan; ṣaɦiiɦ.
independence: ʕistiʕlaal / ʕistiqlaal.
independence day: εiid il-istiqlaal.
index *(in back of book)*: fihris, fahaaris.
index card: fiiʃ (no pl).
India: ʕil-hind.
Indian: hindi, hunuud / hanadwa.
American Indian: hindi ʕaɦmar, hinuud ɦumr.
indignant: mitɣaaẓ, -iin.
individual (n): nafar, ʕanfaar; fard, ʕafraad; ʃaxṣ, ʕaʃxaaṣ.
industrial: ṣinaaεi, -yyiin.
industrious: mugtahid, -iin.
industry: ṣinaaεa, -aat.
inexpensive: rixiiṣ, ruxaaṣ.
to become inexpensive: rixiṣ, yirxaṣ.
infant: ṭifl, ʕaṭfaal.
newborn: mawluud, mawaliid.
infection, inflammation: ʕiltihaab, -aat.
transmission of disease: εadwa.
contamination: talawwus.
infirmary *(clinic)*: εiyaada, -aat.
inflammation: ʕiltihaab, -aat.
inflation *(economic)*: taḍaxxum.
influenza: ʕanfilwanza.
information: maεlumaat.
act of informing: ʕiεlaam.
to ask for information: ʕistaεlim, yistaεlim.
information desk: maktab ʕistiεlamaat.
ingenuity: εabqariyya.
inhabitant: saakin, sukkaan.
injection *(shot)*: ɦuʕna, ɦuʕan.
injury: garɦ, guruuɦ.
ink: ɦibr.
inquire *(about)*: ʕistaεlim, yistaεlim (εan).
inquiries: ʕistiεlamaat.
inscription: kitaaba, -aat.
insect: ɦaʃara, -aat.
insect repellent: ṭaarid li-nnamuus; *(referred to by brand name, e.g. "Off" or "Tus")*.
insecticide: mubiid, aat.
insecure *(situation)*: miʃ maʕmuun, -iin; miʃ maḍmuun.
feeling insecure, worried: ʕalʕaan, -iin.
inside (adj): guwwaani.
inside (adv, prep): guwwa.
insist: ṣammim, yiṣammim; ʕaṣarr, yiṣirr (εala).

insistent, insisting: muṣammim, -iin; muṣirr.
insomnia: ʕaraq; ʕalaʕ.
inspect, search: fattiʃ, yifattiʃ.
inspector: mufattiʃ, -iin.
install (*e.g. a washing machine*): rakkib, yirakkib.
installation: tarkiib, (-a, tarakiib).
installment: ʕisṭ, ʕaʕsaaṭ.
by installment: bit-taʕsiiṭ.
divide into installments: ʕassaṭ, yiʕassaṭ.
instantly: ɦaalan; ʕawaam.
instead of (conj): badal ma (+ verb in imperfect).
instead of (prep): badal.
institute (*scientific*): maɛhad, maɛaahid.
instructions (*steps to follow*): taɛlimaat; ʕirʃadaat.
instructor, teacher: mudarris, -iin; ʕustaaz, ʕasatza.
insult (n): ʕihaana, -aat.
verbal abuse: ʃitiima, ʃataayim; masabba, -aat.
insult (v): ʕahaan / haan, yihiin.
call s.o. names, abuse: ʃatam, yiʃtim; sabb, yisibb.
insurance: taʕmiin, -aat.
intelligent: zaki, ʕazkiya; nabiih, nubaha.
intend: ʕaṣad, yuʕṣud; nawa, yinwi.
intending (part): naawi, -yiin.
intended, meant: maʕṣuud, -iin.
intention: ʕaṣd; niyya, -aat / nawaaya.
interest (n) *benefit, advantage*: maṣlaɦa, maṣaaliɦ.
concern: ʕihtimaam.
interest on money in bank: fawaayid / fawaaʕid.
interested (*in*) (*e.g. sports*): muhtamm, -iin. (bi).
interesting: amazing, strange: ɛagiib, ɛugaab.
amusing, entertaining: musalli, -yiin.
charming: ẓariif, ẓuraaf.
delightful, enjoyable: mumtiɛ, -iin.
exciting: musiir, -iin.
important: muhimm, -iin.
pleasing, delightful: ʃayyiq, -iin; mumtiɛ, -iin.
remarkable, wonderful: mudhiʃ, -iin.
useful: mufiid, -iin.
interior design: dikoor, -aat.
intermediary (n): wasṭa, wasaayiṭ.
to act as an intermediary: ʕitwassaṭ, yitwassaṭ (li); ʕitwaasiṭ, yitwaasiṭ.
intermediate (adj): mutawassiṭ, -iin.
international: dawli, -yyiin.
international book fair: maɛraḍ ik-kitaab id-dawli.
interpretation (*explanation, analysis*): tafsiir, -aat.
simultaneous interpretation: targama fawriyya.

interpreter, translator: mutargim, -iin.
simultaneous interpreter: mutargim fawri.
interrupt (*e.g. a speaker*): ʕaaṭiɛ, yiʕaaṭiɛ.
obstruct: ɛaṭṭal, yiɛaṭṭal.
intersection: taʕaaṭuɛ / taqaaṭuɛ, -aat.
interview (n): *investigation, interrogation*: taɦʕiiʕ, -aat.
reporter's interview: taɦʕiiʕ ṣuɦafi, taɦʕiʕaat ṣuɦafiyya.
private meeting: muʕabla ʃaxṣiyya, muʕablaat ʃaxṣiyya.
introduce: ʕaddim, yiʕaddim.
acquaint: ɛarraf, yiɛarraf.
introducer, (*e.g. of a program*): muʕaddim, -iin.
introduction: muqaddima, -aat.
invade: ɣaza, yiɣzi; ʕiɛtada, yiɛtidi ɛala.
invasion, act or invading: ɣazw; ʕiɛtidaaʕ (ɛala).
an invasion: ɣazwa, -aat.
invention: ʕixtiraaɛ, -aat.
investigate (*e.g. a crime*): ɦaʕʕaʕ, yiɦaʕʕaʕ.
research (*v*): baɦas, yibɦas.
invitation: ɛuzuuma, ɛazaayim.
written, formal invitation: daɛwa, daɛaawi.
invitation card: kart^{e} daɛwa, kuruut daɛwa.
invite (*for*): ɛazam, yiɛzim (ɛala).
invited: maɛzuum, -iin.
invoice, bill (n): fatuura, fawatiir.
receipt: waṣl, wuṣulaat.
Iraq: ʕil-ɛiraaʕ / ʕil-ɛiraaq.
Iraqi: ɛiraaʕI / ɛiraaqi, -yyiin.
iron (n): (*metal*): ɦadiid.
iron for ironing clothes: makwa, makaawi.
iron, press (v) (*clothes*): kawa, yikwi.
ironing board: ṭarabeezit, ṭarabizaat makwa.
ironing person: makwagi, (pl) -yya.
irritable, nervous: ɛaṣabi, -yyiin.
irritate: ɣaaẓ, yiɣiiẓ; daayiʕ, yidaayiʕ.
make nervous: narfiz, yinarfiz.
irritated: mitɣaaẓ, -iin; middaayiʕ, -iin.
to be irritated: ʕitɣaaẓ, yitɣaaẓ; ʕiddaayiʕ, yiddaayiʕ; ʕitnarfiz, yitnarfiz.
Islam: ʕil-ʕislaam.
Islamic: ʕislaami, -yyiin.
island: giziira, guzur.
Ismailia: ʕil-ʕismaɛiliyya.
Israel: ʕisraʕiil.
Israeli (adj. n): ʕisraʕiili, -yyiin.
issue (n) *question, matter*: masʕala, masaaʕil; mawḍuuɛ, mawaḍiiɛ.
cause: ʕaḍiyya, ʕaḍaaya.
it (*as subject*): (m) huwwa; (f) hiyya.

Italian: ṭalyaani, talayna / ṭalayna; ʕiṭaali, -yyiin.
Italy: ʕiṭalya.
its: *see pronominal suffix chart.*
ivory: ɛaag; sinn fiil.
ivy (*climbing plant*): nabaat mutasalliq.
(*creeping plant*): maddaad, -aat.

J

jack (n): kureek.
jacket, *sport coat*: jaakit, -aat / jawaakit; swiitar, -aat.
suit coat: jakitta, -aat.
jail: sign, suguun; ɦabs.
jam, preserves: mirabba, -aat.
janitor, office handyman: farraaʃ, -iin.
January: yanaayir.
Japan: ʕil-yabaan.
Japanese: yabaani, -yyiin.
jar: baṭramaan / barṭamaan, -aat.
jasmine: yasmiin (-a, -aat).
Arabian jasmine: full (-a / -aaya, -aat).
jealous: ɣayraan, -iin.
to be jealous (*of*) (*for*): ɣaar, yiɣiir (min) (ɛala).
jello (*Br.*: *jelly*): jeli.
Jerusalem: ʕil-ʕuds / ʕil-quds.
Jesus: (*Chr*): yasuuɛ; (*Isl*): ɛiisa.
Christ, the Messiah: ʕil-misiiɦ / ʕil-masiiɦ.
Jew, Jewish: yahuudi, yahuud.
jeweler: saayiɣ, saaɣa / suyyaaɣ; gawahirgi, -yya.
jewelry: siiɣa; mugawharaat (invariable plural).
costume jewelry, accessory: ʕaksiswaar.
jewelry store: maɦall saayiɣ.
Jews' mallow: muluxiyya.
job: waẓiifa, waẓaayif; ʃuɣla, -aat.
jogging: riyaaḍit ig-gary.
join (*become a member of*): ʕiʃtarak, yiʃtirik fi.
join a university (*i.e. enter*): daxal, yudxul gamɛa.
joint (*in body*): mafṣal, mafaaṣil.
joke (n): nukta, nukat.
joke (v) (*with*): hazzar, yihazzar (maɛa).
tell jokes: nakkit, yinakkit.
Jordan: ʕil-ʕurdun.
Jordanian: ʕurduni, -yyiin.
journalist: ṣaɦafi, -yyiin.
journey, travel (n): safar.
journey, trip: riɦla, -aat.
joy: faraɦ; ʕinbisaaṭ.
joyful, glad,: farɦaan, -iin; mabsuuṭ, -iin.
to be joyful: firiɦ, yifraɦ; ʕinbasaṭ, yinbisiṭ.
to make s.o. joyful: farraɦ, yifarraɦ; basaṭ, yibsiṭ.
judge (n): ʕaaḍi, ʕuḍaah.
jug, pitcher: dooraʕ, dawaariʕ; ʃafʃaʕ, ʃafaaʃiʕ.
juice: ɛaṣiir.
July: yulyu / yulya.
jump (v): naṭṭ, yinuṭṭ; ʕafaz, yiʕfiz.
June: yunyu /yunya.
jungle, forest: ɣaaba, -aat.
junior high school, prep school: madrasa ʕiɛdadiyya.

junior year (*third year*): sana talta.

junk: karakiib (pl).
piece of junk: karkuuba, karakiib.
old clothes: huduum ʕadiima; rubɑbikya.
junk peddler: bitaaɛ rubɑbikya.

just (adj): ɛaadil, -iin.

just, barely, hardly: yadoob, yadoobak.
just, a moment ago: lissa (+ part) (*e.g. he just left*: lissa xaarig).
just a minute, don't hang up: xallii-k (-ki) maɛayya.

K

kangaroo: kangaruu; ʕil-kunɣur.
keep: *leave* (*s.t. somewhere*):
xalla, yixalli; saab, yisiib.
retain: ʕiħtafaẓ, yiħtifiẓ bi.
keep on (*continue*): fiḍil, yifḍal.
kerosene: gaaz.
kettle (*for tea*): barraad, -aat.
key: muftaaħ, mafatiiħ.
answer-key to test:
waraʕit ʕigaaba.
answer: ʕigaaba, -aat /
ʕagwiba.
keyring: ħalaʕit mafatiiħ,
ħalaʕaat mafatiiħ.
key-money: xiliwwᵉ rigl.
kick (n) (*to a ball*): ʃooṭa, -aat.
(*to a person*): ʃalluut, ʃalaiit.
kick (v) (*a ball*): ʃaaṭ, yiʃuuṭ.
(*a person*): ḍarab,
yiḍrab (*s.o.*) ʃalluut.
(*by an animal*): rafaṣ, yurfuṣ.
kiddingly: bi-hzaar.
kidnap, hijack: xaṭaf, yixṭaf.
kidney (*food*): kilwa, -aat /
kalaawi.
(*part of body*): kilya, kila /
ʕik-kilyiteen.
kidney stone: ħaṣwa fik-kila,
ħaṣaawi fik-kila.
kill: mawwit, yimawwit.
murder: ʕatal, yiʕtil.
kilogram: kiilu, -haat.
kilometer: kiilu, -haat; kilumitr,
-aat.
kind, good-natured (adj): ṭayyib,
-iin; laṭiif, luṭaaf.
kind, tender (*to*):
ħinayyin, -iin (ɛala).
kind, sort (n): nooɛ, ʕanwaaɛ;
ṣanf, ʕaṣnaaf.
what kind: ʕayyᵉ nooɛ.
the best kind:
ʕaħsan nooɛ: ʕaħsan ṣanf.
what brand: markit-u (-ha, etc.)
ʕeeh.
kindergarten: rooḍit ʕaṭfaal;
rooḍa, -aat.
king: malik, muluuk.
kinky (*hair*): mifalfil.
frizzy: ʕakraṭ.
kiss (n): boosa, busaaṭ.
kiss (v): baas, yibuus.
kitchen: maṭbax, maṭaabix.
kitten: ʕiṭeeṭa, ʕaṭaayiṭ; ʕuṭṭa-
sɣayyara / -zɣayyara.
Kleenex: waraʕ kliniks; mandiil
waraʕ, manadiil waraʕ.
knee: rukba, rukab.
kneecap: ṣabuunit ir-rukba.
knife: sikkiina, sakakiin.
pocket knife:
maṭwa, maṭaawi.
knitting: trikooh.
knock (v) (*at a door*): xabbaṭ,
yixabbaṭ.
knock, rattle (v) (*in a
car engine*): saʕʕaf,
yisaʕʕaf.
knocking: tasʕiif.

knock on wood: ʕimsik il-xaʃab.

know: εirif, yiεraf; (part): εaarif, -iin.

knowledge: maεrifa.

Koran: ʕil-qurʕaan.

The Holy Koran: ʕil-qurʕaan il-kariim.

Kuwait: ʕik-kuweet.

Kuwaiti: kuweeti, -yyiin / kawayta.

L

laboratory: maɛmal, maɛaamil.
lacking, *in short supply, out* (*of the market*): naaʕiṣ, -iin.
to be lacking: niʕiṣ, yinʕaṣ.
ladder: sillim, salaalim.
ladle, scoop (n): maɣrafa, maɣaarif; kabʃa, kubaʃ.
ladle, scoop (v): ɣaraf, yiɣrif.
lady: sitt, -aat; madaam (*formal*); haanim, hawaanim (*formal*).
ladies' (*used or worn by ladies*): ɦariimi.
lake: buɦeera, -aat; buɦayra (cl).
lamb, mutton: laɦma ḍaani.
lame: ʕaɛrag, (f) ɛarga, ɛurg.
lamination: taɣliif bil-bilastik.
lamp, ceiling lamp: lamba, -aat / lumaḍ.
chandeliers: nagaf (-a, -aat).
neon lamp: lamba naylun/ niyoon, lumaḍ naylun/ niyoon.
lamp, table lamp: ʕabajuura, -aat.
lamppost: ɛamuud nuur, ɛawamiid nuur.
lampshade: burneeṭit ʕabajuura, baraniiṭ ʕabajuura.
land, descend (v): nizil, yinzil; habaṭ, yuhbuṭ.
land (n): ʕarḍ (f), ʕaraaḍi.
landlord: ṣaahib il-beet / ṣaɦb-il-beet.
language: luɣa, -aat.
lantern: fanuus, fawaniis.
Ramadan lanterns; fawaniis ramaḍaan.
large, big: kibiir, kubaar.
large, roomy, spacious: waasiɛ, -iin.
last (adj): (before n), ʕaaxir,ʕawaaxir; (after n) ʕaxiir, -iin.
last, past, previous: ʕilli faat / faatit (f).
last (v): ʕaɛad, yuʕɛud.
continue: ʕistamaar, yistamirr.
last permanently: daam, yiduum.
late (adj): mitʕaxxar, -iin.
late for: mitʕaxxar ɛala.
to be late: ʕitʕaxxar, yitʕaxxar.
latest, modern, most recent: ʕaɦdas.
late (adv): waxri; mitʕaxxar.
lateness: taʕxiir.
later, afterwards: baɛdeen; baɛd^{e} kida.
Latin: latiini.
laugh (a) (v): diɦik, yidɦak (ɛala).
laughter: diɦk.
laundry: *laundry establishment*: tanturleeh.
washing, clothes to be washed: ɣasiil.
washing and ironing: ɣasiil wi makwa.

laundry man: makwagi, (pl), -yya.
law: qanuun, qawaniin.
(*academic subject*): ɦuʕuuʕ.
Islamic law: ʃariiɛa.
law school, faculty of law: kulliyyit ɦuʕuuʕ.
lawyer: muɦaami, (pl), -yyiin.
laxative (*mild*): mulayyin, -aat.
(*strong*): musahhil, -aat.
layered (*hair*): degradee; midarrag.
lazy: kaslaan, -iin.
extremely lazy, hopeless case: xaayib, -iin.
to feel too lazy (*to do s.t.*): kassil, yikassil.
leader: qaaʕid, quwwaad.
political leader: zaɛiim, zuɛama.
leaf: *leaves*: waraʕ, (-a, -aat)
leak (v): (*water*) xarr, yixurr; to drip: naʕʕaṭ, yinaʕʕaṭ.
(*air, gas*); naffis, yinaffis.
leaky valve: balfᵉ-mnaffis.
leaning (adj): maayil, -iin.
leap year: sana kabiisa.
learn: ʕitɛallim, yitɛallim.
learning: taɛallum.
least, at least: ɛa-l-ʕaʕall.
leather: gild, guluud.
leave (n): *sick leave*: ʕagaaza maraḍiyya.
paid leave: ʕagaaza bi-murattab.
unpaid leave: ʕagaaza min ɣeer murattab.
leave (v) (tr): saab, yisiib.
leave, go away (intr): miʃi, yimʃi.
take leave, excuse oneself: ʕistaʕzin, yistaʕzin.
to be left behind, to remain: fiḍil, yifḍal.
leave / keep s.t. where it is: xalla, yixalli; saab, yisiib.
leave for, travel to: saafir, yisaafir (+ *destination*).
Lebanese: libnaani / lubnaani, -yyiin.
Lebanon: libnaan /lubnaan.
lecture (n): muɦaḍra, -aat.
lecture (v): ɦaaḍir, yiɦaaḍir; ʕidda, yiddi muɦaḍra; ʕalqa, yilqi muɦaḍra (cl).
lecturer: muɦaaḍir, -iin.
leeks: kurraat.
left: *left side*: ʃimaal.
left, remaining: faaḍil, -iin.
political left: ʕil-yasaar.
leg: rigl (f), -een (dual), ruguul.
leg, thigh (meat): faxda, -aat.
thigh (*human*): faxd, fixaad.
(*dark meat, thigh of a rabbit or fowl*): wirk.
drumstick: dabbuus, dababiis.
leg of lamb: faxda ḍaani.
legal: qanuuni, -yyiin.
in accordance with Islamic law: ʃarɛi, -yyiin.
legend, fairy tale: ʕusṭuura, ʕasaṭiir.

leisure time: waʕtᵉ faraaɣ.
lemon juice: ɛaṣiir lamuun.
lemons: lamuun (-a, -aat).
lend: sallif, yisallif.
lentils: ɛads.
less: ʕaʕall (comp. of ʕulaayyil).
less than: ʕaʕallᵉ min.
lesson: dars, duruus.
lest: ʕaɦsan; laɦsan (*e.g. lest he fall*: ʕaɦsan yuʕaɛ).
let: xalla, yixalli.
let, permit, allow: samaɦ, yismaɦ (li).
let in: daxxal, yidaxxal.
let out: xarrag, yixarrag.
let's (*do s.t.*): yalla; yalla biina.
letter: gawaab, -aat.
of alphabet: ɦarf, ɦuruuf.
letter box: sanduuʕ busṭa, sanadiiʕ busṭa.
letter of recommendation: gawaab, gawabaat tawṣiyya.
letter opener: fattaaɦit, fattaɦaat gawabaat.
lettuce: xaṣṣ (-a / -aaya, -aat).
iceberg lettuce: kabutʃa.
level (n): mustawa, -yaat (m).
liar: kaḍdaab / kazzaab, -iin.
liberation: taɦriir.
Liberation Square: midaan it-taɦriir.
library: maktaba, -aat.
Libya: libya.
Libyan: liibi, -yyiin.
lice: ʕaml (-a, -aat).
license: ruxṣa, ruxaṣ.
(*international*) *driving license*: ruxṣit siwaaʕa (dawliyya).
license plate: looɦa, -aat / liwaɦ.
car registration: ruxṣit ɛarabiyya.
lid, cover: ɣaṭa, ɣuṭaan.
lie (n): kizba, -aat.
lie, tell a lie (v): kidib, yikdib (ɛala); kizib, yikzib (ɛala).
lie down: naam, yinaam; itsalṭaɦ, yitsalṭaɦ.
lieutenant colonel: muqaddim, -iin.
life: ɦayaah.
life, lifetime: ɛumr, ʕaɛmaar (*all my life*: ṭuul ɛumri).
lifestyle: ɛiiʃa.
lift (n): (*Am.*: *elevator*): ʕasanseer, -aat.
a ride in a car: tawṣiila, -aat.
light (adj) (*not heavy, not strong, eg. coffee*): xafiif, xufaaf.
light (*color*): faatiɦ, -iin.
light (n): nuur, ʕanwaar.
traffic signal: ʕiʃaara, -aat.
red light: ʕiʃaara maʕfuula; ʕiʃaara ɦamra.
green light: ʕiʃaara maftuuɦa; ʕiʃaara xaḍra.
light (v), **ignite**: wallaɛ, yiwallaɛ.
light bulb: lamba, -aat / lumaḍ.
chandelier bulb: lamba balaɦa.
fluorescent, neon bulb: lamba naylun; niyoon.

nail bulb: lamba musmaar.
screw-in bulb:
lamba ʕalawooz̧.
string of lights:
ɦablᵉ lambaat ziina.
light shaft: manwar, manaawir.
light switch: muftaaɦ nuur, mafatiiɦ nuur.
lighter, cigarette lighter: wallaaɛa, -aat.
lighting (*e.g. in a theater*): ʕiḍaaʕa.
lightning: barʕ.
like (adj) *similar to*: zayy.
look like, resemble:
ʃabah (invar); (bi)yiʃbah.
like this (size): ʕaddᵉ kida.
like (v): ɦabb, yiɦibb; ʕistalṭaf, yistalṭaf.
to be liked by (s.o.), *to please, impress*: ɛagab, yiɛgib
(*I liked him*: ɛagab-ni).
as you like: ɛala keef-ak (-ik).
likely, probable: muɦtamal, -iin.
limit (n): ɦadd, ɦuduud.
line (n): xaṭṭ, xuṭuuṭ.
line in book: saṭr, suṭuur (tusṭur, after nos. 3–10).
line, waiting line, queue:
ṭabuur, ṭawabiir.
linguistics: ɛilm il-luɣa; luɣawiyyaat.
lining (n) (*inside clothing*):
biṭaana, baṭaayin / -aat.
link (n): ɦalaʕa, ɦalaʕaat.
link, connection:
ṣila, -aat; ɛilaaʕa, -aat.
lion: ʕasad, ʕusuud; sabɛ, subuɛa.
lip: ʃiffa, ʃafaayif / ʃafateen (dual, cl).
lipstick: ʕaɦmar ʃafaayif; ṣubaaɛ ruuj.
liquor: xamra, xumuur.
liquorice: ɛirʕᵉ suus.
list (n): lista, lisat; ʕayma, ʕawaayim.
list (v): ɦaṭṭ, yiɦuṭṭ fi lista; ɛamal, yiɛmil lista.
listen: simiɛ, yismaɛ.
literal: ɦarfi, -yyiin.
literally: ɦarfiyyan.
literary: ʕadabi.
literature: ʕadab, ʕadaab.
little (*not much*): ʃiwayya.
little, small: ṣuɣayyar, -iin.
live (*be alive*): ɛaaʃ, yiɛiiʃ.
live, reside (*in a place*):
sikin, yuskun.
(part): saakin, -iin.
liver: kibd / kabid.
(*as food*): kibda.
living room:
formal, for guests:
ʕooḍit ṣaloon.
informal, for family and TV:
ʕooḍit ʕuɛaad.
lizard: siɦliyya, saɦaali.
gecko: burṣ, ʕabraaṣ.
load up (tr, intr): ʃaɦan, yiʃɦan.
to be loaded up (passive):
ʕitʃaɦan, yitʃiɦin.
loaf: riɣiif, ʕirɣifa (tirɣifa after nos. 3–10).

loan (n) (*money*): sulfa, -aat / sulaf; salafiyya, -aat; qarḍ, quruuḍ (cl).
on loan: salaf.
an employee on loan: muɛaar, -iin; muntadab, -iin.
loan (v): sallif, yisallif; ʕidda, yiddi sulfa.
lobby (n), *entrance hall*: madxal, madaaxil.
reception desk: risibsiyoon, -aat; maktab-istiʕbaal.
political lobby: loobi.
local: maɦalli, -yyiin.
local, native: baladi (invar).
lock (n): kaloon, kawaliin.
padlock: ʕifl, ʕiʕfaal.
lock (v): sakk, yisukk.
locksmith: kawalingi, (pl), -yya; kalungi, (pl), -yya.
locusts: garaad (-a, -aat).
logic (*school subject*): ʕil-manṭiq.
logical (adj): manṭiqi / manṭiʕi, -yyiin; maɛʕuul, -iin.
long: ṭawiil, ṭuwaal.
as long as, since (conj): ṭuul ma.
how long?: ʕaddᵉ ʕeeh?
how long have you (m) *been here?*: baʕaa-lak ʕaddᵉ ʕee hina?
long distance phone call: tarank / tarank, -aat.
look (*at s.o.*): baṣṣ, yibuṣṣ li.
(*at s.t.*): baṣṣ, yibuṣṣ fi.
look (*on*) (*from above*): ṭall, yiṭull (ɛala); baṣṣ, yibuṣṣ (ɛala).
look around, take a look (*at*): ʕitfarrag, yitfarrag (ɛala).
look for, search for: dawwar, yidawwar (ɛala).
look like, resemble: ʃabah (invar); (bi)yiʃbah.
look out!: ʕiwɛa, (f) ʕiwɛi, ʕiwɛu; ɦaasib, (f) ɦasbi, ɦasbu.
looking, seeming, appearing: baayin, -iin.
loose (adj): saayib, -iin.
loquats: baʃmala.
Lord (*Our Lord*): rabb-i-na.
lorry (*Am.*: *truck*): luuri, lawaari; ɛarabiyya, ɛarabiyyaat naʕl.
lose: ḍayyaɛ, yiḍayyaɛ.
lose (*money in business, gambling, etc.*): xisir, yixsar.
lose a game: ʕitɣalab, yitɣilib.
lose money: xisir, yixsar.
lose weight: xass, yixiss.
lose one's way: taah, yituuh.
loss: xusaara, xasaayir.
lost (adj): (*of an object*): ḍaayiɛ, -iin.
(*of a person*): taayih, -iin.
to be lost: (*object*): ḍaaɛ, yiḍiiɛ;
(*person*): taah, yituuh.
loud: ɛaali, -yiin.
love (n): ɦubb; maɦabba.
love (v): ɦabb, yiɦibb.
lover: ɦabiib, ɦabaayib / ʕaɦbaab.

low: waaṭi, -yiin; munxafiḍ, -iin.
lower (comp): ʕawṭa (invar).
lower, turn down (v) (*volume*): waṭṭa, yiwaṭṭi.
lubricate: ʃaɦɦam, yiʃaɦɦam.
lubricate with oil:
zayyit, yizayyit.
lubrication: taʃɦiim; tazyiit (*with oil*).
luck: ɦaẓẓ, ɦuẓuuẓ; baxt.
lucky: maɦẓuuẓ, -iin; ɛand-u (-ik, etc.) ɦaẓẓ / baxt.
luggage, baggage (*suitcase*): ʃanṭa, ʃunaṭ.
lunch: ɣada.
to eat lunch:
ʕitɣadda, yitɣadda.
lung: riʕa, -aat. lungs (dual): riʕateen.
lung cancer: saraṭaan ir-riʕa.
lupine seeds: tirmis (-a, -aat).
Luxor: luʕṣur.
luxuries: kamaliyyaat.
lying (n) (*telling lies*): kidb / kizb.

M

M.A. degree: majisteer, -aat.
Maadi: ʕil-maɛaadi.
macaroni: makaroona.
mace (*spice*): bisbaasa.
machine: makana, -aat / makan; ʕaala, -aat.
mackerel (*canned fish*): salamun.
madam: madaam; sitt, -aat; haanim, hawaanim; ʕissayyida + *name* (*polite form of address*).
made of: maɛmuul, -iin, min; maṣnuuɛ, -iin, min.
magazine: magalla, -aat.
magic: siɦr.
magical: siɦri, -yyiin.
magician: saaɦir, saɦara; ɦaawi, ɦuwaa.
maid: ʃaɣɣaala, -aat.
mail (n): busṭa.
air mail: bariid gawwi.
mail (v) (*a letter*): rama, yirmi (gawaab).
mailbox: sanduuʢ, sanadiiʢ busṭa.
mailman: busṭagi, (pl), -yya.
main: ɛumuumi; raʕiisi.
maitre d'hotel: mitr.
maize: dura.
major, specialization (n): taxaṣṣuṣ, -aat.
major, specialize (v): ʕitxaṣṣaṣ, yitxaṣṣaṣ (fi).
majority: ʕaɣlabiyyit in-naas; ʕaɣlabiyya.
make: ɛamal, yiɛmil.
make happy: farraɦ, yifarraɦ.
make it Sunday (*fixing an appointment*): xallii-ha yoom il-ɦadd.
make the bed: waḍḍab, yiwaḍḍab is-siriir.
make up with: ṣaaliɦ, yiṣaaliɦ; ʕitṣaaliɦ, yitṣaaliɦ (maɛa)
make up for, compensate: ɛawwaḍ, yiɛawwaḍ.
make-up, cosmetics: makyaaj.
male (adj) (*plants or animals*): dakar, dukura.
man: raagil, riggaala.
men's (*used or worn by men*): rigaali (invar).
manager: mudiir, -iin.
mangoes: manga (-aaya, -aat).
manicure (*nail polish*): manikyuur.
manners: ʕadab; zooʢ.
well-mannered: muʕaddab, -iin; muhazzab, -iin.
ill-mannered: ʢallil il-ʕadab, ʢullalaat il-ʕadab.
manual (*instructions*): kataloog, -aat.
manuscript: maxṭuuṭ, -aat; maxṭuuṭa, -aat.
many: kitiir, kutaar.
map: xariiṭa, xaraayiṭ.
marble: ruxaam.

March: maaris.
margarine: margariin.
margin: haamiʃ, hawaamiʃ.
marjoram: bardaʕuuʃ / bardaʕooʃ.
mark, put a sign (v): ɛallim, yiɛallim.
marketplace: suuʕ, ʕaswaaʕ.
marketing: taswiiʕ.
marriage: gawaaz; zawaag (cl).
marriage contract signing: katb^e-ktaab.
married: mitgawwiz, -iin.
get married (*to*): ʕitgawwiz, yitgawwiz.
mascara: maskara.
masculine (gr): muzakkar.
mash (v): haras, yihris.
mashed, pureed: biyureeh; mahruus.
mask: qinaaɛ, ʕaqniɛa.
Mass (*church service*): ʕuddaas.
master: sayyid, ʕasyaad.
Master's degree: majisteer, -aat.
mastic: mistika.
mat: ɦaʂiira, ɦuʂr.
matches: kabriit.
matchstick: ɛuud kabriit, ɛidaan kabriit.
matchbox: ɛilbit kabriit, ɛilab kabriit.
match, tournament: matʃ, -aat / mubaraah.
material, *cloth*: ʕumaaʃ, -aat / ʕaʕmiʃa.
material, substance: maadda, mawaadd.
mathematics: riyaaɖa; riyaɖiyyaat.
matte, dull (*in color*): maʈfi (invar).
matter (n): *affair*: ɦikaaya, -aat.
problem, issue: masʕala, masaaʕil.
what's the matter: ʕee-l-ɦikaaya, fii ʕee.
what's the matter with you: maal-ak (-ik, -ku).
mattress: martaba, maraatib.
mausoleum: ɖariiɦ, ʕaɖriɦa.
maximum: ɦadd^e ʕaqʂa.
May: maayu.
may: (*conjecture*): gaayiz; yimkin (both invar).
(*permission, ability*): mumkin (invar).
maybe, possibly: muɦtamal; yimkin; gaayiz (all invar).
mayonnaise: mayuneez.
me: *see pronominal suffix chart.*
mean: *it means*: yaɛni (invar).
to mean, intend: ʕaʂad, yuʕʂud.
what do you (m) *mean*: ʕaʂd-ak ʕee.
I mean: ʕaʂd-i.
meaning: maɛna, maɛaani.
what's the meaning of: yaɛni ʕee (invar).
meant, intended: maʕʂuud, -iin.
meanwhile: fil-waʕt^e da.
measles: ɦaʂba.
German measles: ɦaʂba ʕalmaani.

measure (v): ʕaas, yiʕiis.
meat: laɦma, luɦuum.
mechanic: mikaniiki, (pl), -yya.
mechanical engineering:
handasa mikanikiyya.
medical checkup: kaʃf[e] ṭibbi.
medical treatment: ɛilaag.
medicine (*drug*): dawa (m), ʕadwiya.
medicine, medical profession or field of study: ṭibb.
Mediterranean Sea, the:
ʕil-baɦr il-ʕabyaḍ (il-mutawassiṭ).
medium (adj): mutawassiṭ, -iin.
meet (v) (tr): ʕaabil, yiʕaabil.
(intr): ʕitʕaabil, yitʕaabil (maɛa).
make the acquaintance of: ʕitɛarraf, yitɛarraf (bi).
meeting: ʕigtimaaɛ, -aat.
hold a meeting (*with*): ʕigtamaɛ, yigtimiɛ (maɛa).
informal meeting: muʕabla.
melon: ʃammaam (-a, -aat).
melt: saaɦ, yisiiɦ.
member: ɛuḍw, ʕaɛḍaaʕ; miʃtirik / muʃtarik, -iin (fi).
membership: ɛuḍwiyya, -aat; ʕiʃtiraak, -aat.
memorial, rememberance: zikra, -yaat.
memorize: ṣamm, yiṣumm; ɦafaẓ, yiɦfaẓ.
memory: zaakira.
meningitis: ʕiltihaab suɦaaʕi.
men's (*clothes, etc., pertaining to men*): rigaali (invar).
menstruation: ɛaada, -aat; ɦeeḍ; dawra ʃahriyya.
mention: zakar, yuzkur.
menu: menyu.
meow (n): nawnawa.
meow (v): nawnaw, yinawnaw.
merchant: taagir, tuggaar.
mercy: raɦma.
to have mercy on: raɦam, yirɦam.
may God have mercy on his soul: ʕallaa yirɦamu.
message: risaala, rasaayil.
metal: maɛdan, maɛaadin.
metalwork, bodywork (*on a car*): samkara.
metal worker: samkari, (pl), -yya.
meter (*measure of length*): mitr, ʕamtaar.
(*e.g. electric or in a cab*): ɛaddaad, -aat.
meter reader (*for elect.*): kaʃʃaaf, -iin nuur.
method: ṭariiʕa, ṭuruʕ.
metro: mitru; mitru-l-ʕanfaaʕ.
Mexican: maksiiki / miksiiki, -yyiin.
middle (adj): wisṭaani, -yyiin.
middle (n): wisṭ.
the Middle East: ʕiʃ-ʃarq il-ʕawsaṭ.
midwife: daaya, -aat.
might: mumkin (invar)
milage: kilumitraaj.
military (adj): ɛaskari, -yyiin.
military police: ʃurṭa ɛaskariyya.

milk: laban.
milkman: labbaan; (ʕir-raagil) bitaaɛ il-laban.
minced, ground: mafruum, -iin.
mind (n) (*intellect*): ɛaʕl, ɛuʕuul; zihn, ʕazhaan.
(*opinion*): raʕy, ʕaraaʕ (cl).
mind (v): *do you mind?*: ɛandak (-ik, -uku) maaniɛ?
mine (pronoun): (m) bitaaɛ-i, (f) bitaɛt-i, (pl) bituuɛ-i.
mineral water: mayya maɛdaniyya.
minimum: ʕaʕall; ħadde ʕadna.
minister (*in govt.*): waziir, wuzara.
(*in religion*): ʕassiis, ʕusus.
ministry: wizaara, aat.
minority: ʕaqalliyya, -aat.
mint (*plant*): niɛnaaɛ.
mint tea: ʃaay bi-niɛnaaɛ.
minus: ʕilla.
minute (n): diʕiiʕa, daʕaayiʕ.
two minutes: diʕiʕteen.
miracle: muɛgiza, -aat.
mirror: miraaya, -aat.
miserly, stingy: baxiil, buxala.
Miss: madmuzeel, -aat; ʕaanisa, -aat (*formal*, cl.).
miss: *lack*: niʕiṣ, yinʕaṣ.
I missed the train: ʕil-ʕaṭre fat-ni (v. faat, yifuut).
be missed by: waħaʃ, yiwħaʃ, (part): waaħiʃ.
(*e.g. I missed you* (m): waħaʃt-i-ni)
response: *and* (*I missed*) *you too*: w-inta (w-inti, w-intu) kamaan.
I miss you: waħiʃni (to m.), waħʃaani (to f.).
missing, lost: ḍaayiɛ, -iin.
lacking: naaʕiṣ, -iin.
mist: ʃabbuura.
mistake: ɣalṭa, -aat.
make a mistake: ɣiliṭ, yiɣlaṭ.
mistaken: ɣalṭaan, -iin.
mix (v): xalaṭ, yixliṭ.
mix up, confuse: laxbaṭ, yilaxbaṭ, bargil, yibargil.
mixed up, confused: mitlaxbaṭ, -iin.
mixed, assorted: miʃakkil, -iin.
mixed, blended: maxluuṭ, -iin.
mixture: xalṭa, -aat.
assortment: taʃkiila, -aat.
mobile phone: mubayl, -aat; maħmuul, -aat.
mock, make fun (**of**): ʕittaryaʕ, yittaryaʕ (ɛala).
model, fashion: mudeel, -aat.
fashion model (*person*): manikaan, -aat.
modern: ħadiis, -iin; muɛaaṣir, -iin.
modest: mitwaaḍiɛ, -iin; mutawaaḍiɛ, -iin (cl).
molar: ḍirs, ḍuruus.
molasses: ɛasal ʕiswid.
moldy: miɛaffin, -iin.
moment: laħẓa, -aat.
mommy: maama.
Monaco: munaaku.
monastery, convent: deer, ʕadyira.

Monday: yoom l-itneen.
money: filuus.
mongoose: nims, numuus.
monk: raahib, ruhbaan.
monkey: ʕird, ʕuruud.
month: ʃahr, ʃuhuur / ʕaʃhur (tuʃhur, after nos. 3–10).
monthly (adj): ʃahri, -yyiin.
monuments (*historic*): ʕasaar.
mood: mazaag, ʕamziga; nifs.
I am in no mood for: maliiʃ mazaag / nifs li.
moon: ʕamar, ʕaʕmaar.
moonlight: ʕamara.
mop (n): mamsaɦa, mamaasiɦ.
mop (v): masaɦ. yimsaɦ.
morals: ʕaxlaaʕ.
more (comp): ʕaktar.
more, additional quantity: kamaan.
more, extra: ziyaada (ɛan).
five more minutes: faadil xamas daʕaayiʕ.
morning: ṣubɦ.
in the morning: ʕiṣ-ṣubɦ.
good morning: ṣabaaɦ-ilxeer.
response: ṣabaaɦ-innuur.
Morocco: ʕil-maɣrib.
mortar (*with pestle*): hoon.
mosque: gaamiɛ, gawaamiɛ; masgid, masaagid.
mosquitoes: namuus (-a, -aat).
most, the majority of: muɛẓam; ʕaɣlab; ʕaktar.
mostly, most probably: ɣaaliban.
mother: ʕumm, -ahaat; walda (*formal*).
your mom: mamt-ak (-ik, mamit-ku).
mother-in-law: ɦama (*my mother-in-law*: ɦamaati).
Mother's Day: ɛiid il-ʕumm.
mother-of-pearl, shell: ṣadaf (-a, -aat).
moths, butterflies: faraaʃ (-a, -aat).
clothes moths: ɛitta (ɛitta, ɛitat).
motor, engine: mutoor, -aat.
mountain: gabal, gibaal.
mouse: faar, firaan.
mouth: buʕʕ. (no pl).
move (v) (tr): ɦarrak, yiɦarrak.
transfer, carry: naʕal, yinʕil.
(intr): ʕitɦarrak, yitɦarrak.
move (*in*) (*to a new residence*): ɛazzil, yiɛazzil (fi).
move to a new country: ʕitnaʕal, yitniʕil.
the train moved: ʕil-ʕaṭr^{e} miʃi / ʕil-ʕaṭr^{e} ʕaam.
movie, film: film, ʕaflaam.
movie house: sinima, -aat.
moving (adj) (*emotionally*): miʕassar / muʕassir, iin.
Mr.: ʕis-sayyid; ʕil-ʕustaaz.
Mrs.: madaam.
much: kitiir.
how much (*quantity*): ʕadd^{e} ʕeeh.
this much: ʕadd^{e} kida.
how much (*price*): bi-kaam.
mud: ṭiin.
muffler (*on a car*): ɛilbit ʃakmaan.

mulberries: tuut (-a, -aat).
mule: bayl, biyaal.
female mule: bayla, -aat.
mullet, gray: buuri (-yya, -yaat).
red: barbooni (barbunaaya, -aat).
multiplication table: gadwall ɖarb.
multiply: ɖarab, yiɖrab (by: fi).
mummy (*preserved body*): mumya, -aat / mumawaat.
mumps: ʕiltihaab il-yudda-n-nakafiyya.
muscles: ɛaɖal, (-a, -aat).
museum: matɦaf, mataaɦif.
mushrooms: ɛiʃʃ^e yuraab.
music: mazziika; musiiqa.
musical, musician: musiiqi, -yyiin.
Muslim: muslim, -iin.
must: laazim (invar); yagib ʕinn (cl, invar).
mustache: ʃanab, -aat.
mustard: muʂʈarda; xardal.
musty: *it smells musty*: riɦtu radda.
my: *see pronominal suffix chart*.

N

nag, pester (n): zann, yizinn (fi).
nail (*fingernail*): ɖufr, ɖawaafir.
(*tool*): musmaar, masamiir.
nail file: mabrad ɖawaafir, mabaarid ɖawaafir.
nail polish, varnish: manikyuur.
naive: saazig, -iin / suzzaag; ɛala niyyaat-u (-ha, etc.).
naked: ɛiryaan, -iin / ɛaraaya.
stark naked: ɛiryaan malʈ, ɛiryaniin malʈ.
name: ʕism, ʕasaami / ʕasmaaʕ.
what is your name?: ʕism-ak (-ik) ʕeeh?
nanny: murabbiyya, -aat.
nap (n): taɛsiila, -aat; ɣafwa, -aat.
nap (v) (*take a nap*): ɛassil, yiɛassil;
xad, yaaxud ɣafwa;
xad, yaaxud taɛsiila.
napkin, table napkin: fuuʈa, fuwaʈ; fuuʈit sufra, fuwaʈ sufra.
nappy (*Am.*: *diaper*): kafuula, kawafiil; bambas (*Pampers*).
narrate: ɧaka, yiɧki.
narrow: dayyaʕ, -iin.
nasal congestion: zukaam.
having nasal congestion: mizakkim, -iin.
nation: ʕumma, ʕumam.
homeland: waʈan, ʕawʈaan.
people: ʃaɛb, ʃuɛuub.
national: waʈani, -yyiin; qawmi, -yyiin; ʕahli.
nationalism: qawmiyya, -aat.
Arab nationalism: ʕil-qawmiyya l-ɛarabiyya.
nationalist: qawmi, -yyiin.
nationality: ginsiyya, -aat.
native: baladi (invar);
ʕibn, ʕawlaad balad (*ref. to people*).
natural: ʈabiiɛi, -yyiin.
naturally, of course: ʈabɛan; ʈabiiɛi.
nature: ʕiʈ-ʈabiiɛa.
naughty, mischievous: ʃaʕi, ʕaʃʕiya / ʃuʕaay;
ɛafriit, ɛafariit (*demon*).
nauseous, nauseated: mitʕaaya/ mitʕaayi.
I am feeling nauseous: nifs-i ɣamma ɛalayya.
he is feeling nauseous: nifs-u ɣamma ɛalee.
she is feeling nauseous: nifs-a-ha ɣamma ɛalee-ha.
navy (*military*): baɧriyya.
(*blue color*): kuɧli (invar).
near: ʕurayyib, -iin (li / min).
(*near by, in the vicinity of*): gamb; ɛand.
nearer, nearest: ʕaʕrab.
at the nearest opportunity: fi ʕaʕrab furʂa.
nearly: taʕriiban.

neat: *elegant*: ʃiik (invar).
arranged, orderly: mitsattif; munaẓẓam; mirattib/ murattab, iin.
necessary: ḍaruuri, -yyiin; laazim, -iin.
necessity: luzuum; ḍaruura.; lazma.
there is no necessity for: mafiiʃ luzuum li.
neck: raʕaba, riʕaab.
necklace: ɛuʕd, ɛuʕuud.
necktie: karavatta / garafatta, -aat.
need (n): luzuum.
no need (*for*): mafiiʃ luzuum (li); mafiiʃ daaɛi (*to do s.t.*).
need (v): ʕiɦtaag, yiɦtaag (li); ɛaaz, yiɛuuz.
(part): miɦtaag, -iin; ɛaayiz, -iin.
needle: ʕibra, ʕibar.
negate (gr): nafa, yinfi.
neighbor: gaar, giraan.
neighborhood: manṭiʕa, manaaṭiʕ; ɦitta, ɦitat; ɦayy, ʕaɦyaaʕ.
neither ... nor: la ... wala ...
neon light: lamba naylun / niyoon, lumaḍ naylun / niyoon.
nephew: son of brother / of sister ...: ʕibn axu / uxt ...
nephews of ...: wilaad axu / uxt ...
nervous, irritable: ɛaṣabi, -yyiin.
(*momentarily*): mitnarfiz, -iin.
to get nervous: ʕitɛaṣṣab, yitɛaṣṣab; ʕitnarfiz, yitnarfiz.
nervous breakdown: ʕinhiyaar ɛaṣabi.
nervousness: narfaza; ɛaṣabiyya.
nest: ɛiʃʃ, ɛiʃuuʃ.
net (adj): ṣaafi, -yiin.
net profit: ribɦ^e ṣaafi, ʕarbaaɦ ṣafya.
net (n): *grid* (*for sports, communications*): ʃabaka, -aat.
soccer goal: goon, giwaan / ʕagwaan.
basketball net: salla, silal.
neutral (*in a conflict*): muɦaayid, -iin; ɛala-l-ɦiyaad.
never: ʕabadan (*following negative statements*).
never in my (*his, etc.*) *life*: ɛumri (-u, etc.) ma.
I've never seen him before: ɛumri ma ʃuftu ʕabl^e kida.
never mind, take it easy: maɛliʃʃ.
never mind (*don't*): balaaʃ.
new: gidiid, gudaad.
brand new: gidiid lang.
New Year: raas is-sana.
news: xabar, ʕaxbaar.
what's new?: ʕaxbaar-ak (-ik, etc.) ʕeeh?
newspaper: gurnaal, garaniil; gariida, garaayid.
next, the following: ʕilli gayy / ʕig-gayy, -iin.

next sunday: yoom il-ɦadd illi gayy.
the next one (in a sequence): ʕilli baɛdu.

nice, *pleasant*: laʈiif, luʈɑɑf.
charming: zɑriif, zurɑɑf.
kind, good-natured: ʈɑyyib, -iin.
nice looking: ɦilw, -iin.

nickname: ʕism^e dalaɛ, ʕasaami / ʕasmaaʕ dalaɛ.

niece: *daughter of brother / of sister ...*: bint axu / uxt ...
nieces of ...: banaat axu / uxt ...

night (adj, *e.g. night school*): layli, -yyiin.

night (n): leel (-a, layaali).
at night: bil-leel.
tonight: ʕil-leela; ʕil-lelaa-di.
to pass the night, stay overnight: baat, yibaat; bayyit, yibayyit.

night club: nayt^e klub; malha, malaahi; naadi layli, nawaadi layliyya; naadi-l-leel; kabareeh, -aat.

nightgown: ʕɑmiiṣ noom, ʕumṣɑɑn noom.

Nile, the: ʕin-niil.

nine: tisɛa (tisaɛ, before pl. n).

nineteen: tisɑɛtɑɑʃɑr.

ninety: tisɛiin.

no: laʕ.
no ..., (forbidden): mamnuuɛ.
no smoking: mamnuuɛ it-tadxiin.
there is no ...: mafiiʃ ....

no one, nobody: maɦaddiʃ.
there is no one: mafiiʃ hadd.

noise: dawʃa.

none: *there is none*: mafiiʃ.
it's all gone (finished): xiliṣ.

noodles, pasta: mɑkɑroona.

noon: ɖuhr.
at noon: ʕiɖ-ɖuhr.
afternoon: baɛd iɖ-ɖuhr.

normal, regular, ordinary (adj): ɛaadi, -yyiin.

normally: ɛaadatan; fil-ɛaada.

north: ʃamaal.

northern, northward: ʃamaali, -yyiin.
northerly wind: riyaaɦ ʃamaliyya.
(*seaward, i.e. toward Mediterranean*): baɦari / baɦri.

Norway: ʕin-nirwiig.

nose (*nostrils*): manaxiir (pl).

nosey: fuɖuuli, -iin / -yya; ɦuʃari, -yyiin.

not: miʃ.
(*with some tenses*): ma ... ʃ (*see formation of negatives chart*).
there isn't: mafiiʃ.
not bad: miʃ bɑʈʈɑɑl, -iin; miʃ wiɦiʃ, -iin.

notebook: kurrɑɑsɑ, karariis (*thin*); kaʃkuul, kaʃakiil (*thick*).
loose leaf ring binder: kilaseer, -ɑɑt.
spiral notebook: kaʃkuul silk.

notepad: nuuta / noota, -aat / niwat (*small*); bulukk^e noot (*large*).
nothing: wala ɦaaga.
it's nothing (*said after an accident*): ɦaṣal xeer.
notification: ʕiʃɛaar, -aat; ʕixṭaar, -aat.
novel (n): riwaaya, -aat.
November: nufimbir / nuvimbir.
now: dilwaʕti.
nowadays, these days: ʕil-ʕayyaam di; ʕil-yumeen dool.
nowhere: wala ɦitta.
Nubia: ʕin-nuuba.
Nubian: nuubi, -yyiin.
nuclear: nawawi, -yyiin; zarri, -yyiin (*atomic*).
number: ɛadad, ʕaɛdaad.
designation in a series, e.g. house no.: nimra, nimar.
page no., I.D. no.: raqam, ʕarqaam (cl).
wrong number (*telephone*): ʕin-nimra ɣalaṭ.
nun: rahba / raahiba, rahbaat.
nurse (f): mumarriḍa, -aat.
nurse (m), *hospital orderly*: tamargi, (pl), -yya.
nursery (*for children*): ɦaḍaana, -aat.
(*for plants*): maʃtal, maʃaatil.
nut: (*see also* **nuts**).
nut that goes with bolt: ṣamuula, ṣawamiil.
nutcracker: kassaara, -aat.
nutmeg: gooz iṭ-ṭiib.
nuts, dried seeds: mikassaraat.
nylon (*material*): naylun / naylu.
nylons (*pantyhose*): kuloon; ʃaraab naylun.

O

oasis: waaɦa, -aat.
oatmeal: kweekir.
oats: ʃufaan.
obese, fat: tixiin, tuxaan; simiin, sumaan.
object (v) (to): ʕiεtarad̨, yiεtirid̨ (εala).
objection: ʕiεtiraad̨, -aat.
no objection: mafiiʃ maaniε.
objective, aim (n): hadaf, ʕahdaaf; ʕaṣd.
obligated: mut̨t̨arr, -iin.
to be obligated: ʕit̨t̨arr, yit̨t̨arr.
obligation, duty: waagib, -aat.
obliged: *see* **obligated.**
obscene: ʕabiiɦ, ʕubaɦa.
obscenity: ʕabaaɦa.
obstacle: maaniε, mawaaniε.
obstinate: ṣilib, -iin; εaniid, εunaad;
raas-u (-ha, etc.) naʃfa;
dimaaɣ-u (-ha, etc.) naʃfa.
obstruct, delay (*one's work*): εat̨t̨al, yiεat̨t̨al.
obvious: waad̨iɦ, -iin.
occasion: munasba, -aat.
on the occasion of: bi-munasbit.
occasionally: min waʕtᵉ lit-taani.
occupation, *profession*: mihna, mihan.
trade: ɦirfa, ɦiraf.
military occupation: ʕiɦtilaal.
occupied, *busy*: maʃɣuul, -iin.
occupied militarily: muɦtall.
occupy: ʕiɦtall, yiɦtall.
occupy s.o.'s time, thoughts: ʃaɣal, yiʃɣil.
ocean: muɦiit̨, -aat.
October: ʕuktoobar.
odometer: ik-kilumitr.
of (*partitive*): min.
(*genitive*) *belonging to*: bitaaε (m), bitaaεit (f), bituuε (pl).
of course: t̨abεan.
offer (n): εard̨, εuruud̨.
offer (v): ʕaddim, yiʕaddim; εarad̨, yiεrid̨ (εala).
offer me a cigarette: εazam, yiεzim εalayya bi-sgaara.
office: maktab, makaatib.
doctor's office (*Br.*: *surgery*): εiyaada, -aat.
officer: z̨aabit̨, z̨ubbaat̨.
military officer: z̨aabit̨ geeʃ.
police officer: z̨aabit̨ ʃurt̨a / buliis.
official (adj): rasmi, -yyiin.
official (n) (*in sports match*): muraaʕib, muraʕbiin, mubaraah.
often, quite often: kitiir; saεaat kitiira.
very often: kullᵉ saaεa wi-t-tanya.

oil (n): zeet, zuyuut.
lubricating oil: zeet taʃɦiim.
motor oil: zeet mutoor.
oil can: mazyata, mazaayit.
olive oil: zeet zatuun.
petroleum: bitrool.
oil (v): zayyit, yizayyit.
okay (*agreement*): ṭayyib; maaʃi.
(adj): kwayyis; miʃ bɑṭṭɑal.
okra: bamya.
old (*not new*): ʕadiim, ʕudaam.
to become old (*not new*): ʕidim, yiʕdam.
(*not young*): kibiir, kubɑɑr.
very old person: ɛaguuz, ɛawagiiz.
to grow old: kibir, yikbɑr; ɛaggiz, yiɛaggiz (*grow very old*).
olive (*color*): zatuuni (invar).
dark green: zeeti (invar).
olives: zatuun (-a, -aat).
omelet: ɛigga; ʕumlett.
on (prep): ɛala (ɛalee + *pron suffix*: ɛaleek, -ki *etc. but* ɛalayya *on me*).
on (*e.g. radio*): waaliɛ, -iin; ʃaɣɣaal, -iin.
to turn on: wallaɛ, yiwallaɛ; ʃaɣɣal, yiʃaɣɣal.
once: mɑrrɑ, -ɑɑt.
three times: talat mɑrrɑɑt.
once upon a time there was: kaan yama kaan; kaan fii mɑrrɑ.

one: waaɦid, (f) waɦda.
one (pron): ʕil-waɦda.
one of the girls: bint min il-banaat.
one of a pair: farda, firad (*things, e.g. shoes, gloves*).
one more year: kamaan sana.
one year from now: baɛd^{e} sana.
one after another: waaɦid baɛd it-taani.
one another, each other: bɑɛḍ.
one-fourth: rubɛ, ʕirbaɛ.
one-fourth kilogram: rubɛ^{e} kiilu.
three-fourths: talat tirbaɛ.
one-third: tilt, ʕatlaat.
one-way street: ʃaariɛ b-ittigaah waaɦid.
no right turn: mafiiʃ yimiin.
no left turn: mafiiʃ ʃimaal.
onions: bɑṣɑl (-ɑ / -ɑɑyɑ, -ɑɑt).
only (adj) (*e.g. only son*): waɦiid.
only (adv): bass.
open (v): fataɦ, yiftaɦ.
open ones eyes: fattaɦ, yifattaɦ.
open, opened (adj): maftuuɦ, -iin.
(*referring to store hours*): faatiɦ, -iin.
opener (*can opener*): fattaaɦa, -aat; fattaaɦit ɛilab.
operate (*e.g. a machine*): ʃaɣɣal, yiʃaɣɣal.
operation (*e.g. medical*): ɛamaliyya, -aat.
to have or perform an operation: ɛamal, yiɛmil ɛamaliyya.

opinion: raʕy, ʕaraaʕ.
what is your opinion:
ʕeeh raʕy-ak (-ik, -uku).
opportunity: furṣa, furaṣ.
at the earliest opportunity:
fi-ʕaʕrab furṣa.
opposite, facing: ʕuṣaad; ʕubaal.
opposite, contrary: ɛaks.
opposition: muɛarḍa.
oppress: ẓalam, yuẓlum / yiẓlim.
optional: ʕixtiyaari, -yyiin.
or (*in statements*): ʕaw.
(*in questions*): walla.
or rather: walla.
or else, lest: ʕaḥsan, laḥsan.
or else, otherwise: wa ʕilla.
oral, spoken: ʃafawi.
orange (*color*): burtuʕaani / burtuʕaani (invar).
oranges: burtuʕaan / burtuʕaan (-a, -aat).
navel oranges:
burtuʕaan ʕabu surra.
order (n): *arrangement*: tartiib, -aat.
in order: bit-tartiib.
(*opposite of chaos*): niẓaam.
command: ʕamr, ʕawaamir.
request: ṭalab, -aat.
in order to: ɛaʃaan.
order (v): *command*: ʕamar, yuʕmur.
request: ṭalab, yuṭlub.
orderly (*at hospital*): tamargi, (pl), -yya.
orderly, organized: munaẓẓam, -iin.
ordinary: ɛaadi, -yiin.
oregano, thyme: zaɛtar / zaɛtar.
organization (*abstract*): niẓaam, ʕanẓima.
an organization, group:
munaẓẓama, -aat.
organize: naẓẓam, yinaẓẓam; rattib, yirattib.
organized: munaẓẓam, -iin; mirattib / murattab, -iin.
origin: ʕaṣl, ʕuṣuul.
original: ʕaṣli, -yyiin.
originally: ʕaṣlan.
orphan: yitiim, yutama / ʕaytaam / yataama.
orphanage: malgaʕ ʕaytaam, malaagiʕ ʕaytaam.
orthopedist: duktoor ɛiẓaam.
other, another: taani, -yiin.
other than: ɣeer.
otherwise: wa ʕilla.
our: *see pronominal suffix chart*.
ours: (m) bitaɛ-na, (f) bitaɛit-na, (pl) bituɛ-na.
out: *outside*: barra.
to take out (*for entertainment*):
fassaḥ, yifassaḥ.
there is none: mafiiʃ.
we're out of sugar (*etc.*):
ʕis-sukkar xiliṣ / xaaliṣ.
out of order (*broken*): ɛaṭlaan, -iin; xasraan, -iin.
to be out of order:
ɛiṭil, yiɛṭal; xisir, yixsar.
outing: fusḥa, fusaḥ.
outlet (*electrical socket*): bariiza, baraayiz.

outside (prep, adv): bɑrrɑ.

outside, outer (adj): bɑrrɑɑni,
 -yyiin.
 external: xaarigi (cl).

outstanding: mutafawwiq, -iin.

oval: baydɑɑwi, -yyiin.

oven: furn, ʕafrɑɑn.

over, above: fooʕ.

over, it's over, it's finished:
 xɑlɑɑṣ (invar).
 to be over, to end:
 ʕintaha, yintihi; xiliṣ, yixlɑṣ.

overcoat: bɑlṭu, balɑɑṭi.

overhasty, rash: mutasarriɛ, -iin.
 to be overhasty:
 ʕitsɑrrɑɛ, yitsɑrrɑɛ.

overpass (*Br.*: *flyover*): kubri,
 kabaari.

overseas: bɑrrɑ; fil-xaarig.

oversleep (v): rɑɑɦit, tiruuɦ
 ɛaleeh (-ha, etc.) nooma.

overtime, additional hours:
 saɛaat ʕiḍafiyya.

owe: *I owe you one pound*:
 ɛalayya ginee;
 lak (-ki) ginee; liik (-ki)
 ɛandi ginee.
 you owe me one pound:
 ɛaleek (-ki) ginee;
 liyya ɛandak (-ik) ginee.

owls: buum (-a, -aat).

owner (*of*): ṣɑɑɦib, ʕaṣɦaab
 (+ n / pron).
 owner of house (*landlord*):
 ṣaaɦib il-beet; ṣaɦb-il-beet.
 (*of property*):
 maalik, mullak; ṣaaɦib milk.

ox: toor, tiraan.

P

pack (n): baaku, -haat / -waat / bawaaki; ɛilba, ɛilab.
pack up: laff, yiliff.
(*suitcases*):
waḍḍab, yiwaḍḍab (ʃunaṭ).
package: laffa, -aat / lifaf; baaku, -haat.
mailed or shipped package: ṭard, ṭuruud.
pad of paper: nuuta / noota, -aat / niwat (*small*); bulukkᵉ noot (*large*).
padlock: ʕifl, ʕiʕfaal.
page: ṣafḥa, -aat.
pail, *bucket*: gardal, garaadil.
pain (n): wagaɛ, ʕawgaaɛ; ʕalam, ʕalaam.
pain, give pain to, hurt (v): wagaɛ, yiwgaɛ.
I have pain in my leg.: rigli-btiwgaɛ-ni.
paint (n): buuya, -aat; dihaan.
paint (v): dahan, yidhin.
paint a house, whitewash: bayyaḍ, yibayyaḍ.
paint, draw: rasam, yirsim.
painter (*pictures*): rassaam, -iin. (*walls*): naʕʕaaʃ, -iin; mibayyaḍ, -iin; mibayyaḍaati, (pl), -yya.
painting (n) (*pictures*): ṣuura, ṣuwar; looḥa, luḥaat; rasm, rusumaat.
pair: gooz, ʕagwaaz (tigwaaz, after nos. 3–10).
pajama: bijaama, -aat.
palace: ʕaṣr, ʕuṣuur.
Palestine: filisṭiin / falasṭiin.
Palestinian: filisṭiini / falasṭiini, -yyiin.
Palestinian Authority: ʕis-sulṭa l-filisṭiniyya.
Palestine Liberation Organization: munaẓẓamit it-taḥriir il-filisṭiniyya.
Palestinian National Council: ʕil-maglis il-waṭani il-filisṭiini.
Palm Sunday: ḥadd iz-zaɛaf.
palm oil: zeet naxiil.
palm trees: naxl (-a, -aat).
pan: frying pan: ṭaasa, -aat.
cooking pot: ḥalla, ḥilal.
saucepan: kasarulla / kasaroona, -aat.
milk pan: labbaana, -aat.
panther: nimrᵉ ʕiswid; fahd, fuhuud.
pancakes (*small, to stuff*): ʕaṭaayif.
pantihose: kuloon, -aat.
pants: *trousers, slacks*: banṭaloon, -aat.
underpants, underwear: kulutt / kilutt, -aat.
papaya: babaaya.
paper (n): waraʕ (-a, -aat).
newspaper: gurnaal, garaniil; gariida, garaayid.
research paper: baḥs, buḥuus / ʕabḥaas.

paper clip: kilibs^e, kilibsaat waraʕ;
maʃbak, maʃaabik waraʕ.
paper cutter: maʕaṣṣ^e, maʕaṣṣaat waraʕ.
paperweight: tuʕʕaalit, tuʕʕalaat waraʕ.
papyrus: bardi; waraʕ il-bardi.
Paradise, Heaven: ʕig-ganna.
paralyzed: maʃluul, -iin.
parcel: ṭard, ṭuruud.
pardon (n): ɛafw.
I beg your pardon?: ʕafandim?; naɛam?
pardon (v): ɛafa, yiɛfi (ɛan).
parentheses: qoos, ʕaqwaas.
in parentheses: been quseen.
parents (*family*): ʕahl.
my parents: ʕahli;
ʕabuu-ya w-umm-i;
wald-i w-waldit-i (*formal*).
daddy and mommy: baaba w-maama.
park (n): gineena, ganaayin.
park (v): rakan, yirkin.
parking lot: mawʕaf, mawaaʕif;
makaan rakn.
parquet flooring: barkeeh, -aat.
parsley: baʕduunis.
part time: bartaaym.
by the hour: bis-saaɛa.
temporary, seasonal: ẓuhuraat (adj, invar).
seasonal worker: ɛaamil, ɛummaal taraḥiil.
temporary, short term: muwaʕʕat.

part, section (n): guzʕ, ʕagzaaʕ.
part in a series: ḥalaʕa, -aat.
part in hair: farʕ.
part in a play, movie, etc., role: door, ʕadwaar.
participate: ʕiʃtarak, yiʃtirik (fi).
participating (adj): miʃtirik;
muʃtarik, -iin.
participle, active (*gr*): ʕism il-faaɛil.
participle, passive (*gr*): ʕism il-mafɛuul.
particular, in particular: muɛayyan, -iin; biz-zaat.
particularly: xuṣuuṣan.
parts, spare parts, accessories: ʕaksiswaar, -aat.
party: *celebration*: ḥafla, ḥafalaat.
political party: ḥizab, ʕaḥzaab.
party line (*on phone*): xaṭṭ muʃtarak, xuṭuuṭ muʃtaraka.
pass (v): faat, yifuut; marr, yimurr; ɛadda, yiɛaddi.
pass an exam, succeed: nigiḥ, yingaḥ (fi).
pass away, die: ʕitwaffa, yitwaffa; maat, yimuut.
pass by: faat ɛala, yifuut ɛala; marr, yimurr ɛala.
pass out, faint: ʕuɣma, yuɣma ɛalee (-ha, etc.);
sooraʕ, yisooraʕ.
pass the time (*in some diversion*): ʕitsalla, yitsalla.
passenger: raakib, rukkaab.
Passion Week: ʕusbuuɛ il-ʕalaam.

passive voice (*gr*): ʕil-maghuul; ʕil-mabni lil-maghuul.
Passover: ɛiid il-fiṣɦ.
passport: basboor, -taat; gawaaz, gawazaat safar.
past: *past tense verb*: fiɛl^e maaḍi.
in the past: fil-maaḍi.
pasta, noodles: makaroona.
pastries, sweets: ɦalawiyyaat.
French pastries: gatoo, -haat.
patch (n) (*on clothes*): ruʕɛa, ruʕaɛ.
patch, mend (v): laɦam, yilɦim; lazaʕ, yilzaʕ.
patch clothes: raʕʕaɛ, yiraʕʕaɛ.
patching: liɦaam; lazʕ; tarʕiiɛ.
patent leather shoes: gazma vernii, gizam vernii.
patience: ṣabr.
patient (adj): ṣabuur, -iin.
to be patient (*with*): ṣabar, yuṣbur (ɛala).
patient (n): ɛayyaan, -iin.
pattern (*for dressmaking*): batroon, -aat.
pavement (*Am.*: *sidewalk*): raṣiif, ʕarṣifa.
pay (n) (*e.g. pay day*): ʕabḍ.
pay (v) (*e.g. the price of s.t.*): dafaɛ, yidfaɛ.
pay s.o. (*salary*): ʕabbaḍ, yiʕabbaḍ; naʕad, yunʕud.
to get paid: ʕabaḍ, yiʕbaḍ.
payment: dafɛ.
peace: salaam.
make peace with: ṣaaliɦ, yiṣaaliɦ; ʕitṣaaliɦ, yitṣaaliɦ maɛa.
peace, reconciliation: ṣulɦ.
peace be on you! (formal greeting): (ʕis-) salaamu ɛaleekum! (*response*: wi ɛaleekum is-salaam!).
peaches: xoox (-a, -aat).
peacock: ṭawuus, ṭawawiis.
peanut butter: zibdit fuul sudaani; zibdit is-sudaani.
peanuts: (fuul) sudaani.
pearls: luuli (-yya, -aat).
pears: kummitra (-aaya, -aat).
peas: bisilla (-aaya, -aat).
sweet peas: bisillit iz-zuhuur.
black-eyed peas: lubya.
peasant: fallaaɦ, -iin.
peat moss: ṭiin ṣinaaɛi.
fertilizer: samaad, ʕasmida.
pecans: bikaan.
pedagogy: ʕuṣuul it-tarbiya; ṭuruʕ it-taɛliim.
pedal (n): baddaal, -aat.
clutch pedal: baddaal dibriyaaj.
pedestrians: muʃaah.
pedestrian crossing: ɛubuur il-muʃaah.
peel (v): ʕaʃʃar, yiʕaʃʃar.
pen (n): ʕalam, ʕiʕlima / ʕiʕlaam (tiʕlaam, after nos. 3–10)
pencil (n): ʕalam ruṣaaṣ, ʕiʕlaam ruṣaaṣ.
pencil sharpener: barraaya, -aat.

pension: maεaaʃ.
on pension: εal-maεaaʃ.
to be put on pension, to retire: ʕitɦaal, yitɦaal εal-maεaaʃ.
Pentecost: εiid il-εanṣara.
people: naas.
a people, nation: ʃaεb, ʃuεuub; ʕumma, ʕumam.
people's, pertaining to the common people: ʃaεbi, -yyiin.
people of (*e.g. a city*): ʕahl, ʕahaali.
person: ʃaxṣ, ʕaʃxaaṣ; nafar, ʕanfaar (tinfaar, after nos. 3–10).
pepper, black: filfil ʕiswid.
white: filfil ʕabyaḍ.
red hot powdered pepper: ʃaṭṭa.
peppers, peppercorns: filfil (-a, -aat).
chili peppers: filfil baladi.
hot peppers: filfil ɦarraaʕ.
long green peppers: filfil ʕaxḍar.
long red peppers: filfil ʃaṭṭa.
red peppers: filfil ʕaɦmar.
sweet green bell peppers: filfil ruumi.
peppermint: niεnaaε.
per: fi- (*e.g. per night*: fil-leela).
percent: fil-miyya.
perfume: barfaan / parfaan; εiṭr, εuṭuur.
perhaps: yimkin; gaayiz.
period: (*in punctuation, Br: full stop*): nuʕṭa, nuʕaṭ.
time: mudda, mudad; fatra, -aat.
for a period of: li-muddit.
menstruation: εaada, -aat / εawaayid; ɦeeḍ; dawra ʃahriyya.
class period, session: ɦiṣṣa, ɦiṣaṣ.
permanent: daayim, -iin.
to be permanent: daam, yiduum.
permanently: εala ṭuul: bi-ṣifa mustadiima.
permission: ʕizn.
to ask permission: ʕistaʕzin, yistaʕzin.
with your permission: εan / baεd^e ʕizn-ak (-ik, etc.).
you have permission to: masmuuɦ-lak (-lik, etc.).
permit (n): taṣriiɦ, taṣariiɦ; ʕizn, ʕuzunaat.
work permit: taṣriiɦ εamal.
permit (v): samaɦ. yismaɦ (li).
persimmons: kaaki.
person: ʃaxṣ, ʕaʃxaaṣ; nafar, ʕanfaar (tinfaar, after nos. 3–10).
each person: kull^e ʃaxṣ; kull^e waaɦid.
personal: ʃaxṣi, -yyiin.
personality: ʃaxṣiyya; -aat.
personally: ʃaxṣiyyan.
personnel: muwaẓẓafiin.
(*staff*): mustaxdimiin; εaamiliin.

pessimism: taʃaaʕum.
pessimistic: mutaʃaaʕim, -iin.
to be pessimistic: ʕitʃaaʕim, yitʃaaʕim (min).
petits fours: bitifuur (-a, -aat).
petrol: banziin.
petroleum: bitrool.
petty cash: fakka.
pewter: *metal*: maεdan, maεaadin.
assortment of metals: taʃkiilit maεaadin.
pewter: *tin*: ʕaṣdiir.
Ph.D.: dukturaa, -haat.
pharaoh: farεoon, faraεna.
pharaonic: farεooni, -yyiin.
pharmacist: ṣaydali, (f) ṣaydalaniyya, ṣayadla.
proprietor of a pharmacy: ʕagzagi, (pl), -yya.
pharmacology: ṣaydala.
pharmacy, drugstore, chemist's: ʕagzaxaana, -aat; ṣaydaliyya, -aat.
philosopher: faylasuuf, falasfa; mufakkir, -iin.
philosophy: falsafa, -aat.
phone me: ʕiḍrab-li tilifoon.
phonetics: εilm il-ʕaṣwaat.
photocopy, photograph (n): ṣuura, ṣuwar.
photocopy, photograph (v): ṣawwar, yiṣawwar.
photocopying, photographing (n): taṣwiir.
photographer: miṣawwaraati, (pl), -yya.
phrase, expression: εibaara, -aat; taεbiir, -aat.
physical education: tarbiya riyaḍiyya; tarbiya badaniyya.
physical therapy: εilaag ṭabiiεi.
physics: ṭabiiεa.
piaster: ʕirʃ, ʕuruuʃ.
five piasters: xamsa saaɣ; ʃilin, -aat.
ten piasters: εaʃara saaɣ; bariiza, baraayiz.
twenty piasters: εiʃriin ʕirʃ; riyaal, -aat.
pick, choose, select: ʕixtaar, yixtaar; naʕaḍ, yunʕuḍ; naʕʕa, yinaʕʕi.
pick up, lift, carry (v): ʃaal, yiʃiil.
pickles: ṭurʃi; mixallil.
pickpocket: naʃʃaal, -iin.
pickup (n) (*engine power*): ʕiwwit il-mutoor.
pickup truck: nuṣṣ^{e} naʕl.
picture: ṣuura, ṣuwar.
piece: ɦitta, ɦitat.
piece, morsel (*e.g. of bread*): luʕma, -aat / luʕam.
pig: xanziir, xanaziir.
pork: laɦma xanziir.
pigeonhole (*mail box*): busṭa; sanduuʕ, sanadiiʕ busṭa; xaana, -aat.
pigeons: ɦamaam (-a, -aat).
pile, heap (n): koom, ʕakwaam.
pile, heap (v): kawwim, yikawwim.
pilgrim: ɦagg, ɦuggaag.
pilgrimage: ɦigg.

lesser pilgrimage: ɛumra.
to go on a pilgrimage: ɦagg, yiɦigg.
pill: ɦabbaaya, ɦubuub.
sleeping pills: ɦubuub munawwima.
pillow: *for bed*: maxadda, -aat.
large cushion to sit on, on floor or sofa: ʃalta, ʃilat.
pillow to lean against on sofa: xudadiyya, -aat.
pillowcase: kiis maxadda.
pimple: dimmil, damaamil; fasfuusa, fasafiis.
pin (n): dabbuus, dababiis.
straight pin: dabbuus ʕibra.
safety pin: dabbuus maʃbak; dabbuus ingiliizi.
hair pin: dabbuus ʃaɛr.
pin (v): dabbis, yidabbis.
pinch (v): ʕaraṣ, yuʕruṣ.
pine nuts: ṣinoobar / ṣineebar (-a, -aat).
pineapple: ʕananaas.
pink: bamba (invar).
pipe (*plumbing*): masuura, mawasiir; ʕanbuuba, ʕanabiib.
(*smoking*): biiba.
piquant food: ʕakl ɦaami / ɦarraaʕ.
pistachios: fuzduʕ (-a, -aat).
piston: bistim, basaatim.
piston ring: binz il-bistim.
pit, hole, ditch: goora, -aat / guwar; ɦufra, ɦufar.
pit (*in fruit*): nawa (nawaaya, -aat).
pitcher, jug: dooraʕ, dawaariʕ; ʃafʃaʕ, ʃafaaʃiʕ.
pitcher with a spout, ewer: ʕabriiʕ, ʕabariiʕ.
pitiable, poor: maskiin, masakiin.
place (n): makaan, ʕamaakin; maɦall, -aat; maṭraɦ, maṭaariɦ.
section (*of a city*): ɦitta, ɦitat; manṭiʕa, manaaṭiʕ.
plain (adj): saada (invar).
plainclothes policeman: muxbir, -iin.
plan (n): xiṭṭa, xiṭaṭ.
plan (v): xaṭṭaṭ, yixaṭṭaṭ.
planet: kawkab, kawaakib.
plant (v): zaraɛ, yizraɛ.
plants (v): zarɛ (-a, -aat).
plaster (*bandaids, for wounds*): bilastar (no pl).
(*for walls, etc.*): ʕasmant.
plaster, gypsum: gibs.
plastic: bilastik (invar).
plastic bag: kiis naylun, ʕakyaas naylun.
plate: ṭabaʕ, ʕaṭbaaʕ (tiṭbaaʕ, after nos. 3–10); ṣaɦn, ṣuɦuun.
platform (*railway*): raṣiif, ʕarṣifa.
(*review stand, dais*): manaṣṣa, -aat.
platter: sirviis, -aat.
play (n) *stage play*: masraɦiyya, -aat.
radio / TV play: tamsiliyya, -aat.

play (v): liεib, yilεab.
play maliciously with (e.g. prices): ʕitlaaεib, yitlaaεib bi.
play music: εazaf, yiεzif; liεib, yilεab.

playful: ʃaʕi, ʃuʕaay / ʕaʃʕiya.

playing field: malεab, malaaεib.

plaza, square (*in a city*): midaan, mayadiin.

pleasant: laṭiif, luṭaaf; ẓariif, ẓuraaf.

please: min faḍl-ak (-ik, -uku); wi-ɦyaat-ak (ik, -ku) (*informal*).
if you please, if you permit: law samaɦt (-i, -u).
please go ahead, take, etc. (*in offering s.t.*): ʕitfaḍḍal (-i, -u).

please (v) *impress*: εagab, yiεgib.
make happy: basaṭ, yibsiṭ; farraɦ, yifarraɦ.

pleasure, whim, mood: mazaag, ʕamziga; keef.
pleasure, enjoyment: mutεa, mutaε.
with pleasure: bi-kull^e suruur.

pliers: binsa, -aat / binas; zarradiyya, -aat. kullaaba, -aat.

plot (n): (*in a play*): ɦabka; qiṣṣa, qiṣaṣ.
(*of land*): ɦittit ʕarḍ.
scheme: muʕamra, -aat.

plug (n) (*stopper, for sink*): saddaada, -aat; ṭabba, -aat.
electric plug (*male*): fiiʃa, fiyaʃ.
electric socket (*female*): bariiza, baraayiz.
extension cord: waṣlit kahraba.
extension cord with multi-sockets: muʃtarak bis-silk.
multi-socket plug: muʃtarak.

plug (v): *plug in* (*electricity*): ɦaṭṭ il-fiiʃa, yiɦuṭṭ it-fiiʃa.
plug up, block: sadd, yisidd.
plugged up (*part*): masduud, -iin.

plumber: sabbaak, -iin.

plums: barʕuuʕ (-a / -aaya, -aat).

plunger (*for drains*): sallaakit hooḍ; ʃaffaaṭa; kawitʃ^e tasliik.

plural: gamε.

pneumonia: ʕiltihaab riʕawi.

pocket: geeb, guyuub.

podium, *rostrum, raised platform*: manaṣṣa, -aaṭ.

poem: ʕaṣiida, ʕaṣaayid.

poet: ʃaaεir. ʃuεara.

poetry: ʃiεr.

poinsettia: bint il-ʕunṣul.

point (n): nuʕṭa, nuʕaṭ.

point (to) (v): ʃaawir, yiʃaawir, (εala).

points (*on a car*): ʕablatiin (-a, -aat).

poison (n): simm, sumuun.

poison (v): sammim, yisammim; samm, yisimm.

poisoning (*food poisoning*): tasammum.

poisonous, toxic: saamm.
pole, post: ɛamuud, ɛawamiid / ʕaɛmida.
electric pole: ɛamuud nuur.
telephone pole, lamp pole: kazaka, -aat.
police: buliis; ʃurṭa.
officer: ẓaabiṭ, ẓubbaṭ.
tourist police: ʃurṭit siyaaɦa.
traffic police: ʃurṭit muruur.
police station: ʕism, ʕaʕsaam (ʃurṭa; buliis).
policeman: ɛaskari, ɛasaakir (buliis); ʕamiin, ʕumanaaʕ ʃurṭa.
traffic policeman: ɛaskari, ɛasaakir muruur.
policy: siyaasa, -aat.
polish (n): warniiʃ.
nail polish, nail varnish: manikyuur.
polish (v): lammaɛ, yilammaɛ.
polite: muʕaddab, -iin.
refined: muhazzab, -iin.
politeness: ʕadab.
lacking in politeness: ʕaliil ʕadab, ʕulalaat ʕadab.
political, diplomatic (adj): siyaasi, -yyiin.
political science: ɛuluum siyasiyya.
politics: siyaasa.
pollute: lawwis, yilawwis.
polluted: mulawwas; miʃ niḍiif.
pollution: talawwus.
poloneck sweater (*Am.*: *turtleneck sweater*): biluuvar bi-raʕaba.
pomegranates: rummaan (-a, -aat).
pony: siisi (siisi, sayaasi).
pony tail (*hair*): deel ɦuṣaan.
pool: ɦammaam, ɦammamaat sibaaɦa; bisiin.
poor (*not rich*): faʕiir, fuʕara.
pitiable: maskiin, masakiin; ɣalbaan, ɣalaaba.
popcorn: fiʃaar / fuʃaar.
Pope, the: ʕil-baaba.
(*Coptic*) *patriarch*: ʕil-ʕamba (*title before pope's name*).
popular (*liked*): maɦbuub, -iin.
popular, pertaining to the common people: ʃaɛbi, -yyiin.
population: sukkaan.
total number of inhabitants: ɛadad (is-) sukkaan.
pork: laɦma xanziir.
port (*harbor*): miina, mawaani.
porter (*for suitcases*): ʃayyaal, -iin.
doorkeeper: bawwaab, -iin.
possible: mumkin, -iin; gaayiz.
possible, believable: maɛʕuul, -iin.
post, pole: ɛamuud, ɛawamiid / ʕaɛmida.
post office: busṭa; maktab, makaatib busṭa / bariid.
the main post office: ʕilbusṭa-l-ɛumumiyya.
post office box: sanduuʕ, sanadiiʕ bariid.
postage stamp: ṭaabiɛ, ṭawaabiɛ (busṭa); waraʕit, waraʕ busṭa.

postbox, mailbox: sanduuʕ busṭa, sanadiiʕ busṭa.
postcard: kart^{e}, kuruut bustaal.
posters, notices: mulṣaʕaat.
postman: busṭagi, (pl), -yya.
postpone: ʕaggil, yiʕaggil.
pot: *cooking pot*: ɦalla, ɦilal.
flowerpot, plantpot: ʕaṣriyya, -aat / ʕaṣaari (zarɛ).
frying pan: ṭaasa, -aaṭ.
milk pan: labbaana, -aat.
saucepan: kasarulla / kasaroona, -aat.
teapot: barraad, -aat (ʃaay).
potassium permanganate: birmanganaat.
potato chips (*Br.*: *crisps*): ʃibs; ʃibsi.
potatoes: baṭaaṭis (f) (baṭaṭsaaya, -aat).
sweet potato: baṭaaṭa (-aaya, -aat).
French fries (*Br.*: *chips*): baṭaaṭis miɦammara.
pothole: maṭabb, -aat.
pound (n) (*money*): ginee, -haat.
pound (v): daʕʕ, yiduʕʕ; saɦaʕ, yisɦaʕ.
pour: ṣabb, yuṣubb.
powder: budra.
powdered sugar: sukkar budra.
talcum powder: budrit talk.
power (*strength*): ʕuwwa / ʕiwwa.
(*electricity*): kahraba.
(*in telephones*): ɦaraara.
engine power: ʕiwwit mutoor.
practical: ɛamali, -yyiin.
practically: ɛamaliyyan.
practice (n): tamriin, tamariin.
practice (v): ʕitmarran, yitmarran (ɛala).
praise (v): madaɦ, yimdaɦ.
praise, thanks (n): ɦamd.
praise to God, thank God: ʕil-ɦamdu li-llaah.
pray: ṣalla, yiṣalli.
pray (*for*): daɛa, yidɛi (li).
prayer: ṣala / ṣalaah, ṣalaat / ṣalawaat.
private petition prayer: duɛa, ʕadɛiya.
Friday noon prayers: ṣalaat ig-gumɛa.
the five times of daily prayer in Islam:
dawn: ṣalaat il-fagr.
noon: ṣalaat iḍ-ḍuhr.
afternoon: ṣalaat il-ɛaṣr.
sunset: ṣalaat il-maɣrib.
dark ($1^{1}/_{2}$ *hours after sunset*): ṣalaat il-ɛiʃa.
prayer beads, rosary: sibɦa, sibaɦ.
prayer mat: miṣalliyya, -aat.
precede: sabaʕ, yisbaʕ.
prefer: faḍḍal, yifaḍḍal.
preferable: mufaḍḍal, -iin.
pregnant: ɦaamil, ɦawaamil; ɦibla, ɦabaala.
to become pregnant: ɦimlit, tiɦmal; ɦiblit, tiɦbal.
to bear (*children*): xallif, yixallif.

prepare: gahhiz, yigahhiz;
ḥaddar, yiḥaddar.

prescribe: katab, yiktib dawa;
katab, yiktib ruʃitta.

prescription (*for medicine*):
ruʃitta, -aat.
(*set of instructions*): waṣfa,
-aat.

present (adj): mawguud, -iin.
*present tense, imperfect
verb*: fiɛle muḍaariɛ.
present time: ʔiz-zaman
il-ḥaadir; ʔil-waʕt il-ḥaadir.
to be present at, attend:
ḥaḍar, yiḥḍar.

present (v): ʕaddim, yiʕaddim.
give a research paper:
ʕaddim, yiʕaddim baḥs.

present, gift (n): hidiyya,
hadaaya.

presentation: taʕdiim.
oral presentation in class:
ʔinʃa ʃafawi.

president: raʕiis, ruʕasa.
the President (*informally*):
ʔir-rayyis.

press (n) (*newspaper*): saḥaafa.
press, printing house:
maṭbaɛa, maṭaabiɛ.

press (v): daɣaṭ, yidɣaṭ.
press a button:
daas, yiduus (ɛala zuraar).
press, iron (*clothes*):
kawa, yikwi.

press-studs: kabsuun (-a, -aat).

presser (*of clothes*): makwagi,
(pl), -yya.

pressure (n): daɣṭ, duɣuuṭ (ɛala).
air pressure: daɣṭ il-hawa.
blood pressure: daɣṭ id-damm.
water pressure: daɣṭ il-mayya.

prestige, status: gaah;
ʔiftiraam; heeba.

prestigious: muḥtaram, -iin.

pretend: ʔitzaahir, yitzaahir;
ɛamal, yiɛmil nafs-u
(+ bi- form of verb).

pretext, excuse: ḥigga, ḥigag.
on the pretext: bi ḥiggit …

pretty: ḥilw, -iin.

prevent: manaɛ, yimnaɛ.

price (n): taman, ʔatmaan.
price, rate: siɛr, ʔasɛaar.

prickly: miʃawwik.

prickly pears: tiin ʃooki (tiina
ʃooki, tiinaat ʃooki).

priest: ʔassiis, ʔusus.

prince: ʔamiir, ʔumara.

principal (adj), *main*: raʔiisi;
ʔasaasi.

principal, headmaster: naazir,
nuzzaar.
headmistress: nazra, -aat.

print (v): ṭabaɛ, yitbaɛ.
printing: ṭibaaɛa.
a printing, edition: ṭabɛa, -aat.

printed (*cloth*): manʃuuʃ, -iin.

printer (*person*): maṭbaɛgi,
(pl) -yya.
(*for a computer*): printar.

printing press: makanit,
makanaat ṭibaaɛa,
maṭbaɛa.

prison: sign, suguun.

prisoner: masguun, -iin / masagiin.
prisoner of war: ʕasiir, ʕasra.
private (*personal*): xuṣuuṣi, -yyiin; xaaṣṣ, -iin.
(*not public*): xaaṣṣ, -iin.
private lessons: duruus xuṣuṣiyya.
the private sector: ʕil-qiṭaaɛ il-xaaṣṣ.
prize, reward: gayza, gawaayiz.
probability: ʕiḥtimaal, -aat.
probable: muḥtamal, -iin; mumkin, -iin.
probably: muḥtamal.
most probably: ɣaaliban; fil-ɣaalib.
problem: muʃkila, maʃaakil.
procession, music for wedding: zaffa.
funeral procession: ganaaza, -aat.
profession: mihna, mihan.
professional (n) (*as opposed to amateur*): muḥtarif, -iin.
professor: (m) ʕustaaz, ʕasatza, (f) ʕustaaza, -aat.
professors' ranks in Egypt: *demonstrator* (*with B.A.*): muɛiid, -iin.
instructor (*with M.A.*): mudarris musaaɛid.
instructor (*with Ph.D.*): mudarris, -iin, *then* ʕustaaz musaaɛid,
full professor: ʕustaaz.
profit (n): ribḥ, ʕarbaaḥ; maksab, makaasib.
profit (v): kisib, yiksab; ribiḥ, yirbaḥ.
profit, benefit (*from*): ʕistafaad, yistafiid (min).
program (n): birnaamig, baraamig.
progress (n): taʕaddum / taqaddum (cl).
progress (v): ʕitʕaddium, yitʕaddim.
project (n): maʃruuɛ, -aat / maʃariiɛ.
promise (n) waɛd, wuɛuud.
promise (v): waɛad, yiwɛid.
promote: raʕʕa, yiraʕʕi.
to be promoted: ʕitraʕʕa, yitraʕʕa.
promotion: tarʕiya, -aat.
pronoun (gr): ḍamiir, ḍamaayir.
pronounce: naṭaʕ, yinṭaʕ; lafaẓ, yulfuẓ.
pronounciation: nuṭʕ; lafẓ.
proof: ʕisbaat, -aat; burhaan, barahiin; daliil, ʕadilla.
proof reading: murageɛa.
proper: *to be proper, appropriate*: ṣaḥḥ, yiṣaḥḥ (*used impersonally*).
prophet: nabi, ʕanbiya.
The Prophet: ʕin-nabi.
in the Prophet's name (*oath*): wi-n-nabi.
the Prophet's birthday: ʕil-muulid; muulid in-nabi; ʕil-mawlid in-nabawi (cl).

proportional: mutanaasiq, -iin.
props (*in theater*): ʕaksiswaar, -aat.
protect: ɦama, yiɦmi.
protection, safety, security: ʕamaan.
act of protecting: ɦimaaya.
protest (n): ʕiɦtigaag, -aat.
demonstration: muẓahra, -aat.
protest (v): ʕiɦtagg, yiɦtagg.
protocol, regulations: burutukuul, aat.
proud, feeling pride (*in a good sense*) (adj): faxuur, -iin.
to feel pround: ʕiftaxar, yiftixir.
conceited: maɣruur, -iin.
prove: barhan, yibarhan (ɛala); dall, yidill; ʕasbat, yisbit.
proverb: masal, ʕamsaal.
maxim, wise saying: ɦikma, ɦikam.
prunes: ʕaraṣya (ʕaraṣyaaya, -aat) .
psychiatrist: ṭabiib nafsaani; duktoor ʕamraaḍ nafsiyya / ɛaṣabiyya.
psychiatry: ṭibbᵉ nafsi.
psychological: nafsi.
psychology: ɛilmᵉ nafs.
public (*general*) (adj): ɛumuumi, -yyiin; ɛaamm.
public, popular (*common*): ʃaɛbi, -iin.
public relations: ɛilaʕaat ɛamma / ɛaamma.
public speech: xiṭaab, -aat.
the public sector: ʕil-qiṭaaɛ il-ɛaamm.
public (n) (*general public*): ʕil-ɛamma; ɛammit iʃ-ʃaɛb; iʃ-ʃaɛb.
public opinion: ʕir-raʕy il-ɛaamm.
publish: naʃar, yunʃur.
publisher: naaʃir, -iin.
pudding (*blancmange, a milk pudding*): mahallabiyya.
flan (*caramel*) *pudding*: kireem karamill.
pull: saɦab, yisɦab.
pull hard: ʃadd, yiʃidd.
pulpit: mambar, manaabir.
pulse (n): nabḍ (-a, -aat).
take one's pulse: gassᵉ, yigissᵉ nabḍ-u (-aha, etc.).
pump (n): turumba / ṭurumba / ṭulumba, -aat.
air, hand pump: munfaax, manafiix.
fuel pump: turumbit banziin.
oil pump: turumbit zeet.
pump in toilet tank: makanit sifoon.
water pump: ṭurumbit mayya.
pumpkin: ʕarɛᵉ ruumi.
punctual: mawaɛiid-u (-ha etc.) maẓbuuṭa.
punctured: maxruum, -iin.
punish: ɛaaqib, yiɛaaqib; zannib, yizannib; gaaza, yigaazi.

punishment: εiqɑɑb; giza / gazaaʕ (cl).
pupil (*in school*): tilmiiz, talamiiz / talamza.
pureed: biyureeh; mahruus.
purple, violet: banafsigi (invar).
dark purple: bidingaani / bitingaani (invar).
purse (n) (*ladies' bag*): ʃɑnʈɑ, ʃunɑʈ.
(*money bag*): kiis filuus.
push (n): zaʕʕa, -aat.
push (v): zaʕʕ, yizuʕʕ.
pushing (*act of pushing*): zaʕʕ.
push (*a button*): daas, yiduus (εala zurɑɑr)
put: ɦɑʈʈ, yiɦuʈʈ.
put off, postpone: ʕaggil, yiʕaggil.
put on, dress: libis, yilbis.
put out, extinguish: ʈɑfɑ, yiʈfi.
pyramid: hɑrɑm, ʕɑhrɑɑm / ʕɑhrɑmɑɑt.
Pyramid Street: ʃaariε ʕil-hɑrɑm.
Pyramid Street area: ʕil-hɑrɑm.

Q

quail: simmaan / sammaan (-a, -aat).
qualifications (*e.g. for a job*): muʕahhil, -aat.
quality: guuda.
good type: ṣanfᵉ kwayyis, ʕaṣnaaf kwayyisa.
better quality: nawɛiyya ʕaḥsan.
quantity: kimmiya, -yyaat.
how much?: ʔaddᵉ ʕeeh?
this much: ʔaddᵉ kida.
quarrel (n): xinaaʔa, -aat.
act of quarreling: xinaaʔ.
quarrel (v): ʕitxaaniʔ, yitxaaniʔ (maɛa).
quarter (n) (*one-fourth*): rubɛ, ʕirbaɛ / ʕarbaaɛ.
three-quarters: talat tirbaɛ.
question: suʕaal, ʕasʕila.
queue: ṭabuur, ṭawabiir.
quick: sariiɛ, suraaɛ.
quickly, rapidly: ʔawaam; bi-surɛa.
quiet: haadi, -yiin.
quiet, silent: saakit, -iin.
to be quiet: hidi, yihda; sikit, yuskut.
quilt (n): liḥaaf, liḥifa.
quit (*e.g. smoking*): baṭṭal, yibaṭṭal (+ n or imperf. v).
be no longer: baʔa (neg + imperf) (*e.g. he doesn't come anymore*: ma-baʔaa-ʃ yiigi).
quotation: ʕiqtibaas.
quote (v): ʕiqtabas, yaqtabis (cl).

R

rabbit: ʕarnab, ʕaraanib.
rabid (adj): saεraan, -iin.
rabies (n): saεar; marad̦ ik-kalb.
race (n) (*horse, car*): sabaʕ / sibaaʕ, -aat.
rack (*for hanging clothes*): manʃar, manaaʃir.
(*on top of a car*): ʃabaka, -aat.
racket, paddle: mad̦rab, mad̦aarib.
radiator (*on a car*): radyateer, -aat.
radio: radyu, -haat.
radishes: figl (-a, -aat).
rag (*torn piece of clothing*): xirʕa, xiraʕ.
dust rag, wiping rag: fuuţa şafra, fuwaţ şafra.
floor rag: xeeʃa, -aat; fuuţit, fuwaţ masɦ.
railroad: sikka ɦadiid, sikak ɦadiid.
rain (n): maţar, ʕamţaar.
rain (v): maţţarit, timaţţar (usu. with ʕid-dinya as subject).
raincoat: balţu maţar, balaaţi maţar.
raise (n) (*in salary*): εalaawa, -aat.
raise (v) (*grow s.t.*): rabba, yirabbi.
raise, lift: rafaε, yirfaε.
raising, upbringing, education: tarbiya.
raisins: zibiib (-a, -aat).
rank, grade: daraga, -aat; rutba, rutab.
rape (n): ʕiɣtişaab, -aat.
rape (v): ʕiɣtaşab, yiɣtişib; ʕiεtada, yiεtidi εala.
rapist: muɣtaşib, -iin.
rare, rarely: naadir.
rash, reckless, (adj): mutasarriε, -iin; mutahawwir, -iin; ţaayiʃ, -iin; mundafiε, -iin.
rashness: tasarruε; tahawwur.
rat: faar, firaan.
rate (*price*): siεr, ʕasεaar.
at any rate, anyway: εala-l-εumuum; εala kull^{e} ɦaal.
rather than (conj): badal ma.
rather than (prep): badal.
rather, prefer (v): fad̦d̦al, yifad̦d̦al.
ration (n): tamwiin, -aat.
rationing book: biţaaʕit tamwiin, biţaʕaat tamwiin.
raw (*food*): nayy, -iin.
razor: muus, ʕamwaas.
reach (v): wişil, yiwşal.
reaction: radd^{e} fiεl, ruduud fiεl.
read: ʕara, yiʕra.
reading (n): ʕiraaya / qiraaʕa (cl).
ready (*for*): musta εidd, -iin (li).
completed, ready-made: gaahiz, -iin.
to be ready (*e.g. food*): gihiz, yighaz.
to get ready: ʕistaεadd, yistaεidd.

real: haʕiiʕi, -yyiin.
realist: waaqiɛi, -yyiin.
really: ṣaɦiiɦ; ɦaʕiiʕi.
rear (adj) (*back*): warraani, -yyiin; ʕilli wara.
reason, cause: sabab, ʕasbaab.
no reason: min ɣeer sabab; min ɣeer lee.
reasonable: maɛʕuul, -iin.
recall, ask for the return of: ʕistaradd, yistaridd.
receipt: waṣl, wuṣulaat.
invoice, bill: fatuura, -aat / fawatiir.
receive (*formally, e.g. against receipt*): ʕistalam, yistilim.
welcome (e.g. a guest): ʕistaʕbil, yistaʕbil.
I received a letter: gaa-li gawaab.
recently: min ʕurayyib; min mudda-ʕurayyiba.
reception (*desk in hotel*): maktab ʕistiʕbaal.
reception (party): ɦaflit ʕistiʕbaal, ɦaflaat ʕistiʕbaal.
recharge card: kart ʃaɦn, kuruut ʃaɦn.
recipe: waṣfa, -aat.
recognize (*e.g. a person*): ɛirif, yiɛraf; ʕitɛarraf, yitɛarraf ɛala.
recommend, suggest (v): ʕiqtaraɦ, yaqtariɦ (cl).
recommendation (*letter of*): gawaab, gawabaat tawṣiyya.
reconfirm (*a reservation*): ʕakkid, yiʕakkid (ɦagz).
record (n) (*music*): ʕisṭiwaana, -aat.
register: sigill, -aat.
record (v): saggil, yisaggil.
record player: bikab / funuɣraaf.
recorder: musaggil, -aat; rikurdar, -aat; gihaaz, ʕaghizit tasgiil.
recover (*from illness*): xaff, yixiff; ṭaab, yiṭiib; ʃifi, yiʃfa.
rectangle: mustaṭiil, -aat.
red: ʕaɦmar, (f) ɦamra, ɦumr.
the Red Sea: ʕil-baɦr il-ʕaɦmar.
reduce (*photocopy*): ṣaɣɣar, yiṣaɣɣar.
(*price*): xaffaḍ, yixaffaḍ.
reduction (*photocopy*): taṣɣiir.
(*price*): taxfiiḍ, -aat.
discount: xaṣm, xuṣumaat.
reeds: buuṣ (-a, -aat).
reef (*coral reef*): ʃiɛba, ʃiɛab.
referee (v): ɦakkim, yiɦakkim.
referee, umpire (n): ɦakam, ɦukkaam.
reference (*book*): margiɛ, maragiɛ.
(*letter of conduct and behavior*): ʃahaadit seer wi-suluuk.
refined, high class (adj): raaʕi, raʕyiin.
well-mannered: muhazzab, -iin; muʕaddab, -iin.
refreshing: munɛiʃ, -iin.
refrigerator: tallaga, -aat.

refugee: laagiʕ, -iin.
refuse (v): rafaḍ, yurfuḍ.
regard, consider: ʕiεtabar, yiεtibir.
region: manṭiʕa, manaaṭiʕ.
register (n): sigill, -aat.
register (v): saggil, yisaggil.
registrar: musaggil, -iin.
registration: tasgiil.
car registration: ruxṣit εarabiyya.
registration fee: rasm, rusuum tasgiil.
school registration: tasgiil ṭullaab.
regular (*oil, gas*): εaadi, -yyiin; εaada (invar).
regularly: bi-ntiẓaam.
regulator (*e.g. on a car*): munaẓẓim, -aat.
rejoice, to be jubilant: firiɧ, yifraɧ.
to have great fun: hayyaṣ, yihayyaṣ.
relation: εilaaʕa, -aat.
in relation to, with regard to: bin-nisba li.
in relation to me, as far as I am concerned: bin-nisbaa-li.
relative (adj): nisbi, -yyiin.
it's a relative matter: di masʕala nisbiyya.
relative (n): ʕariib, ʕaraayib.
close relatives: ʕahl (*family*: εeela, -aat).
relatively: nisbiyyan.
reliable, sturdy: ṣulb; yuεtamad εalee (-ha, etc.); maḍmuun.
strong, hard, durable: matiin, mutaan; gaamid, -iin.
relieve: rayyaɧ, yirayyaɧ.
to be relieved (from): ʕirtaaɧ, yirtaaɧ (min).
religion: diin, ʕadyaan; diyaana, -aat.
religious: diini, -yyiin.
(*of a person*) mutadayyin, -iin.
rely (*on*): ʕiεtamad, yiεtimid / yaεtamid εala; ʕittakal, yittikil (εala).
remain; fiḍil, yifḍal; biʕi, yibʕa.
remaining (part): faaḍil.
remainder, rest: baaʕi, -yiin.
remember: ʕiftakar, yiftikir.
(part): faakir, -iin.
do you (m) *remember?*: ʕinta faakir?
remind: fakkar, yifakkar.
remove: ʃaal, yiʃiil; zaal, yiziil.
renaissance: nahḍa, -aat.
renew: gaddid, yigaddid.
renewal: tagdiid.
renovate: gaddid, yigaddid.
renovation: tagdiid, -aat.
rent (n): ʕigaar, -aat.
rental fees: kira; ʕugra, ʕuguur / ʕugar.
rent, hire (v): ʕaggar, yiʕaggar; kara, yikri.
repair (n): taṣliiɧ, -aat.
repair (v): ṣallaɧ, yiṣallaɧ.

repeat: ɛaad, yiɛiid.
repeat several times: karrar, yikarrar.
repetition: tikraar; ʕiɛaada.
reply (n): radd, ruduud.
reply (v): radd, yirudd (ɛala); gaawib, yigaawib.
report (n): taqriir, taqariir.
republic: gumhuriyya, -aat.
Arab Republic of Egypt: gumhuriyyit maʂr il-ɛarabiyya.
reputation: sumɛa.
request (n): ṭalab, -aat.
request (v): ṭalab, yuṭlub (min).
requirements: maṭlubaat; mutaṭallabaaṭ lawaazim.
research (n): baɦs, buɦuus / ʕabɦaas.
to do research: baɦas, yibɦas; ɛamal, yiɛmil baɦs.
resemble (imperfect only): yiʃbih / yiʃbah.
resemblance: ʃabah.
she resembles you (f): hiyya-btiʃbih-lik; hiyya ʃabah-ik.
reservation, booking: ɦagz.
may I make a reservation?: mumkin ʕaɛmil ɦagz?
reserve (v): ɦagaz, yiɦgiz.
reserved (*e.g. a seat*): maɦguuz, -iin.
(*personality*): mutaɦaffiẓ.
reside: sikin, yuskun (part): saakin, -iin.
residence permit: taʂriiɦ ʕiqaama, taʂariiɦ ʕiqaama.
residential hotel: pansiyoon / bansiyoon, -aat.
resign: ʕistaʕaal, yistaʕiil; ʕistaqaal, yistaqiil.
resignation: ʕistiʕaala / ʕistiqaala, -aat.
resistor (*electric*): rizistans.
resort (*summer*): maʂyaf, maʂaayif.
(*winter*): maʃta, maʃaati.
respect (n): ʕiɦtiraam.
respect (v): ʕiɦtaram, yiɦtirim.
respectable: muɦtaram, -iin; *well-behaved*: muhazzab, -iin.
respectful (*of*): miɦtirim, -iin. (+ obj.).
responsibility (*for*): masʕuliyya, aat (ɛan).
responsible (*for*): masʕuul, -iin (ɛan).
rest (n) (*from work*): ʕistiraaɦa.
rest, remainder: baaʕi, -yiin / bawaaʕi.
rest (v): ʕistirayyaɦ, yistiraayyaɦ; ʕirtaaɦ, yirtaaɦ.
restaurant: maṭɛam, maṭaaɛim.
resthouse: ʕistiraaɦa, -aat.
restroom: ɦammaam; tiwalitt.
result: natiiga, nataayig.
retain a lawyer: wakkil muɦaami, yiwakkil muɦaami.
retire: ṭiliɛ, yiṭlaɛ ɛal-maɛaaʃ.
retired (adj): ɛa-lmaɛaaʃ; mutaqaaɛid.
retirement: maɛaaʃ, -aat; taqaaɛud.

return (v) (tr), *bring or take back*: raggaɛ, yiraggaɛ. (intr), *come or go back*: rigiɛ, yirgaɛ.
return, round trip (n): raayiɦ gayy; zihaab wa ʕiyaab / ɛawda. *round trip ticket*: tazkara zihaab wi-ɛawda.
reverse gear: marʃ-aryeer.
review (n): muragɛa, -aat.
review (v): raagiɛ, yiraagiɛ.
revise: raagiɛ, yiraagiɛ.
revolution: sawra, -aat.
reward, prize: gayza, gawaayiz. *bonus*: mukafʕa, -aat.
rhetoric (*subject*): balaaɣa.
ribbon: ʃiriiṭ, ʃaraayiṭ.
rice: ruzz.
rich: ɣani, ɣunaay / ʕaɣniya. (*of food*): dasim. *well-off*: mabsuuṭ, -iin.
riddle (n): fazzuura, fawaziir.
ride (n) (*lift*) tawṣiila. *give a ride*: rakkib, yirakkib. *can you* (m) *give me a ride*: mumkin tiwaṣṣal-ni; mumkin tirakkib-ni maɛaa-k.
ride (v): rikib, yirkab. *to go horseback riding*: rikib, yirkab xeel. *riding horses, horseback riding*: rukuub xeel.
right (adj), *correct*: mazḅuuṭ, -iin; ṣaɦɦ (invar). *you are right*: ɛandak ɦaʕʕ; ʕil-ɦaʕʕ^e maɛaa-k. *to be right, appropriate*: ṣaɦɦ, yiṣaɦɦ (*used impersonally*). *is that right! is that so!*: win-nabi!; ṣaɦiiɦ? *to set right, adjust*: zabaṭ, yuzḅuṭ.
right (n): ɦaʕʕ, ɦuʕuuʕ. *right side* (*direction*): yimiin. *political right*: ʕil-yimiin / ʕil-yamiin.
right away, immediately: ɦaalan; fil-ɦaal; ɛala ṭuul. (*response to order or request*): ɦaaḍir (invar).
rim (*of wheel*): janṭ, junuṭa.
ring (n): xaatim, xawaatim. (*in a chain*): ɦalaʕa, -aat. *engagement ring*: dibla, dibal.
ring (v) (*a bell*): ḍarab, yiḍrab (garas); daʕʕ, yiduʕʕ (garas).
Ring Road, the: ʕiṭ-ṭariiʕ id-dayri / id-daaʕiri.
riot (n): ʃaɣab
riot (v): ʃaaɣib, yiʃaaɣib.
ripe: mistiwi, -yyiin.
rise, get up: ʕaam, yiʕuum. *rise high* (*eg. sun, plane*): ʕirtafaɛ, yirtifiɛ.
river: nahr, ʕanhaar. *riverside road*: kurniiʃ / kurneeʃ.
roach: ṣurṣaar, ṣaraṣiir.
road: ṭariiʕ, ṭuruʕ; sikka, sikak.
roast (n): rustu.

roast (v): ʃawa, yiʃwi.
  (e.g. nuts, etc.): ɧammaṣ,
  yiɧammaṣ.
  roasted, grilled (meat, corn):
  maʃwi;
  roasted (nuts, coffee, bread):
  miɧammaṣ.
roast beef: ruzbiif.
rob, steal: saraʕ, yisraʕ.
robber: ɧaraami, (pl) -yya.
robbery, theft: sirʕa, sariʕaat.
  armed robbery:
  sirʕa bil-ʕikraaɧ.
robe: roob, ʕarwaab.
  traditional robe:
  gallabiyya, galaliib.
rock, boulder: ṣaxr (-a, ṣuxuur).
  a piece of rock, a stone:
  ɧagar, ʕaɧgaar / ɧigaara;
  ṭuub (-a, -aat).
rocket: ṣaruux, ṣawariix.
role: door, ʕadwaar.
rollers (hair curlers): bigudii;
  buklaat; rulooɧ.
romantic: rumantiiki, -yyiin.
roof terrace: suṭuuɧ.
room (e.g. of a house): ʕooḍa,
  ʕuwaḍ.
  room, space: makaan,
  ʕamaakin; maṭraɧ,
  maṭaariɧ.
rope: ɧabl, ɧibaal.
rosemary: ɧaṣalbaan.
roses: ward (-a, -aat).
rostrum: manaṣṣa, -aat.
rotten: miʕaffin, -iin; baayiz̧,
  -iin.

rouge: ruuj.
rough, coarse: xiʃin, -iin.
  rough draft:
  miswadda, -aat.
round (shape); midawwar, -iin.
round trip: raayiɧ gayy; zihaab
  wa ʕiyaab / ʕawda.
  round trip ticket:
  tazkara zihaab wi-ʕawda.
roundabout (Am.: traffic circle):
  ṣaniyya, ṣawaani.
  intersection: taʕaaṭuʕ, -aaṭ.
row (n): ṣaff, ṣufuuf.
row (v): ʕaddif, yiʕaddif.
rowing: taʕdiif; tagdiif.
rubber (material): kawitʃ.
rubber band: ʕastik, ʕasaatik.
rubber eraser: ʕastiika, ʕasatiik;
  gooma.
rubber plant: fiikus dikoora.
rubbing alcohol: sibirtu naʕi;
  kuɧuul naʕi / naqi.
rubbish: see garbage.
rude: waqiɧ, -iin; ʕaliil ʕadab,
  ʕulalaat ʕadab.
rug: siggaada, sagagiid.
ruin (v): bawwaz̧, yibawwaz̧.
ruined (adj): baayiz̧, -iin.
  to be ruined, spoiled:
  baaz̧, yibuuz̧.
ruins: *historical monuments:*
  ʕasaar.
  wrecked area:
  xaraaba, -aat / xaraayib.
rule, law (n): qanuun, qawaniin.
ruler (of a country): ɧaakim,
  ɧukkaam.

(*measuring*): masṭara, masaaṭir.
rumor: ʕiʃaaɛa, -aat.
run: giri, yigri.
to run over: daas, yiduus.
running, jogging: gary.
Russia: rusya.
USSR: ʕil-ʕittiɦaad is-suvyetti.
Russian: ruusi, ruus.
rust (n): ṣada.
rust (v): ṣadda, yiṣaddi.
rust, copper color (adj): naɦaasi (invar).
rusty (adj): miṣaddi, -yiin.

S

sabbatical: *I'm on leave to do research*: ʕana fi ʕagaazit tafarruɣ ɛaʃaan ʕaɛmil baɦs.
sack, bag: kiis, ʕakyaas.
sacrifice (n): ɖaɦiyya, ɖaɦaaya.
sacrifice (v): ɖaɦɦa, yiɖaɦɦi.
sad: zaɛlaan, -iin; ɦaziin, ɦazaana.
to become sad: ziɛil, yizɛal; ɦizin, yiɦzan.
safe (n): xazna, xizan.
safety: salaama.
security: ʕamaan; ʕamn.
saffron: zaɛfaraan / zaɛfaraan.
sage (*herb*): maryamiyya.
sailboat: markib ʃiraaɛi, maraakib ʃiraɛiyya.
large sailboat on Nile, felucca: filuuka, falaayik.
sailor: baɦɦaar, -iin.
boatman: marakbi, -yya (pl).
sake, for the sake of: ɛaʃaan; ɛaʃaan xaaʈir.
for your (m) *sake*: ɛaʃaan xatr-ak.
salad: salaʈa, -aat.
salary: mahiyya, -aat / mahaaya; murattab, -aat.
sale (*reduced prices*): ʕukazyoon, -aat; taxfiiɖ, -aat.
for sale: li-l-beeɛ.
sales manager: mudiir mabiɛaat, -iin mabiɛaat.
salesman, vendor: bayyaaɛ, -iin.
clerk, shop assistant, employee: muwaẓẓaf, -iin.
lemon (etc.) salesman: bitaaɛ il-lamuun (etc.).
salt: malɦ.
salty: mimallaɦ, -iin; ɦaadiʕ, -iin.
same: nafs (+ def. noun or pronoun suffix).
the same man: nafs ir-raagil; ʕir-raagil nafs-u.
the same day: nafs il-yoom.
at the same time: fi nafs il-waʕt;
while we are at it: bil-marra.
the same (*as each other*): zayy^{e} baɛɖ.
sample (n): ɛayyina, -aat.
sand: raml.
sandal: ʂandal, ʂanaadil.
sandpaper (n): waraʕ ʂanfara (-it, -aat ʂanfara).
sandstorm: ɛaaʂifa ramliyya, ɛawaaʂif ramliyya.
duststorm: ɛaaʂifa turabiyya, ɛawaaʂif turabiyya.
sandwich: sandawitʃ, -aat.
sanitary napkins: fuwaʈ ʂiɦɦiyya.
sapphire: zaɛfar / zaɛfar.
sarcasm: suxriya.
satellite: ʕamar ʂinaaɛi, ʕaʕmaar ʂinaɛiyya.
satellite dish: diʃʃ, -aat.
satisfaction, pleasure: ʕirtiyaaɦ; qanaaɛa.

satisfied (*full of food*): ʃabɛaan, -iin.
pleased, happy: mɑbsuuṭ, -iin; muqtaniɛ, -iin.
Saturday: yoom is-sabt.
Holy Saturday: sabt in-nuur.
sauce: ṣɑlṣɑ.
saucepan: kɑsɑrullɑ / kɑsɑroona, -aat.
saucer: ṣɑɦnᵉ fingaan, ṣuɦuun fanagiin.
Saudi Arabia: ʕis-suɛudiyya.
Saudi Arabian: suɛuudi, -yyiin.
sausage: suguʔʔ (-a / -aaya, -aat).
save (*e.g. time, money*): wɑffɑr, yiwɑffɑr.
hoard: ɦawwiʃ, yiɦawwiʃ.
save (*a life*): ʕɑnqɑz, yinqiz.
(*on a computer*): sayyif/sayyiv, yisayyif/yisayyiv.
saving (*n*): tawfiir.
savings bank book: dɑftɑr, dafaatir tawfiir.
savings club: gamɛiyyit, -yyaat iddixɑɑr.
saw (n): munʃɑɑr, manaʃiir.
sawdust: niʃɑɑrit xaʃab.
say: ʔaal, yiʔuul / yuʔuul.
scald, burn (v): ɦaraʔ, yiɦraʔ.
to be burnt: ʕitɦaraʔ, yitɦiriʔ.
scale (n) (*weighing*): mizaan, mawaziin.
scarce: ʔulayyil, -iin.
scared (adj): mitxawwif, -iin; xaayif, -iin.
scared, *to be scared* (intr): ʕitxawwif, yitxawwif; xaaf, yixaaf.
scarf: *Arab men's headdress*: ɣuṭrɑ, ɣuṭɑr
(*held in place by ring called* ɛuʔaal, -aat).
cloth wound around a skullcap to make a turban: ɛimma, ɛimam.
men's, women's winter wool neck type: kufiyya, -aat.
shawl: ʃaal, ʃilaan.
women's large Islamic covering: ṭɑrɦɑ, ṭurɑɦ; ɦigaab.
women's scarf: ʕiʃɑrb, -ɑɑt.
scene: manẓɑr, mɑnɑɑẓir.
schedule: gadwal, gadaawil.
scholarship, grant: minɦa, minaɦ.
scholarship abroad, mission: biɛsa, -aat.
scholastic: dirɑɑsi, -yyiin.
school: madrasa, madaaris.
elementary school: madrasa ʕibtidaʕiyya.
preparatory school: madrasa ʕiɛdadiyya.
high, secondary school: madrasa sanawiyya.
science: ɛilm, ɛuluum.
scientific: ɛilmi, -yyiin.
scientist: ɛaalim, ɛulama / ɛulamaaʕ (cl).
scissors: mɑʔɑṣṣ, -ɑɑt.
scissors for feathering hair: mɑʔɑṣṣᵉ flaaʃ.

scold, reprimand: zaεεaʕ, yizaεεaʕ li; wabbax, yiwabbax.
scorch, burn: lasaε, yilsaε.
score (n): natiiga, nataayig.
score (v) (*to make a goal*): gaab, yigiib gọon.
scowl (n): gahaama; takʃiir; takʃiira.
scowl (v): gahhim, yigahhim; kaʃʃar, yikaʃʃar.
scrambled eggs: beeḍ skraambild; beeḍ maḍruub.
scratch (n): xadʃ, xuduuʃ.
from scratch: min il-ʕawwil xaaliṣ.
scratch (v): xadaʃ, yixdiʃ.
scratch with claws, e.g. a cat: xarbiʃ, yixarbiʃ.
scream (n): sarxa / ṣarxa, -aat / -aat.
screaming (n): ṣuwaat; sarx / ṣarx / ṣuraax.
scream (v): ṣawwat, yiṣawwat; sarax / ṣarax, yuṣrux.
screen (*for window*): silk.
(*for movie*): ʃaaʃa, -aat.
screw (n): musmaar ʕalawooẓ, masamiir ʕalawooẓ.
screwdriver: mifakk, -aat.
philips screwdriver: mifakk^{e} fiilibs.
scrub (n): masaɦ, yimsaɦ.
scrub hard: daεak, yidεak.
sea: baɦr, biɦaar / buɦuur.
seaside road: kurniiʃ / kurneeʃ.
sea bass, grouper: waʕaar (-a, -aat).
seagull: ṭeer, ṭuyuur in-nooras.
seal (n): *animal*: kalb il-baɦr, kilaab il-baɦr.
stamp: xitm, ʕaxtaam.
seal (v): lazaʕ, yilzaʕ; ʕafal, yiʕfil.
seam (*sewing, stitching, of a seam*): xiyaaṭa.
seamstress: xayyaaṭa, -aat.
(*male seamster, for women, does dresses only*): xayyaaṭ, -iin.
(*does coats too*): tarzi, -yya; tarzi ɦariimi.
search (*for*): baɦas, yibɦas (εan); dawwar, yidawwar (εala).
season: muusim, mawaasim.
(*one of four seasons of the year*): faṣl, fuṣuul.
seat (n) (*chair*): kursi, karaasi; maʕεad, maʕaaεid.
there are no seats available: mafiiʃ makaan; mafiiʃ ʕamaakin faḍya.
seat belt: ɦizaam, ʕaɦzimit ʕamaan.
seatcover: ɣaṭa kursi, ɣuṭyaan karaasi.
seaweed: ʕaεʃaab baɦriyya (pl).
second: (*in a series*): taani, -yiin.
(*in time*): sanya, sawaani.
"just a second": sawaani. (*pl. of* sanya)
(*dates—use cardinal no., e.g. 2 September*: ʕitneen sibtimbir).

second-hand, used: mustaɛ mal, -iin.
secondary: saanawi, -yyiin.
secondary school: madrasa sanawiyya, saanawiyya.
seconded: muntadab, -iin.
secondly: saaniyan.
secret (adj): sirri, -yyiin.
secret (n): sirr, ʕasraar.
secret police: buliis sirri.
police informant, plainclothes policeman: muxbir, -iin.
secretary (f): sikirteera, -aat.
section: guzʕ, ʕagzaaʕ; qism, ʕaqsaam.
security: ʕamn.
safety: ʕamaan.
security forces: quwwaat il-ʕamn.
see: ʃaaf, yiʃuuf.
see off, bid farewell: waddaɛ, yiwaddaɛ.
seed, grain: ɦabba, / ɦabbaaya, ɦabbaat.
(coll): ɦabb, ɦubuub.
seeds (*edible*): libb (-a, / -aaya, -aat).
white (*pumpkin*) *seeds*: libb abyaḍ.
dark seeds: libb asmar.
seeds, pips, stones: bizr (-a, -aat); naʕa.
seem: baan, yibaan; ẓahar, yiẓhar.
it seems (*that*): baayin; yiẓhar (ʕinn).
it seems to me (*etc.*): biyithayyaʕ-li (-lak, etc.).
you (*etc.*) *seem to be*: baayin ɛaleek (-ki, etc.).
select: ʕixtaar, yixtaar; naʕʕa, yinaʕʕi.
self: nafs.
yourself, myself, etc.: nafs-ak (-ik), nafs-i, etc.
self-esteem: ɛizziyyit nafs; ɛizzit nafs.
selfish: ʕanaani, -yyiin.
sell: baaɛ, yibiiɛ.
semester: simastir (invar); tirm, -aat; faṣl^{e} diraasi, fuṣuul dirasiyya.
send: baɛat, yibɛat.
deliver, send: waṣṣal, yiwaṣṣal.
senior year (*fourth year*): sana rabɛa; ʕaaxir sana.
sentence (n): (*group of words*): gumla, gumal.
(*by a court of law*): ɦukm, ʕaɦkaam.
separate (v); faṣal, yifṣil.
September: sibtimbir.
serial, soap opera: musalsal, -aat; tamsiliyya, -aat.
series: silsila.
serious, serlousness: gadd (invar).
serious, grave, critical: xaṭiir.
seriously: bi-gadd; gadd.
servant: xaddaam, -iin; ʃaɣɣaal, -iin.
serve: xadam, yixdim.

service: xidma, xadamaat.
I'm at your service: taɦt^{e} ʕamr-ak (to m), taɦt ʕamr-ik (to f), taɦt ʕamr-uku (to pl).
church service (*Catholic, Orthodox*): ʕuddaas, -aat / ʕadadiis.
church service (*Protestant*): xidma (no pl).
military service (n): xidma ɛaskariyya.

service station: maɦaṭṭit banziin, banziina.

serviette (*Am.*: *table napkin*): fuuṭa, fuwaṭ; fuuṭit, fuwaṭ sufra.

sesame (*seeds*): simsim (-a, -aat).

sesame seed paste: ṭiɦiina.

session, shift: fatra, -aat.,
morning session: fatra ṣabaɦiyya.
evening session: fatra masaʕiyya.
session, meeting, sitting: galsa, -aat

set (n) (*hair*): mizamplii; tasriiɦa.
(*tea, bedding, writing set, etc.*): ṭaʕm, ʕaṭʕum.

set, fix (v) (*e.g. a time for*): ɦaddid, yiɦaddid.

settle account with: ɦaasib, yiɦaasib; ʕitɦaasib, yitɦaasib maɛa.

settlements, residences: mustawṭanaat.

seven: sabɛa; sabaɛ (before pl. no.).

seventeen: sabaɛtaaʃar.

seventy: sabɛiin.

severe: ʃidiid, ʃudaad; gaamid, -iin.

severence pay: mukafʕa, -aat; mukafʕit nihaayit il-xidma.

sew: xayyaṭ, yixayyaṭ.

sewing machine: makanit xiyaaṭa.

sex: gins (no pl).
the two sexes: ʕig-ginseen.

shade, shadow: ḍill.

shake (v) (*e.g., a rug, a tree, feelings*): hazz, yihizz.
churn, agitate (*milk*): xaḍḍ, yixuḍḍ.
shake (*a bottle*), *to mix contents*: ragg, yirugg.
shake out (*a rug*): naffaḍ, yinaffaḍ.

shake hands with: ṣaafiɦ, yiṣaafiɦ; sallim, yisallim (bil-ʕiid) ɛala.

shame (n): ɛeeb; ɦaraam.
shame on you (m) (*for a shameful act*): ɛeeb ɛaleek.
shame on you (m) (*for a cruel act*): ɦaraam ɛaleek.

shame (v): kasaf, yiksif.
shame on you: ʕallaah yiksif-ak (-ik, -ku).

shampoo: ʃampuu.

shape (n): ʃakl, ʕaʃkaal.

share (n): ɦiṣṣa, ɦiṣaṣ; naṣiib, ʕanṣiba.

share (v), *distribute, divide up*: ʕitʕaasim, yitʕaasim.
join with, participate with (tr): ʃaarik, yiʃaarik.
join, participate (intr): ʕitʃaarik, yitʃaarik (maɛa).
shark: samak ʕirʃ.
sharp (adj): ɦadd / ɦaadd.
sharp, pungent: ɦaami, -yiin.
sharp knife: sikkiina ɦamya.
sharpen: (*a knife*): sann, yisinn.
(*a pencil*): bara, yibri.
sharpener: (*knife*): misannᵉ sikkiina.
(*pencil*): barraaya, -aat.
shave (v): ɦalaʕ, yiɦlaʕ.
shaving cream: kireem ɦilaaʕa; maɛguun ɦilaaʕa.
shawl: ʃaal, ʃilaan.
she: hiyya.
sheep: xaruuf, xirfaan; ɣanam (-a, ʕaɣnaam).
sheer, transparent: ʃaffaaf, -iin.
sheet (*cloth*): milaaya, -aat.
(*paper*): waraʕa, -aat.
shelf: raff, rufuuf / ʕurfuf.
shell (n), *mother-of-pearl*: ṣadaf (-a, -aat).
shell, peel (v): ʕaʃʃar, yiʕaʃʃar.
Shiite: ʃiiɛi, ʃiiɛa.
shine (n): lamɛa.
shine (v) (*to polish shoes*): lammaɛ, yilammaɛ.
ship (n): markib, maraakib.
steam boat: baaxira, bawaaxir; safiina, sufun.
shirt: ʕamiiṣ, ʕumṣaan.
shish kebab: kabaab.
shiver (v): ʕitraɛaʃ, yitriɛiʃ.
shock (n): ṣadma, -aat.
shock (v): ṣadam, yuṣdum / yiṣdim; xaḍḍ, yixuḍḍ.
to be shocked: ʕitṣadam, yitṣidim.
shock absorber: musaaɛid, -iin.
shoehorn: labbiisa, lababiis; labbiisit gazma.
shoelace: rubaaṭ, ʕarbiṭa.
shoemaker: gazmagi, (pl) -yya.
shoes, pair of: gazma, gizam (*one shoe*: fardit gazma).
shoeshine man: massaaɦ ig-gizam; buhyagi, (pl), -yya.
shoot, fire a shot: ḍarab, yiḍrab ṭalʕa/naar.
to shoot s.o.: ṭaxx, yiṭuxx.
shop (n) (*Am.*: *store*): maɦall, -aat; dukkaan, dakakiin.
workshop: warʃa, wiraʃ.
shop assistant (*store employee*): muwaẓẓaf, -iin; bayyaaɛ, -iin.
shopkeeper: bayyaaɛ, -iin.
shopwindow: vatriina, -aat / vatariin.
short (adj): ʕuṣayyar, -iin.
short-circuit (n): maas.
shorten: ʕaṣṣar, yiʕaṣṣar.
shorts (*sportswear*): ʃurṭ, -aat.
shot (n) (*as from a gun*): ṭalʕa, -aat.
injection: ɦuʕna, ɦuʕan.

should (*supposed to*): mafruuḍ / ʕil-mafruuḍ (invar).
  (*necessary*): laazim / ḍaruuri (invar + imperf. v).
shoulder: kitf, kitaaf.
shout: zaɛɛaʕ, yizaɛɛaʕ.
show (n) (*movie*): film, ʕaflaam.
  the one o'clock show: ɦaflit is-saaɛa waɦda.
  display, exhibition: maɛraḍ, maɛaariḍ.
  musical show, revue: ʕistiɛraaḍ.
  stage show, performance, etc.: ɛarḍ, ɛuruuḍ.
show (v): warra, yiwarri; farrag, yifarrag (*someone*) ɛala.
show off, put on airs (v): ʕitmanẓar, yitmanẓar.
  showing off (n): manẓara.
shower: duʃʃ, ʕadʃaaʃ.
shredded-wheat dessert: kunaafa.
shrimp: gambari.
shrink: kaʃʃ. yikiʃʃ.
shutters: ʃiiʃ.
shy: xaguul, -iin (*permanent*); maksuuf, -iin (*temporary*).
  become shy: ʕitkasaf, yitkisif.
siblings: ʕixwaat.
sick: ɛayyaan, -aat.
  to get sick: ɛiyi, yiɛya.
  tired, worn out, sick: taɛbaan, -iin.
  seriously or chronically ill: mariiḍ, muraḍa.
  sick person (n): mariiḍ, marḍa / muraḍa.
  to get sick, tired, bored (*of/with*): zihiʕ, yizhaʕ; ʕirif, yiʕraf; tiɛib, yitɛab (min).
side: naɦya, nawaaɦi.
  this side: ʕin-naɦyaa-di (ʕin-naɦya di).
  the other side: ʕin-naɦya-t-tanya.
  on the wrong side: fin-naɦya-l-ɣalaṭ.
  side (*as compared with front or back*): gamb, ginaab.
  on the sides: fig-ginaab.
side-effects: muḍaɛafaat.
sideboard (*Am.*: *buffet*): bufeeh, -aat.
sideburns: sawaalif.
sidewalk (*Br.*: *pavement*): raṣiif, ʕarṣifa.
sign (n): ʕiʃaara, -aat.
  advertising sign: ʕiɛlaan, -aat.
  road sign, shop sign: yafṭa, yufaṭ.
  astrological sign: burg, ʕabraag.
sign (v) (*e.g. a letter*): maḍa, yimḍi.
signal (*traffic, wave*): ʕiʃaara, -aat.
signature: ʕimḍa, ʕimḍaʕaat.
silence, quiet (n): huduuʕ; sukuut; ṣamt (cl).
  silence!: sukuut!
  don't make a noise: balaaʃ dawʃa.

silencer (*on a car*) (*Am.: muffler*): ɛilbit ʃakmaan.
silent, not talking: saakit, -iin.
to be silent: sikit, yuskut.
silk: ɦariir.
sill (*window*): ʕaɛdit, ʕawaaɛid ʃibbaak.
silly: saxiif, suxafa, baayix, -iin.
to act silly: habbil, yihabbil.
don't be silly!: balaaʃ ɛabaṭ!
silver (n and adj) (*material*); faḍḍa.
(*color*): faḍḍi.
silvery: mifaḍḍaḍ.
similar to: ʃabah; zayy.
a little different: muxtalif ʃiwayya.
simple: basiiṭ, busaṭa / busaaṭ.
Sinai: siina.
Mount Sinai: gabal muusa.
Sinai Day: ɛiid siina.
since (conj): min waʕt^{e} ma (*e.g. since she came*: min waʕt^{e} ma gat).
as long as: madaam; ṭuul ma.
since (prep): min (*e.g. since yesterday*: min imbaariɦ).
sinful act: ɦaraam.
sing: ɣanna, yiɣanni.
singer: muɣanni, -yyiin; muṭrib, -iin.
single (*unmarried*): ɛaazib, ɛuzzaab; miʃ mitgawwiz, -iin.
(*room in hotel*): ʕooḍa li-ʃaxṣ^{e} waɦid; ʕooḍa li-fard^{e} waaɦid.
singular: mufrad.
sink (n): ɦooḍ, ʕaɦwaaḍ.
sip (n): ʃafṭa, -aat.
sip (v): ʃafaṭ, yuʃfuṭ.
siphon (v): ʃaffaṭ, yiʃaffaṭ.
Sir!: ya bee; ya ʕustaaz; ya-fandim.
siren: sariina, -aat.
sister: ʕuxt, ʕixwaat.
sit: ʕaɛad, yuʕɛud / yuɛɛud.
sitting (part): ʕaaɛid, -iin.
sitting (n): ʕuɛaad.
situation (*a particular situation, case*): ɦaala, -aat.
six: sitta; sitt (before pl n).
sixteen: sittaaaʃar.
sixth: saadis / saatit.
sixty: sittiin.
size: ɦagm, ʕaɦgaam.
numbered size (*of clothing items*): maʕaas, -aat.
it's not my size: miʃ ʕadd-i; miʃ maʕaas-i.
this size: ʕadd^{e} kida; ʕil-maʕaas da.
the same size: nafs il-maʕaas.
(*they are*) *the same size*: (humma) ʕadd^{e} baɛḍ.
ski (v): *waterski*: ʕitzaɦlaʕ, yitzaɦlaʕ ɛala-l-mayya.
snowski: ʕitzaɦlaʕ, yitzaɦlaʕ ɛala-t-talg.
skill: mahaara, -aat.
skillful: ʃaaṭir, -iin.
skin: gild, guluud.
skip a line: saab, yisiib saṭr.

skirt: jiiba, -aat; jupp, -aat; gunilla, -aat.
skullcap: ṭaʕiyya, ṭawaaʕi. (*peasant style*): libda, libad.
sky: sama, samawaat.
sky-blue: samaawi.
skylight: ʕamariyya, -aat.
slacks, trousers: banṭaloon, -aat.
slap (n): ʕalam, ʕIʕlaam; ṣafɛa, -aat (cl).
slap (v): ḍarab, yiḍrab ʕalam.
slaughter (*by cutting the throat, e.g. animals for food*): dabaɦ, yidbaɦ.
sleep (n): noom.
sleep (v): naam, yinaam.
put to sleep (*e.g. a child*): nayyim, yinayyim.
sleeping, asleep (part): naayim, -iin.
sleeping pills: ɦubuub munawwima.
sleepy: naɛsaan, -iin; minaɛwis, -iin.
to become sleepy: niɛis, yinɛas.
sleeve: kumm, kumaam.
sleeveless: kaṭṭ; min ɣeer kumaam.
slice (n): taranʃ, -aat; ɦitta, ɦitat; xarṭa, xuraṭ; ʃariiɦa, ʃaraayiɦ.
slice (v): xarraṭ, yixarraṭ; ʕaṭṭaɛ, yiʕaṭṭaɛ taranʃaat.
sliced (adj) (*e.g. bread*): mitʕaṭṭaɛ, -iin; mitʕaṭṭaɛ ṭaranʃaat.
slide (n) (*photograph, microscope*): ʃariiɦa, ʃaraayiɦ.
slim, thin (adj): rufayyaɛ, -iin.
slingshot (*Br.: catapult*): nibla, nibal.
slip (n) (*ladies' clothing*): kumbiin, -aat.
slip (v) (intr): ʕitzaɦlaʕ, yitzaɦlaʕ.
slippers, pair of: ʃibʃib, ʃabaaʃib (one: fardit ʃibʃib).
slippery (adj): mizaɦlaʕ; biyzaɦlaʕ / bitzaɦlaʕ.
slow: baṭiiʕ, buṭaaʕ.
my watch is slow: saɛt-i-mʕaxxara.
slowly: biʃweeʃ; ɛala mahl-ak (-ik, etc.) (*at your ease, slow down*).
sluggish (*on a car*): taɛbaan, -iin.
small: ṣuɣayyar, -iin.
smaller: ʕaṣɣar / ʕazɣar (invar).
smallpox: gudari.
smart, clever: ʃaaṭir, -iin; naaṣih, -iin; gadaɛ, gidɛaan.
smear (n): ʃalfaṭa, -aat.
smear (v): ʃalfaṭ, yiʃalfaṭ.
smell (v): ʃamm, yiʃimm.
(part): ʃaamim, (f) ʃamma, ʃammiin.
(*e.g. I* (m) *smell gas*: ana ʃaamim riiɦit ɣaaz).
it smells good/bad: riɦt-u (f. riɦit-ha) kwayyisa / wiɦʃa.
smell, scent (n): riiɦa, rawaayiɦ.
smoke (n): duxxaan.

smoke (v): daxxan, yidaxxan.
smoke cigarettes:
ʃirib, yiʃrɑb sagaayir.
smoking: tadxiin.
no smoking:
mamnuuɛ it-tadxiin.
smooth, silky: naaɛim, -iin.
snack (n): tɑṣbiirɑ.
snake (n): ɦayya, -aat; tiɛbaan, taɛabiin.
snakeskin: gild^{e} ɦayya; gild^{e} tiɛbaan.
snaps (n) (*on clothing*): kabsuun (-a, kabasiin).
snapshot: lɑʕţɑ, -ɑɑt; ṣuurɑ, ṣuwɑr.
sneeze (v): ɛɑţɑs, yiɛţɑs.
snobbish, arrogant: ʕɑliiţ, ʕulɑţɑ.
snore (v): ʃɑxxɑr, yiʃɑxxɑr.
snorkeling: snoorkiling.
snow (n): talg.
so (*in this manner*): kida.
therefore: ɛaʃaan kida.
and so, then (conj): fa.
so what?: ţɑb wi baɛdeen?; wi ʕee yaɛni?
so on and so forth:
kaza-w-kaza
soap: ṣɑbuun (-ɑ, -ɑɑt).
soap opera: tamsiliyya, -aat; musalsal, -aat.
soccer: koorɑ; kurt il-ʕadam / il-qɑdam.
social, sociable: ʕigtimaaɛi, -yyiin.
social service: xidma-gtimaɛiyya.
socialism: ʕiʃtirɑkiyya.
socialisṭ: ʕiʃtirɑɑki, -yyiin.
society: mugtamaɛ, -aat.
(*an association*):
gamɛiyya, -aat.
sociology: ɛilm il-igtimaaɛ.
socket (*electric outlet*): bariiza, baraayiz.
(*light bulb*): dawaaya, -aat.
socks, pair of: ʃɑrɑɑb, -ɑɑt (*one sock*: fardit ʃɑrɑɑb).
sofa: kanaba, -aat / kanab (coll).
soft: (*squeezable*): ţɑri, ţurɑɑy.
(*smooth*): naaɛim, -iin.
soft drink (*something cold*):
ɦaaga saʕɛa.
soft-boiled (*eggs*): biriʃt / buruʃt.
softness: ţɑrɑɑwɑ: nuɛuuma.
solar heater: saxxaan, saxxanaat ʃamsi.
solder, weld: laɦam, yilɦim.
soldering: liɦaam.
soldier: ɛaskari, ɛasaakir.
sole (*of shoe*): naɛl, niɛaal.
solid (adj): gaamid, -iin.
solid (plain) color:
saada (invar).
solution (*of a problem*): ɦall, ɦuluul.
solve (*a problem*): ɦall, yiɦill.
some: bɑɛḍ (+ def. n); ʃwayyit (+ indef. n).
some of them: bɑɛḍuhum; ʃwayya minhum.
someone: ɦadd (invar); waaɦid (m), waɦda (f).
something: ɦaaga, -aat.
something else: ɦaaga tanya.

sometimes: ʕaɦyaanan.
son: ʕibn, ʕawlaad / wilaad.
song: ɣinwa / ʕuɣniya, ʕaɣaani.
soon, in the near future: ʕurayyib.
right away: ɦaalan; ɛala ṭuul.
sophomore year (*second year*): sana tanya.
sore throat: ʕiltihaab fiz-zoor.
I have a sore throat: zoor-i byiwgaɛ-ni; zoor-i multahib.
sorry: mutaʕassif, -iin; ʕaasif, -iin.
I'm sorry: maɛliʃʃ; (m) mutaʕassif / ʕaasif, (f) ʕasfa.
I'm sorry (*condolences on a death*): ʕil-baʕiyya-f-ɦayaat-ak (-ik, -ku).
to feel sorry (*grieved*) *for*: ziɛil, yizɛal ɛala.
I felt sorry for him: ziɛilt^e ɛalee / ɛaʃaan-u; ṣiɛib (yiṣɛab) ɛalayya.
sort (n): nooɛ, ʕanwaaɛ; ṣanf ʕaṣnaaf.
sound (adj): saliim, sulaam.
sound (n): ṣoot, ʕaṣwaat.
sound and light show: ʕiṣ-ṣoot wiḍ-ḍooʕ.
soup: ʃurba.
soup spoon: maɛlaʕit ʃurba.
sour cream: ʕiʃṭa; ʕiʃṭa fallaɦi; ʕiʃṭa miziz.
source: mawrid, mawaarid; maṣdar, maṣaadir.
south: ganuub.
southern: ganuubi, -yyiin; ʕibli, -yyiin.
space shuttle: makkuuk faḍaaʕ.
spacious, wide: waasiɛ, -iin.
spaghetti: ʕizbakitti; makaroona-zbakitti.
Spain: ʕaspanya / ʕasbanya.
Spanish: ʕaspaani / ʕasbaani, ʕaspaan (*Spaniards*).
spanner (*Am.*: *wrench*): muftaaɦ, mafatiiɦ.
spare parts, accessories: qiṭaɛ ɣiyaar; ʕaksiswaar, -aat.
spare tire: ʕistibn, -aat.
spark plug: bujee, bujehaat.
speak (*with*): ʕikkallim, yikkallim; ʕitkallim, yitkallim (maɛa).
speak to/with: kallim, yikallim.
speaker (*for radio, tape player, etc.*): sammaaɛa, -aat.
special: xuṣuuṣi, -yyiin; maxṣuuṣ, -iin; xaaṣṣ, -iin.
specialist (in): ʕaxiṣṣaaʕi, -yyiin; mutaxaṣṣiṣ, -iin (fi).
specialization, specialty: taxaṣṣus, -aat.
specialize (*in*): ʕitxaṣṣaṣ, yitxaṣṣaṣ (fi).
specialized: mutaxaṣṣiṣ.
specially: xuṣuuṣan; xaaṣṣatan (cl).
specific, particular: muɛayyan, -iin.
specifications: muwaṣafaat.
speech: kalaam.
lecture: muɦaḍra, -aat.

public speech, address: xiṭaab, -aat.
oration: xuṭba, xuṭab.
speed: surεa, -aat.
speed bump: maṭabbᵉ ṣinaaεi, maṭabbaat ṣinaεiyya.
speedometer: ʕambeer surεa; εaddaad surεa.
spell (v): ʕistahagga, yistahagga.
spelling: higaaya.
spend: (*money*): ṣaraf, yiṣrif.
(*time*): ʕaḍḍa, yiʕaḍḍi; ʕaḍa, yiʕḍi.
spend the (*late*) *evening* (*out*): sihir, yishar.
spend the night, stay overnight: baat, yibaat; bayyit, yibayyit.
spend the summer: ṣayyif, yiṣayyif.
spend the winter: ʃatta, yiʃatti.
Sphinx, the: ʕabu l-ḥool.
spice and herb vendor: εaṭṭaar, -iin.
spices: tawaabil; buharaat;
mixture of pounded spices: duʕʕa.
spicy: mitabbil.
spicy, hot: ɦaami, -yiin; ɦarraaʕ, -iin.
spider: εankabuut, εanaakib.
spill (v): dalaʕ, yudluʕ; kabb, yikubb.
spin (v) (*fibers with thread*): ɣazal, yiɣzil.
rotate: laff, yiliff.
spinach: sabaanix.
spirit (n): ruuɦ, ʕarwaaɦ.
spit (v): taff, yitiff.
spite (*in spite of*): bir-raɣmᵉ min.
splinter, thorn, fork: ʃooka, -aat.
spoil: *ruin*: bawwaẓ, yibawwaẓ.
pamper: dallaε, yidallaε.
spoiled: *ruined*: baayiẓ, -iin.
to be spoiled (*ruined*): baaẓ, yibuuẓ.
pampered: mitdallaε / middallaε, -iin.
sponge (n): safinga, -aat.
bathing sponge: luufa, liifa.
spoon, spoonful: maεlaʕa, maεaaliʕ.
teaspoon: maεlaʕit ʃaay.
soupspoon: maεlaʕit ʃurba.
large strainer scoop: maʕṣuuṣa, -aat.
spoon (v): ɣaraf, yiɣrif.
sportive: riyaaḍi, -yyiin.
sports: riyaaḍa.
sportsman: riyaaḍi, -yyiin.
spot, stain (n): buʕεa, buʕaε.
spray (n) (*hair*): spree.
spray (v): raʃʃ, yiruʃʃ.
spread (v) (tr): faraʃ, yifriʃ.
spread out (intr): ʕintaʃar, yintiʃir.
spring (n) (*season*): ʕir-rabiiε.
(*water*): εeen
(*mayya*): εuyuun.
(*coil*): susta, susat.
spy (n): gasuus, gawasiis.
spy (*on*) (v): ʕitgassis, yitgassis (εala).

square (n) (*geometrical sense*):
murabbaɛ, -aat.
plaza (*in a city*):
midaan, mayadiin.
squash: (*orange type*): ʕarɛ^e ɛasali (-a, -aat ɛasali).
pumpkin: ʕarɛ^e ruumi.
zucchini (*Br. courgette*):
koosa / kuusa (-aaya, -aat).
squeeze (v): zanaʕ, yuznuʕ.
squeeze juice (*out of a fruit*): ɛaṣar, yuɛṣur.
squeeze, crush: faɛaṣ, yifɛaṣ.
stable (n): ʕiṣṭabl, -aat.
stadium: ʕistaad, -aat.
stage (n) (*of development*):
marɦala, maraaɦil.
(*in a theater*): xaʃabit il-masraɦ; masraɦ, masaariɦ.
stain, spot (n): buʕɛa, buʕaɛ.
stain, spot (v): baʕʕaɛ, yibaʕʕaɛ.
stainless steel: ʕistenlis-stiil.
stairs, stairway: sillim, salaalim.
stairwell area for garbage, light shaft: manwar, manaawir.
stale (*not fresh*): baayit, -iin.
stamp (n) (*postage*): ṭaabiɛ, ṭawaabiɛ; waraʕit, waraʕ busṭa. (waraʕaat, with nos. nos. 3–10).
date stamp: xitm^e tariix.
seal: xitm, ʕaxtaam.
stamp (v): xatam, yixtim.
stamp pad: xattaama, -aat.
stand (v): wiʕif, yuʕaf (part: waaʕif, -iin; imperative: ʕuʕaf).
stand, bear, tolerate:
ʕistaɦmil, yistaɦmil; ṭaaʕ, yiṭiiʕ.
he stood me up:
ʕiddaa-ni maʕlab.
standard (adj): ɛaada (invar); ɛaadi, -yyiin.
standard time, winter time:
tawqiit / tawʕiit ʃitwi.
staple (n): dabbuus dabbaasa, dababiis dabbaasa.
stapler: dabbaasa, -aat.
star: nigma, nuguum.
movie star: nagm, (f) nagma, nuguum.
planet: kawkab, kawaakib.
starch (n): niʃa.
starch (v): naʃʃa, yinaʃʃi.
starched (adj) (*e.g. a collar*):
minaʃʃi / mitnaʃʃi, -yyiin.
starchy (*e.g. food*): niʃawi.
starchy foods: niʃawiyyaat.
stare (v): baɦlaʕ, yibaɦlaʕ.
start (v): badaʕ, yibdaʕ; ʕibtada, yibtidi.
(*start over*) *from the beginning*:
min ʕawwil wi-gdiid; min il-bidaaya.
starter, ignition: marʃ, -aat; kuntakt / kuntaak.
state (n) (*a particular situation, case*): ɦaala, -aat.
(*condition*): ɦaal, ʕaɦwaal.
(*country*): dawla, duwal.
(*one of the U.S. states*): wilaaya, -aat.

The United States: ʕilwilayaat il-muttaɦida.
station (n): maɦaṭṭa, -aat.
gas station: maɦaṭṭit banziin.
radio station: maɦaṭṭit ʕizaaɛa.
Ramses (railway) Station: baab il-ɦadiid; maɦaṭṭit ramsiis.
train station: maɦaṭṭit ʕaṭr.
stationery store: maktaba, -aat.
stationery, writing paper: waraʕ kitaaba.
air mail paper: waraʕ ṭayyaara.
statistic: ʕiɦṣaʕiyya, -aat.
statistics (*academic subject*): ʕiɦṣa.
statue: timsaal, tamasiil.
stay (v): ʕaɛad, yuʕɛud.
stay at a hotel: nizil, yinzil (fi).
stay overnight: baat, yibaat; bayyit, yibayyit.
stay up late at night: sihir, yishar (part): sahraan, -iin.
steak (*filet*): fileeh, -aat.
steal: saraʕ, yisraʕ.
steam (n): buxaar.
steel: ṣulb.
steering column: ɛamuud diriksiyoon.
steering wheel: diriksiyoon, aat.
stem (*for winding a watch*): ɛamuud, ɛawamiid.
step by step: daraga daraga.
step on, squash, press: daas, yiduus / yuduus (ɛala).
steps, stairway, ladder: sillim, salaalim.
stereo record player: ʕistiryu, -haat.
sterilization: taɛqiim.
sterilize: ṭahhar, yiṭahhar; ɛaqqam, yiɛaqqam.
stew: ṭabiix yaxni (*kind of stew referred to by name of main vegetable used in it*).
stewed meat: kabaab ɦalla.
stick (n) *thin piece of wood*: ɛaṣaaya, ɛuṣyaan.
heavy stick, club: nabbuut, nababiit.
stiff, dry: naaʃif, -iin.
stiff, starchy: minaʃʃi, -yyiin.
still (adv): lissa.
sting (v): ʕaraṣ, yuʕruṣ.
stipulation, condition: ʃarṭ, ʃuruuṭ.
stock (n) (*financial*): sahm, ʕashum.
(*broth*): maraʕa; ʃurba.
stock market: burṣa, -aat.
stockings, pair of: ʃaraab, -aat (*one stocking*: fardit ʃaraab).
stolen: *to be stolen*: ʕitsaraʕ, yitsiriʕ.
stomach: miɛda, -aat.
abdomen: baṭn (f), buṭuun.
stomach ache: maɣaṣ.
my stomach hurts: baṭn-i-btiwgaɛ-ni; miɛdit-i-btiwgaɛ-ni.

stone: ɦagar, ɦigaara / ʕaɦgaar.
kidney, gall bladder stone: ɦaşwa, ɦaşaawi.
stop (n): mawʕif, mawaaʕif.
bus stop: mawʕif il-ʕutubiis.
bus station: maɦaţţa, -aat.
stop (v) (intr): wiʕif, yuʕaf, (imperative: ʕuʕaf).
(tr): waʕʕaf, yiwaʕʕaf.
stop (a habit, e.g. smoking): baţţal, yibaţţal.
stop, refrain, brake oneself: farmil, yifarmil.
stop at (on the way to some place): faat, yifuut ɛala; ɛadda, yiɛaddi ɛala; marr^e, yimurr^e ɛala.
stop talking: sikit, yuskut.
store (v): xazzin, yixazzin.
store, shop (n): maɦall, -aat.
storehouse: maxzan, maxaazin.
story: ɦikaaya, -aat; qişşa, qişaş.
short story: qişşa qaşiira (cl).
stove, butane stove: butagaaz, -aat.
straight: *straight ahead*: duɣri; ţawwaali; ɛala ţuul.
straight hair: ʃaɛr^e naaɛim.
straight line: xaţţ^e mustaqiim.
straight (good, upright) man: raagil mustaqiim.
straighten up, put in order: waɖɖab, yiwaɖɖab.
straightforward (*frank*): duɣri.
straightforward man: raagil duɣri.
strain (v) (*through a strainer*): şaffa, yişaffi.
strainer: maşfa, maşaafi.
strange: ɣariib, ɣuraab.
how strange!: yȧ salaam!; ɣariiba!
stranger: ɣariib, ɣurb / ʕaɣraab.
foreigner: ʕagnabi, ʕagaanib.
Westerner: (m) xawaaga, (f) xawagaaya, (pl) xawagaat.
straw (*hay*): ʕaʃʃ (-a, -aat).
drinking straw: ʃalumoo; ʃaffaaţa, -aat.
strawberries: farawla (-aaya, -aat).
street: ʃaariɛ, ʃawaariɛ.
streetcar, tram: turmaay / turumwaay, -aat.
strengthening: taʕwiya / taqwiya (cl).
stretch (v) (tr): madd, yimidd; maţţ, yumuţţ.
to stretch oneself (to lie down): ʕitmaddid, yitmaddid.
strict: ʃidiid, ʃudaad; mutaʃaddid, -iin.
strike (n): ɖarba, -aat.
strike, abstaining from work: ʕiɖraab, -aat.
strike, hit (v): ɖarab, yiɖrab; xabaţ, yixbaţ.
strike, go on strike: ʕaɖrab, yiɖrib; ɛamal, yiɛmil ʕIɖraab.
string (n): dubaara (no pl).
striped: miʕallim, -iin; mixaţţaţ, -iin.

stroll, take a walk: ʕitmaʃʃa, yitmaʃʃa; ʕitfassaɦ, yitfassaɦ.
strong: ʃidiid, ʃudaad; gaamid, -iin; qawi, ʕaqwiya (cl). (*drink*): tiʕiil, tuʕaal (*lit*: *heavy*).
stubborn: ɛaniid, -iin; raas-u / dimaaɣ-u (-ha, *etc.*) naʃfa.
stuck, wedged in: maznuuʕ, -iin. *to be stuck* (v): ʕitzanaʕ, yitziniʕ.
student: (m): ţaalib, ţullaab / ţalaba. (f): ţaaliba, ţullaab / ţalaba / ţalibaat.
study (n) (*course of study*): diraasa, -aat. (*research*): baɦs, buɦuus / ʕabɦaas. *graduate study*: dirasaat ɛulya.
study (v) (*take a course of study, learn*): daras, yidris. (*a lesson, do homework etc.*): zaakir, yizaakir.
studying (*act of studying, doing homework, etc.*): muzakra.
stuff (v): ɦaʃa, yiɦʃi.
stuffed vegetables: maɦʃi.
stupid: ɣabi, ʕaɣbiya. *stupid, dull*: baliid, bulada.
style (n): ʕusluub, ʕasaliib. *hair style*: tasriiɦa, -aat.
stylish: ʃiik (invar).
stylist (*hair*): kwafeer, -aat.
subject (n) (*topic*): mawɖuuɛ, mawaɖiiɛ. (*gr, when before verb, or in non-verbal sentence*): mubtadaʕ. (*gr, when after verb*): faaɛil, -iin (*doer, agent*).
submerged, drowned, absorbed: ɣarʕaan, -iin.
submit, present: ʕaddim, yiʕaddim.
subscribe (*e.g. to a magazine*): ʕiʃtarak, yiʃtirik (fi).
subscription, subscription fee: ʕiʃtiraak, -aat.
subsidized: mudaɛɛam, -a.
substitute teacher: mudarris (-iin) ʕiɦtiyaaţi (-yyiin).
suburb, district: ɖaaɦiya, ɖawaaɦi.
subway (*underground passage, tunnel*): nafaʕ, ʕanfaaʕ. *underground train*: mitru-l-ʕanfaaʕ.
succeed (*e.g. in an exam*): nigiɦ, yingaɦ.
success: nagaaɦ.
successful: naagiɦ, -iin.
such and such: kaza-w-kaza; keet wi keet.
Sudan: ʕis-sudaan.
Sudanese: sudaani, -yyiin.
suddenly: fagʕa.
Suez Canal: qanaal is-siwees; qanaat is-siwees.
sufficient, enough: kifaaya (invar). *to be sufficient*: kaffa, yikaffi; ʕaɖɖa, yiʕaɖɖi.

sugar: sukkar.
crystallized, in chunks: sukkar nabaat.
cubes: sukkar ʕawaalib.
granulated: sukkar sanṭarafiiʃ.
powdered, confectioners, icing: sukkar budra.
raw, unrefined: sukkar xaam.
sugar bowl: sukkariyya, -aat.
sugar cane: ʕaṣab.
suggest: ʕiqtaraɦ, yiqtariɦ.
suggestion: ʕiqtiraaɦ, -aat.
suicide: ʕintiɦaar.
to commit suicide: ʕintaɦar, yintiɦir.
suit (n): badla, bidal.
women's suit, outfit: tayyeer, -aat.
bathing suit: mayoo, -haat.
suit, fit (v): naasib, yinaasib.
suitable: munaasib, -iin.
more suitable: ʕansab.
suitcase: ʃanṭa, ʃunaṭ; ʃanṭit safar.
sum (*of money*): mablaɣ, mabaaliɣ.
sumac: simmaaʕ.
summarize: laxxaṣ, yilaxxaṣ.
summary: mulaxxaṣ -aat.
summer (n): ʕiṣ-ṣeef.
(adj) *summer style*: ṣeefi, -yyiin.
to spend the summer (in a resort): ṣayyif, yiṣayyif.
to start wearing summer clothes: ṣayyif, yiṣayyif.
summit: qimma, qimam.
sun: ʃams (f), ʃumuus.
sunbathe: ʕitʃammis, yitʃammis; xad, yaaxud ɦammam ʃams.
Sunday: yoom-il-ɦadd.
sunglasses: naḍḍaara, -aat; naḍḍaarit ʃams.
Sunni (adj, n): sunni, -yyiin.
sunset: ʕil-ɣuruub.
time of sunset: ʕil-maɣrib.
suntanned: *to get suntanned*: ʕismarr, yismarr.
superb: haayil, -iin.
supervisor: muʃrif, -iin.
suppose: faraḍ, yifriḍ.
let's suppose that…: nifriḍ ʕinn…
I suppose…: ʕaẓunn…
supposed (*to be, to do*): mafruuḍ / ʕil-mafruuḍ… (invar).
sure (*with personal subject*): mutaʕakkid, -iin.
indisputable (*with non-personal subject*): ʕakiid, -iin.
surgery: giraaɦa.
clinic (*Am.*: *doctor's office*): ɛiyaada, -aat.
operation: ɛamaliyya, -aat.
surprise (n): mufagʕa, -aat.
surprise (v): faagiʕ, yifaagiʕ.
surprised, astonished: mistaɣrab, -iin.
to be surprised: ʕistaɣrab, yistaɣrab.

surrounding, around: ɦawaleen (+ n);
ɦawalee- (+ pron suffix).
around me: ɦawalay-ya.
suspenders (*Br. braces*): ɦammalaat.
suspension (*on a car*): susat.
swan: wizz^{e} (-a, -aat) -ɛiraaʕi.
swear, give an oath: ɦilif / ɦalaf, yiɦlif.
(*formal, e.g. in court*): ɦilif, yiɦlif yimiin.
sweat (n): ɛaraʕ.
sweat (v): ɛiriʕ, yiɛraʕ.
sweating, perspiring: ɛarʕaan, -iin.
sweater: *pullover*: biluuvar, -aat.
cardigan: biluuvar maftuuɦ.
Sweden: ʕis-siwiid.
Swedish: siwiidi, -yyiin.
sweep: kanas, yuknus.
sweet: ɦilw, -iin.
sweet person, charming, very likable: laziiz, luzaaz.
sweetheart: ɦabiib, ɦabaayib.
sweets (*Am.*: *candy*): bunboon (-a, -aat).
(*pastry*): ɦalawiyyaat.
swell up: wirim, yiwram.
swollen: waarim, -iin.
swim: ɛaam, yiɛuum; sabaɦ, yisbaɦ (cl).
swimming: ɛoom; sibaaɦa.
swimming pool: ɦammaam sibaaɦa; pisiin / bisiin.
swimming suit: mayooh, -haat.
Swiss: siwisri, -yyiin.
switch: muftaaɦ, mafatiiɦ.
switch off, (*lights, radio, TV*): ʈafa, yiʈfi; ʕafal, yiʕfil.
(*water*): ʕafal, yiʕfil.
switch on, turn on: ʃaɣɣal, yiʃaɣɣal.
(*lights, TV, radio*): wallaɛ, yiwallaɛ.
(*water, TV, radio*): fataɦ, yiftaɦ.
switchboard, switchboard operator: siwitʃ, -aat.
Switzerland: siwisra.
syllable: maqʈaɛ / maʕʈaɛ, maqaaʈiɛ / maʕaaʈiɛ.
syllabus: xiʈʈa, xiʈaʈ; muqarrar, -aat.
sympathize with: ʕitɛaaʈif, yitɛaaʈif maɛa.
sympathy: ɛaʈf; (*mutual*) taɛaaʈuf.
symptom: ɛaraɖ, ʕaɛraaɖ.
synthetic: ʂinaaɛi, -yyiin.
Syria: surya
Syrian (n & adj): suuri
syringe: siringa, -aat.
system: niʐaam, ʕanʐima.

T

T-shirt: fanilla, -aat; tii ʃirt, -aat.
table: ţarabeeza, -aat.
dining room table: sufra, sufar.
table-cloth: mafraʃ, mafaariʃ.
tablespoon: maεlaʕit ʃurba, maεaaliʕ ʃurba.
taboo: ɦaraam; muɦarram, -iin; maɦẓuur, -iin.
tack (*thumb tack*): dabbuus rasm, dababiis rasm.
tact (n): siyaasa.
tactfully: bis-siyaasa.
tail: deel, diyuul.
tailor (*for men*): tarzi, (pl), -yya; tarzi rigaali.
(*for women*): xayyaaţ, -iin; tarzi ɦariimi.
take: xad / ʕaxad, yaaxud.
take, escort (*e.g. s.o. home*): waṣṣal, yiwaṣṣal.
take a trip: εamal, yiεmil riɦla; raaɦ, yiruuɦ riɦla.
take a vacation: xad, yaaxud ʕagaaza.
take advantage of (*s.o.*): ʕistaɣall, yistaɣill; xamm, yixumm.
take apart: fakk, yifukk.
take away, transport (*to s.o. or someplace*): wadda, yiwaddi.
take-away (*food, to go*): tikawee.
take care of, treat (*doctor*): εaalig, yiεaalig.
take care of, watch over: xad, yaaxud baal-u (-ha, *etc.*) min; xalla, yixalli baal-u (-ha, etc.) min.
take off (*e.g. an airplane*): ʕaam, yiʕuum.
take off (*clothes*): ʕalaε, yiʕlaε.
take out: (*s.o. for entertainment, etc.*): fassaɦ, yifassaɦ.
take out, remove: ţallaε, yiţallaε barra.
take pictures: ṣawwar, yiṣawwar.
take place, happen: ɦaṣal, yiɦṣal.
take up: *carry up*: ţallaε, yiţallaε fooʕ.
take up time: ʕistaɣraʕ, yistaɣraʕ waʕt; xad, yaaxud waʕt.
talented: mawhuub, -iin; εand-u (-aha, *etc.*) mawhiba.
talk (v): ʕikkallim, yikkkallim; ʕitkallim, yitkallim.
talk to (*someone*): kallim, yikallim.
talk, conversation (n): ɦadiis, ʕaɦadiis.
talk, public speech: xiţaab, -aat; xuţba, xuţab; ɦadiis, ʕaɦadiis.
talking (n); kalaam.
to stop talking: sikit, yuskut.

tall: ṭawiil, ṭuwaal.
to become tall: ṭiwil, yiṭwal.
taller (comp): ʕaṭwal (invar).
tamerind: tamr^e hindi.
tampon: tambuun, -aat.
tangerines: yusafandi / yustafandi (-yyaay, -aat).
tap, faucet: ɦanafiyya, -aat.
tape (*cassette, video*): ʃiriiṭ, ʃaraayit / ʕaʃriṭa.
cellotape, scotch tape: seluteep.
electrical tape, welding tape: ʃiriiṭ liɦaam.
tape measure: mazuura, mawaziir.
tape recorder: gihaaz tasgiil, ʕaghizit tasgiil; musaggil.
tapered (*hair style*): midarrag; degradee.
tar, pitch (n): zift.
target, objective (n): hadaf, ʕahdaaf.
tarragon: ṭarxuun.
taste (n): ṭaεm.
aesthetic taste: zooʢ, ʕazwaaʢ.
taste (v): daaʢ, yiduuʢ / yuduuʢ.
it tastes good/bad: ṭaεm-u (-aha) kwayyis / wiɦiʃ.
to let someone taste: dawwaʢ, yidawwaʢ.
tax (n): ḍariiba, ḍaraayib.
income tax: ḍariibit daxl.
taxi: taks / taksi, taksaat / taksiyyaat.
tea: ʃaay.
teach: darris, yidarris; εallim, yiεallim.
teacher: mudarris, -iin; muεallim, -iin; ʕustaaz, ʕasatza.
teaching (n): tadriis; taεliim.
team: fariiʢ, firaʢ.
teapot: barraad, -aat (ʃaay).
tear (v): ʢaṭaε, yiʢṭaε.
tear up (*to pieces*): ʢaṭṭaε, yiʢaṭṭaε.
tears (n): damε (-a, dimuuε).
tease: εaakis, yiεaakis.
teasing (*hairstyle*): krepaaj / kiribaaj.
teaspoon: maεlaʢit ʃaay, maεaaliʢ ʃaay.
technical: fanni, -yyiin.
technician: fanni, -yyiin.
tedious, boring: mumill, -iin.
telegram, telegraph: tilliɣraaf, -aat.
telephone (n): tilifoon, -aat.
telephone call: mukalma, -aat; tilifoon; mukalma tilifuniyya.
television: tilivizyoon / tilfizyoon, -aat.
tell: *inform* (*say to*): ʢaal, yiʢuul li.
report to (*e.g. the police*): ballaɣ, yiballaɣ.
tell a story, narrate: ɦaka, yiɦki.
temperature: ɦaraara.
degree: daragit il-ɦaraara.
how hot is it?: daragit il-ɦaraara kaam?

temple (*place of worship*): maεbad, maεaabid.
temporarily: muwaʕʕatan / muʕaqqatan (cl).
temporary, seasonal: ẓuhuraat (invar).
seasonal worker: εaamil, εummaal taraɦiil.
short term: muwaʕʕat.
ten: εaʃara; εaʃar (before pl n.).
ten piaster coin: bariiza, baraayiz.
tenant: saakin, sukkaan.
tennis: tinis.
tension (*stress*) (n): tawattur.
tent: xeema, xiyam / xiyaam.
tentmaker: xiyami/ xiyaami, (pl), -yya.
street of the tentmakers: ʃaariε il-xiyamiyya.
tenure:
to be hired on a permanent basis: ʕitsabbit, yitsabbit.
tenured: mitsabbit.
terrible: faẓiiε, fuẓaaε; ʃaniiε, ʃunaaε.
terrorism: ʕirhaab.
terrorist: ʕirhaabi, -yyiin.
terry cloth: baʃkiir.
test (n): ʕimtiɦaan, -aat; ʕixtibaar, -aat.
medical test (*e.g. blood*): taɦliil, taɦaliil.
test, examine (v): ʕimtaɦan, yimtiɦin.
tetanus: titanoos.
than: min (after comp); εan (after regular adj).
bigger than: ʕakbar min; kibiir εan.
thank (*for*): ʃakar, yuʃkur (εala).
I thank you: ʕaʃkur-ak (-ik, -ku).
thanks: ʃukran mirsii; mutʃakkir, -iin (agreement with subj.).
thanks for your visit: ʃukran εala ziyart-ak, -ik, ziyarit-ku.
thanks for telling me: ʃukran εala ʕinnak ʕult-ili / ʕinnik ʕultii-li
thanks for the meal: sufra dayma (*i.e. may your dining table be always spread*).
a thousand thanks: ʕalf^{e} ʃukr.
I (m) *can't thank you* (m) *enough*: miʃ εaarif aʃkurak izzaay.
thank God: ʕil-ɦamdu li-llaah.
that (conj): ʕinn.
that (demonst. adj): da (m), di (f); dukha (m), dikha (f).
that's why, for that reason: εaʃaan kida.
the: ʕil-
(*l assimilates to* t, ṭ, d, ḍ, n, s, ṣ, z, ẓ, r, ʃ, *optionally to k and g*).
theater: masraɦ, masaariɦ.
movie theater: sinima, -aat; siima, siyam.
theft, robbery: sirʕa, sariʕaat.
armed robbery: sirʕa, bi-l-ʕikraah.

embezzlement: ʕixtilaas, -aat.
grand theft, swindling:
naṣb.
pickpocketing: naʃl.
their: *see pronominal suffix chart*.
theirs: (m) bitaɛ-hum, (f) bitaɛit-hum, (pl) bituɛ-hum.
them: *see pronominal suffix chart*.
then: *at that time*: waʕt-aha, fil-waʕt^e da.
afterward: baɛdeen;
baɛd^e kida.
in that case: ʕummaal (*usually in questions*).
therefore, in this case: fil-ɦaala di; ɛala kida;
yibʕa (*preposed*):
baʕa (*postposed*); ʕizan.
theoretical: naẓari, -yyiin.
theoretically: naẓariyyan.
theory: naẓariyya, -aat.
there: hinaak.
there is / are: fii.
therefore: yibʕa (*preposed*);
baʕa (*postposed*);
ɛala kida; ʕizan; ɛaʃaan kida.
thermometer: mizaan ɦaraara.
thermos: tirmus, taraamis.
thermostat: tirmustaat, -aat.
these: dool; di (*in ref. to non-humans*).
thesis, dissertation: risaala, rasaayil.
they: humma; hiyya (*in ref. to non-humans*).
thick: tixiin, tuxaan; samiik, sumaak (cl).
thief: ɦaraami, (pl), -yya.
thigh: faxd (f), fixaad.
(*cut of meat*); faxda, -aat.
(*of rabbit or fowl*):
wirk, wiraak / ʕawraak.
thimble: kustibaan, -aat.
thin: rufayyaɛ, -iin.
thing: ɦaaga, -aat.
think (*of, about*): fakkar, yifakkar (fi).
believe (*that*): ʕiftakar, yiftikir;
ẓann, yiẓunn (ʕinn).
I think so: ʕaftikir kida:
ʕaẓunn^e kida.
thinker, philosopher: mufakkir, -iin; faylasuuf, falasfa.
thinner (*for paint*): tinar.
third (*of a series*): taalit.
one-third: tilt.
thirdly (adv): saalisan.
thirsty: ɛaṭʃaan, -iin.
to get thirsty: ɛiṭiʃ, yiɛṭaʃ.
thirteen: talattaaʃar.
thirty: talatiin.
this: da (m), di (f).
like this: zayy^e kida.
thongs (*shoes held on between toes*):
ʃibʃib, ʃabaaʃib zannuuba.
thorns: ʃook, (-a, -aat).
those (*humans*): dool; dukhum.
(*non-humans*): di; dikha.
though, although (conj): maɛa ʕinn; bir-raɣm^e min (ʕinn).
though, however: maɛa zaalik; bir-raɣm^e min kida.

thousand: ʕalf, ʕuluuf / ʕalaaf (talaaf after nos. 3–10)
two thousand: ʕalfeen.
four thousand: ʕarbaɛ talaaf.
a hundred thousand: miit ʕalf.

thread (n): xeeṭ, xuyuuṭ / xiṭaan.

three: talaata; talat (before pl n).

throat: zoor, zuwaar / ʕizwaar.
sore throat: ʕiltihaab fiz-zoor.

through: *by way of*: ɛan ṭariiʕ.
through, finished: xalaaṣ.
to be through, finished: xiliṣ, yixlaṣ.

throughout: ṭuul.
throughout the day, all day long: ṭuul in-nahaar.

throw: rama, yirmi; zaʕaf, yuzʕuf.

throw up, vomit: raggaɛ, yiraggaɛ.

thumb: ʕibhaam, -aat.

thumb tack: dabbuus rasm, dababiis rasm.

thunder: raɛd, ruɛuud.

Thursday: yoom il-xamiis.
Holy Thursday, Maundy Thursday: xamiis il-ɛahd.

thyme, oregano: zaɛtar / zaɛtar.

ticket: tazkara, tazaakir.
buy a ticket: ʕaṭaɛ, yiʕṭaɛ tazkara.
ticket man, conductor: kumsaari, (pl), -yya.
ticket for traffic offense: muxalfa, -aat.

tie, string (n) (*e.g. shoe string*): rubaaṭ, -aat / ʕarbiṭa.
necktie: karavatta / garafatta, -aat.
tie (*in sports*): taɛaadul.

tie (v): rabaṭ, yurbuṭ.
(*in sports*): ʕitɛaadil, yiɛaadil.

tiger: nimr, numuur.

tight (*e.g. clothes*): dayyaʕ, -iin.
tight with money, stingy: baxiil, buxala.

tighten: rabaṭ, yurbuṭ (kwayyis).

tights (*Am.: pantyhose*): kuloon, -aat.

tiles: balaat (-a, -aat).
ceramic tiles: ʕiʃaani.

till, until (prep): liɦadd; liɣaayit; li.
(conj): liɦadd^{e} ma; liɣaayit ma.

time: waʕt, ʕawʕaat.
a long time ago: min zamaan.
at the same time: fi nafs il-waʕt; bil-marra (*while we're (you're etc.) at it*).
at the time: waʕt-aha; fil-waʕt^{e} da; (fi) saɛit-ha; yum-ha (*on that day*).
by the time: ɛala ma; ɛala baal ma.
during Nasser's time: fi ɛahd^{e} gamaal ɛabd in-naaṣir.
from time to time: min waʕt^{e} lit-taani.

he has been in Egypt a long time: baʕaal-u zamaan fi maṣr.
last time: ʕil-marra-lli faatit.
modern times: ʕil-ɛaṣr il-ɦadiis.
next time: ʕil-marra-g-gayya / ʕil-marra-lli gayya.
on time: fil-maɛaad.
one time, once: marra.
three times: talat marraat.
period of time: mudda, mudad.
for (a period of time): li-muddit.
scheduled time: maɛaad, mawaɛiid.
standard time, winter time: tawqiit ʃitwi.
summer time, daylight saving time: tawqiit ṣeefi.
this time: ʕil-marraadi / ʕil-marra di.
time, the times (e.g. in which we live): zaman, ʕazmina.
time flies: ʕil-waʕt^e biyfuut bisurɛa; ʕil-waʕt^e biyṭiir.
what time is it?: ʕis-saaɛa kaam?

timetable, list of times: mawaɛiid.
airline schedule booklet: gadwal, gadaawil.

tin (*Am.: can*) (n): ɛilba, ɛilab.

tip (n) (*money*): baʕʃiiʃ.
(*e.g. of a shoe*): buuz, buwaaz.
(*e.g. of an island*): raas (f), ruus.

tires (n): ɛagal (-a, -aat); kawitʃ, -aat.

tire, trouble (v) (tr): taɛab, yitɛib.

tired, worn out, sick: taɛbaan, -iin.
sleepy: naɛsaan, -iin; minaɛwis, -iin.
to get tired: tiɛib, yitɛab.

tiring, troublesome: mutɛib, -iin.

tissue (*kleenex*): mandiil waraʕ, manadiil waraʕ.

title (*e.g. of a book*): ɛinwaan, ɛanawiin.

to: li.

toast (*dry rusk*): buʕsumaaṭ.

toast, sandwich bread: tust; ɛeeʃ tust.

tobacco: duxxaan, ʕadxina.

today: ʕin-naharda.

toe: ṣubaaɛ rigl, ṣawaabiɛ rigl.

together: sawa, maɛa baɛḍ.

toilet: tiwalitt; tuwalitt, -aat; ɦammaam, -aat.

toilet pump: makanit sifoon.
bulb in toilet tank: ɛawwaama.

toilet tank: sifoon, -aat.

tolerate: ʕistaɦmil, yistɦmil; ṭaaʕ, yiṭiiʕ.

tomatoes: ʕuuṭa (-aaya, -aat); ṭamaaṭim (ṭamaṭmaaya, -aat).

tomb, grave: ʕabr, ʕubuur.
ancient tomb, grave: maʕbara, maʕaabir.
graveyard: maqaabir.

tomorrow: bukra.
day after tomorrow: baɛd^e bukra.

tongue: lisaan, lisina.
tonight: ʕil-leela; ʕil-lilaadi / ʕil-leela-di.
too (*also*): kamaan; bardu.
 (*excessively*): ʕawi;
 ziyaada ʕan il-luzuum;
 ʕaktar min il-laazim.
tool, instrument: ʕadaah, ʕadawaat.
tools, equipment: ɛidad.
 set of tools: ɛidda, ɛidad.
tooth: sinna, sinaan; dirs, diruus (*molar*).
toothache: wagaɛ sinaan.
 my teeth hurt: sinaan-i-btiwgaɛ-ni.
toothbrush: furʃit sinaan.
toothpaste: maɛguun sinaan.
toothpick: xilla xillit sinaan.
top: *cover, lid*: ɣaṭa, ɣuṭyaan.
 (*e.g. of the class*):
 ʕil-ʕawwil (m), ʕil-ʕuula (f).
 ʕil-ʕawaaʕil (pl).
 at the top of something:
 fooʕ.
 pajama top: jakittit bijaama.
 top, upper (adj):
 fuʕaani, -yyiin.
topic: mawduuɛ, mawadiiɛ.
Torah, the: ʕit-tawraa.
torch (*Am.: flashlight*) (n):
 baṭṭariyya, -aat.
torn: maʕtuuɛ, -iin.
 torn up: miʕaṭṭaɛ, -iin.
total: magmuuɛ, magamiiɛ.
touch (v): lamas, yilmis.

touch, to get in touch: ʕittaṣal, yittiṣil (bi).
tour, trip: riɧla, -aat.
 short trip (*e.g. round city*):
 laffa, -aat; gawla, aat.
tourism: siyaaɧa.
tourist: saayiɧ, suwwaaɧ.
touristic: siyaaɧi, -yyiin.
 touristic site: manṭiʕa
 siyaɧiyya, manaaṭiʕ siyaɧiyya.
tow (v): ʕaṭar, yuʃṭur; ʃadd, yiʃidd.
toward: ɛala naɧyit; naɧyit;
 fi-ttigaah.
towel: fuuṭa, fuwaṭ.
towel rack: fawwaaṭa, -aat.
tower: burg, ʕabraag.
town: balad (f), bilaad.
toy: liɛba, liɛab.
 children's toys: liɛab ʕaṭfaal.
track (*e.g. of train*): xaṭṭ, xuṭuuṭ.
tradition, custom: taqliid,
 taqaliid / taʕaliid.
traditional (adj): taʕliidi / taqliidi.
 local style (*dress, food, etc.*):
 baladi (invar).
traffic: muruur.
 traffic circle, (Br.: roundabout):
 ṣaniyya, ṣawaani.
 traffic jam: zaɧmit muwaṣlaat.
 traffic signal: ʕiʃaara, -aat;
 ʕiʃaarit muruur.
 traffic violation: muxalfa, -aat.
train (n): ʕaṭr, ʕuṭuraat / ʕuṭura.
 train station: maɧaṭṭit ʕaṭr
 Ramsis (railway) Station:
 baab il-ɧadiid; maɧaṭṭit
 ramsiis.

train (v) (tr): marran, yimarran; darrab, yidarrab.
(intr): ʕitdarrab, yitdarrab.
teach a habit: waxxid, yiwaxxid (*s.o.* ɛala *s.t.*); ɛawwid, yiɛawwid (*s.o.* ɛala *s.t.*).
trainer: mudarrib, -iin.
training: tamriin; tadriib.
training suit: badlit tadriib; treening suut; trink.
tramway: turmaay / turumwaay, -aat.
tranquilizer, sedative: muhaddiʕ, -aat.
transfer (n): naʕl.
transfer (v): naʕal, yinʕil; ɦawwil, yiɦawwil.
to be transferred: ʕitnaʕal, yitniʕil.
transformer: tarans, -aat; muɦawwil, -aat.
translate: targim, yitargim.
translation: targama, -aat.
translator: mutargim, -iin.
transmission shaft: ɛamuud kirdaan.
transparent: ʃaffaaf, -iin.
transport (v): wadda, yiwaddi; waȿȿal, yiwaȿȿal.
transport, carry: naʕal, yinʕil.
transportation (*means of*): muwaȿla, muwaȿlaat.
trap (n): maȿyada, maȿaayid.
trash (n): zibaala.
trash can: ȿafiiɦit zibaala, ȿafaayiɦ zibaala.
trash collector: zabbaal, -iin.
trash dump: maʕlab zibaala.
travel (n): safar, ʕasfaar; safariyyaat (pl).
traveling (part): misaafir, -iin.
travel (v): saafir, yisafir.
travel agency: maktab siyaaɦa, makaatib siyaaɦa.
tray: ȿaniyya, ȿawaani.
treading water: wuʕuuf fil-ɣariiʕ.
treasure: kinz, kunuuz.
treat (n):
it's my treat; I'm inviting you (m to m): ʕana ɛazm-ak.
let this be on me: xalli da ɛalayya.
treat (v) (*deal with*): ɛaamil, yiɛaamil.
(*pay for*): ɛazam, yiɛzim.
treat medically: ɛaalig, yiɛaalig.
treaty: muɛahda, -aat; ʕittifaqiyya / ʕittifaʕiyya, -aat.
trees: ʃagar (-a, -aat), ʕaʃgaar (pl of coll).
trial (*attempt*): muɦawla, -aat.
(*in a court of law*): muɦakma, -aat.
experiment: tagriba, tagaarib.
triangle: musallas, -aat.
trick (n): liɛba, ʕalɛaab.
trick, ruse: ɦiila, ɦiyal.
trick, swindle: xidɛa, xidaɛ; ʕiɦtiyaal.
trick (v): xadaɛ, yixdaɛ.
trickery, fraudulence: talaaɛub; taɦaayul.
trigonometry: ɦisaab musallasaat.

trim (v): saawa, yisaawi; waḍḍab, yiwaḍḍab.
cut hair just a little: ʕuṣṣ iʃ-ʃaɛr^e ʃwayya bass.
Trinity (*The Holy Trinity*) (*Chr*): ʕis-saluus il-ʕaqdas.
trip (n): riɦla, -aat.
business trip: maʕmuriyya, -aat.
trip (v): ʕitʃankil, yitʃankil.
trombone: taramboon, -aat.
trophy: kaas, kasaat.
trouble (n): taɛab, mataaɛib.
I don't want any trouble: miʃ ɛaayiz (ɛayza) maʃaakil.
thanks for your (m) *trouble*: ʃukran ɛala ṭaɛab-ak maɛaaya.
what's the trouble?: ʕeeh il-mawḍuuɛ?; ʕeeh il-muʃkila?
trouble (v): ṭaɛab, yitɛib.
I am sorry I troubled you (m): ʕana taɛabt-ak maɛaaya.
troublemaker: muʃaaɣib, -iin.
troublesome: mutɛib, -iin.
trousers: banṭaloon, -aat.
truce: hudna, -aat.
truck (*Br.*: *lorry*): luuri, lawaari; ɛarabiyya, ɛarabiyyaat naʕl.
pickup truck: nuṣṣ^e naʕl.
true: ɦaʕiiʕi, -yyiin; ṣaɦiiɦ.
it's the truth (*by God*): w-allaahi.
truly: ṣaɦiiɦ.
trumpet: turumba, -aat.
trunk (*of a car*): ʃanṭa, ʃunaṭ; ʃanṭit ɛarabiyya.
metal suitcase: sanduuʕ ɦadiid, sanadiiʕ ɦadiid.
trust (v): wasaq, yasiq fi (cl).
truth (*reality, fact*): ɦaʕiiʕa, ɦaʕaayiʕ.
(*correctness, rightness*): ɦaʕʕ.
try (v) (*attempt*): ɦaawil, yiɦaawil;
(*in a court of law*): ɦaakim, yiɦaakim.
try on (*for size*): ʕaas, yiʕiis.
try out, test (*something*): garrab, yigarrab.
tuberculosis: sull; daran.
Tuesday: yoom it-talaat.
tumor: waram, ʕawaraam.
benign: ɦamiid.
malignant: xabiis.
tuna: tuuna.
tune (v) (*engine, musical instrument, etc.*): ẓabaṭ, yuẓbuṭ.
tuning: tiyuuning.
tune-up: ɛamra.
Tunis, Tunisia: tuunis.
Tunisian: tunsi /tuunisi, tawansa.
tunnel (n): nafaʕ, ʕanfaaʕ.
Turkey: turkiyya.
turkey: diik ruumi, duyuuk ruumi.
Turkish: turki, ʕatraak.
turmeric: kurkum.
turn (n) (*e.g. my turn*): door, ʕadwaar.
whose turn is it ?: door miin?

turn, road curve: laffa, -aat; ɦawadaaya, -aat.
turn (v) (intr, tr): ɦawad, yiɦwid; ɦawwid, yiɦawwid.
turn around: laff, yiliff.
cause to turn around: dawwar, yidawwar.
turn down (*volume*): waṭṭa, yiwaṭṭi.
turn into (*become*): baʕa, yibʕa.
turn off (*lights, radio, stove, TV*): ṭafa, yiṭfi.
turn off (*water, radio, TV*): ʕafal, yiʕfil.
turn on: ʃaɣɣal, yiʃaɣɣal; dawwar, yidawwar.
turn on (*lights, radio, stove, TV*): wallaɛ, yiwallaɛ.
turn on (*water, radio, TV*): fataɦ, yiftaɦ.
turn out to be: ṭiliɛ, yiṭlaɛ.
turn up (*volume*): ɛalla, yiɛalli.
turn-up (*Am.*: *trouser cuff*): tanyit, tanyaat banṭaloon.
turnips: lift (-a, -aat).
turpentine: tarabantiina.
turquoise (*stone*): faruuz / faruuz.
(*color*): turkuwaaz / turukwaaz.
turtle: zuɦlifa, zaɦaalif.
turtleneck collar: koola maʕluuba (*turned*).
turtleneck sweater: biluuvar biraʕaba.
tutor (*private teacher*): mudarris xuṣuuṣi, mudarrisiin xuṣuṣiyyiin.
tweezers: mulʕaaṭ, malaʕiiṭ.
twelve: ʕitnaaʃar.
twenty: ɛiʃriin.
11:40: ʕitnaaʃar illa tilt.
12:20: ʕitnaaʃar wi tilt.
twice: marriteen.
twin: tawʕam, tawaaʕim.
two: ʕitneen.
two (*books*): (kitab)een.
two-way street: ʃaariɛ ittigaheen.
type (v): katab, yiktib ɛala-l-makana; ṭabaɛ, yiṭbaɛ.
type, kind (n): nooɛ, ʕanwaaɛ; ṣanf, ʕaṣnaaf.
typewriter (v): makana, -aat; ʕaala katba, ʕalaat katba.
typhoid fever: tayfuud.
tyres (n): ɛagal (a, -aat); kawitʃ, -aat.

U

ugly: wiɦiʃ, iin.
ulcer: ʕurɦa, ʕuraɦ; qurɦa, quraɦ.
umbrella: ʃamsiyya, -aat / ʃamaasi.
unbelievable: miʃ maɛʕuul, -iin.
uncle (*paternal*): ɛamm, ɛimaam.
(*maternal*): xaal, xilaan.
under: taɦt.
underdeveloped: mutaxallif, -iin.
underground, tube (*Am.*: *subway*): mitru-l-ʕanfaaʕ.
underpants: kulutt / kilutt, -aat; libaas, libisa (*often considered crude*);
silibb, -aat.
undershirt, T-shirt: fanilla, -aat; tii ʃirt, -aat.
understand: fihim, yifham.
(part): faahim, -iin.
understanding (n): fahm.
general understanding (of a book, essay, etc.): ʕistiɛaab.
mutual understanding: tafaahum.
to have mutual understanding with:
ʕitfaahim, yitfaahim maɛa.
understood (part): mafhuum, -iin.
underwater sports: riyaaḍit il-ɣaṭs.
underwear: malaabis / huduum daxiliyya;
huduum taɦtaniyya.
undo, release: fakk, yifukk / yifikk.
undoubtedly: min ɣeer ʃakk; biduun ʃakk.
unemployed: ɛaaṭil, -iin; miʃ biyiʃtaɣal;
ma-ɛand-uu-ʃ ʃuɣl, xaali ʃuɣl.
unemployment: biṭaala.
unfortunately: li-l-ʕasaf.
unite (intr): ʕittaɦad, yittiɦid.
(tr): waɦɦid, yiwaɦɦid.
united: muttaɦid, -iin.
the United Nations: ʕil-ʕumam il-muttaɦida.
the United States: ʕil-wilayaat il-muttaɦida.
university: gamɛa, -aat.
University of Cairo: gamɛit il-qaahira.
unjust: (*biased*): mutaɦayyiz, -iin.
(*oppressive*): ẓaalim, -iin.
to treat unjustly, oppress: ẓalam, yiẓlim.
unplug (*the drain-hole*): sallik, yisallik (il-ballaaɛa).
(*the electricity*): ʃaal, yiʃiil il-fiiʃa.
unsuccessful (*in an exam*): saaʕit, -iin.
a total failure: faaʃil, -iin; xaayib, -iin.
until (conj): liɦadd^{e} ma; liɣaayit ma; ɛala ma (*by the time that*).

until (prep): liɦadd. liɣaayit.
up, upstairs: fooʕ.
Upper (*southern*) **Egypt**: ʕiṣ-ṣiɛiid; ʕil-wagh il-ʕibli.
Upper Egyptian: ṣiɛiidi, ṣɑɛɑydɑ.
upper (adj): fuʕaani, -yyiin.
uprising (*e.g. against occupation forces*): ʕintifɑɑḍɑ, -ɑɑt.
upset (adj): zaɛlaan, -iin; middayiʕ, -iin.
to get upset: ziɛil, yizɛal; ʕiddayiʕ, yiddayiʕ.
upset stomach: miɛdit, -u (-ha, *etc.*) maʕluuba.
upset (v): zaɛɛal, yizaɛɛal; daayiʕ, yidaayiʕ.
upside-down: bil-maʕluub; bil-miʃaʕlib.
urine: bool.
us: *see pronominal suffix chart*.
use (n): ʕistiɛmaal, -aat.
usefulness, benefit: fayda, fawaayid.
it's no use: ma-fii-ʃ fayda.
use (v): ʕistaɛmil, yistaɛmil.
used to, accustomed to: mitɛawwid, -iin ɛala.
to get used to: ʕitɛawwid, yitɛawwid ɛala.
used, second-hand: mustaɛmal, -iin.
useful: mufiid, -iin.
to be useful: nafaɛ, yinfaɛ.
useless, there's no use: ma-fiiʃ fayda; miʃ naafiɛ.
usual: ɛaadi, -yiin.
usually: ɛaadatan; fil-ɛaada.
uterus: rɑɦim.
utter (v): nɑṭɑʕ, yinṭɑʕ.

V

vacant: faaḍi, -yiin.
vacation: ʕagaaza, -aat.
vaccine, serum: maṣl, ʕamṣaal.
vacuum cleaner: maknasa, makaanis kahraba.
valley: waadi, widyaan.
Valley of the Kings (*in Luxor*): waadi-l-muluuk.
value: ʢiima, ʢiyam.
it's of little value: ʢimt-u ʢaliila.
it's of personal value: ʢimt-u ʢayyima.
it's expensive: ʢimt-u ɣalya.
valve: balf, buluuf; ṣimaam, -aat; maħbas, maħaabis.
vanilla: fanilya / vanilya.
various: mutanawwiɛ, -iin; muxtalif, -iin; kaza (+ sing. n).
vase: faaza / vaaza, -aat; zuhriyya, -aat.
veal: laħma-btillu.
vegetables: xuḍaar; xuḍra.
vegetable vendor: xuḍari, -yya; bitaaɛ il-xuḍaar.
vegetarian: nabaati, -yyiin.
veil (n): *complete covering including face*: niqaab.
head covering excluding face: ħigaab, ʕiħgiba.
head covering including chest: ximaar (invar).
wedding veil: ṭarħa, ṭuraħ.
veiled (adj): muħaggaba, -aat.
vein: ɛirʢ, ɛuruuʢ.
velvet: ʢaṭiifa.
vendor: *lemon vendor*: bitaaɛ il-lamuun.
butagas man: bitaaɛ il-ɣaaz.
ventilate: hawwa, yihawwi.
ventilation: tahwiyya.
ventilator: hawwaaya, -aat.
verb (gr): fiɛl, ʕafɛaal.
verbal noun (gr): maṣdar, maṣaadir.
verdure, greenery: xaḍaar, xuḍra.
verify, confirm: ʕakkid, yiʕakkid.
ascertain, make sure: ʕitʕakkid, yitʕakkid (min).
very: ʢawi; giddan; xaaliṣ.
vest: (*Br.*: *waistcoat*): jilee, -haat; ṣideeri.
(*Am.*: *undershirt*): fanilla, -aat.
veterinarian: duktoor biṭari, dakatra biṭariyyiin.
veterinary clinic: ɛiyaada, -aat biṭariyya.
veterinary medicine: ṭibb^e biṭari.
vexed, angry: mitɣaaẓ, -iin; ɣaḍbaan, -iin.
view, scene: manẓar, manaaẓir.
viewpoint: wughit naẓar, wughaat naẓar.
viewpoint, aspect: naħya, nawaaħi.
villa: villa, -aat / vilal.
village: qarya, qura.
villager, peasant: fallaaħ, -iin; qarawi, -yyiin.

vinegar: xall.
violate (*a law*): xaalif, yixaalif.
violation: muxalfa, -aat.
violence: ɛunf.
violet (adj): banafsigi (invar).
violin: kamanga, -aat.
virus: fairus / fayruus.
microbe(*s*): mikroob, (-a, -aat).
visa: taʕʃiira, -aat; viiza, -aat.
visit (n): ziyɑɑrɑ, -ɑɑt.
visit (v): zɑɑr, yizuur.
visitor, guest: ḍeef, ḍuyuuf; zaayir, zuwwɑɑr.
vitamin: vitamin / fitamiin, aat.
vocabulary, lexical items: mufrɑdɑɑt / mufradaat (pl).
vocabulary word: kilma, kalimaat.
vocabulary class: ɦiṣṣit mufradaat; dars^e mufradaat.
vocational science: taɛliim fanni; taɛliim mihani.
voice: ṣoot, ʕɑṣwɑɑt.
volleyball: koora ṭɑyrɑ; vuli bool.
voltage: guhd (no pl).
voltage regulator: staabilayzir; munɑẓẓim guhd.
current regulator: munɑẓẓim it-tɑyyɑɑr.
volume (*part of a book*): guzʕ, ʕagzaaʕ.
(*bound book*): mugallad, -aat.
sound: ṣoot, ʕɑṣwɑɑt.
vomit (v): raggaɛ, yiraggaɛ; ʕitʕaaya, yitʕaaya; ʕistafraɣ, yistafraɣ.
vote (n): ṣoot, ʕɑṣwɑɑt.
vote (v): ʕintaxab, yintixib; ṣɑwɑɑt, yiṣɑwwɑt.
vowel (n): ɦaraka, -aat; ɦɑrf mutaɦɑrrik, ɦuruuf mutaɦɑrrika.
vowel (v): ʃakkil, yiʃakkil.
voweling (n): taʃkiil, (*using the short vowel markers in Arabic*)

W

wage: mahiyya, -aat / mahaaya; murattab̧, -aat.
waistcoat (*Am.*: *vest*): jilee, -haat; ṣideeri.
wait (v): ʕistanna, yistanna; ʕintaẓar, yintiẓir.
waiting (part): mistanni, -yyiin.
waiter: garsoon, -aat.
maitre d': mitr.
waiter! (*to get his attention*): ya rayyis!; ya mitr!
waitress: garsoona, -aat; muḍiifa, -aat (*hostess*).
waitress! (*to get her attention*): ya madmuzeel!; ya madaam!
wake up (intr): ṣiɦi, yiṣɦa.
(tr): ṣaɦɦa, yiṣaɦɦi.
walk (v): miʃi, yimʃi.
to take someone on a walk: maʃʃa, yimaʃʃi.
to go for a walk: ʕitmaʃʃa, yitmaʃʃa.
walking (part): maaʃi, -yiin.
wall: ɦeeṭa, ɦiṭaan.
wall surrounding a garden: suur, ʕaswaar.
wallet: maɦfaẓa, maɦaafiẓ.
walnuts: gooz (-a, -aat); ɛeen (ig-) gamal.
want (v): ɛaaz, yiɛuuz / yuɛuuz.
(part): ɛaayiz, -iin; ɛaawiz, -iin.
war: ɦarb (f), ɦuruub.
wardrobe: dulaab, dawaliib huduum.
warehouse: maxzan, maxaazin.
warm (*room, weather*): daafi, -yyiin.
(*people, animals feeling warm*): dafyaan, -iin.
wash, laundry (n): ɣasiil.
wash (v): ɣasal, yiɣsil.
wash cloth, face towel: fuuṭit wiʃʃ, fuwaṭ wiʃʃ.
washer (*e.g. of a faucet*): gilda, -aat.
washer lady: ɣassaala, aat.
washing machine (*electric*): ɣassaala, -aat, (kahraba).
wasp: dabbuur, dababiir.
waste (v): (*time, money*): ḍayyaɛ, yiḍayyaɛ (waʕt, filuus).
throw away (*food*): rama, yirmi (ʕakl).
wastebasket: sabat, ʕisbitit zibaala.
watch (n): saaɛa, -aat.
my watch is slow: saɛt-i-mʕaxxara.
my watch is right: saɛt-i-mazbuuṭa.
my watch is fast: saɛt-i-mʕaddima.
watch (v): ʕitfarrag, yitfarrag ɛala.
keep an eye on: xad, yaaxud baal-u min.
watch out!, be careful! (m): xalli baal-ak (-ik, -ikum)!; ʕiwɛa!; ɦaasib!

water (n): mayya.
boiled water: mayya maɣliyya.
distilled water: mayya-mʕaṭṭara.
fresh water: mayya ɦilwa.
glass of water: kubbaayit mayya.
hot water: mayya suxna.
ice-cold water: mayya saʕɛa; mayya-mtalliga.
mineral water (*bottled*): mayya maɛdaniyya.
room-temperature water: mayya barda.
salt water: mayya malɦa.
tap water: mayyit ɦanafiyya; mayya min il-ɦanafiyya.
water pressure: ḍaɣṭ il-mayya.
water with ice: mayya bi-talg.
water (v): saʕa, yisʕi.
water buffalos: gamuus (-a, gawamiis).
water heater: saxxaan, -aat.
watermelon: baṭṭiix (-a, -aat).
waterpipe, hookah, narghile: ʃiiʃa, -aat / ʃiyaʃ.
waterproof (adj): miʃammaɛ; wootar biruuf.
waterski: ɛamal, yiɛmil ski ɛala-l-mayya; ʕitzaɦlaʕ, yitzaɦlaʕ ɛala-l-mayya.
waterwheel: saʕya, sawaaʕi.
wave (n): (*signal*): ʕiʃaara, -aaṭ.
waves (*water*): moog (-a, -aat / ʕamwaag).
wave (v) (*signal*): ʃaawir, yiʃaawir li.
wavy hair: mimawwig; ʕundulee.
wax (n): ʃamɛ.
the wax museum: matɦaf iʃ-ʃamɛ.
polish for shoes: warniiʃ.
wax (v): ʃammaɛ, yiʃammaɛ.
polish, shine: lammaɛ, lammaɛ; masaɦ, yimsaɦ.
way: ṭariiʕ, ṭuruʕ; sikka, sikak.
way, method: ṭariiʕa, ṭuruʕ.
by way of: ɛan ṭariiʕ.
by the way: ɛala fikra.
we: ʕiɦna.
week: ḍaɛiif, ḍuɛaaf / ḍuɛafa.
wealthy: ɣani, ɣunaay / ʕaɣniya.
weapon: silaaɦ, ʕasliɦa.
weapons of mass destruction: ʕasliɦit id-damaar iʃ-ʃaamil.
wear: libis, yilbis.
to start wearing summer clothes: ṣayyif, yiṣayyif.
to start wearing winter clothes: ʃatta, yiʃatti.
weasel: ɛirsa, ɛiras.
often called nims, numuus (*mongoose*).
weather: gaww; ṭaʕs.
wedding: faraɦ, ʕafraaɦ.
Wednesday: yoom l-arbaɛ.
week: ʕusbuuɛ, ʕasabiiɛ.
weekly (adj): ʕusbuuɛi, -yyiin.
weep: ɛayyaṭ, yiɛayyaṭ; baka, yibki.
weigh: wazan, yiwzin.

weight: wazn, ʕawzaan.
to gain weight: tixin, yitxan.
to lose weight: xass, yixiss.
welcome (*greeting*): ʕahlan; ʕahlan wa-sahlan.
(*response*: ʕahlan biik (-ki, -ku)).
welcome back (*from journey, after illness*): ɦamdilla ɛas-salaama (*response*: ʕallaa-ysallim-ak (-ik, -ku)).
you're welcome (*after thanks*): ɛafwan; ʕil-ɛafw; ɛala ʕeeh (*for what*); mafiiʃ ɦaaga (*for nothing*).
welcome (v): raɦɦab, yiraɦɦab bi.
receive a newcomer: ʕistaʕbil, yistaʕbil.
weld, solder: laɦam, yilɦim.
welding: liɦaam.
welder: laɦɦaam, -iin.
well (adj) *in good health*: kwayyis, -iin; fi-ṣiɦɦa kwayyisa.
to get well: xaff, yixiff.
well (adv): kwayyis.
well (n): biir, ʕabyaar.
well-behaved: ɛaaʕil, -iin; muʕaddab, -iin.
well-being: xeer.
well-known: maɛruuf, -iin.
west: ɣarb.
West Bank, the: ʕiḍ-ḍaffa l-ɣarbiyya.
western: ɣarbi, -yyiin.
wet: mabluul, -iin.
what (interrog): ʕee / ʕeeh.
what (rel pron): ʕilli.
whatever: ʕilli.
whatever you say: ʕilli-tʕuulu.
wheat: ʕamɦ.
cracked wheat: burɣul.
wheelchair: kursi mutaɦarrik, karaasi mutaɦarrika.
wheels: ɛagal (-a, -aat).
when (conj): lamma; waʕtᵉ ma.
when (interrog): ʕimta.
whenever (*any time that …*): waʕtᵉ ma.
(*every time that …*): kullᵉ ma.
where (interrog): feen.
where are you going, where to: ɛala feen?
where from: mineen; min feen.
wherever (conj): maṭraɦ ma.
which (interrog) ʕayy; ʕanhi / ʕanhu.
which one?: ʕanhi waaɦid / waɦda (f)?
that one, the one which, those which: ʕilli.
which (rel pron): ʕilli (*used only when antecedent is definite*).
whichever: ʕilli.
while (conj): lamma; wi + pronoun.
while I was there: lamma kuntᵉ-hnaak; w-ana-hnaak.
while there (*at the same time, while we're at it*): bil-marra.
while (n): *a short while ago*: min ʃiwayya.
after a while: baɛdᵉ ʃwayya.

whim, fancy: mazaag, ʕamziga.
whiskey: wiski.
whisper (n): waʃwaʃa.
whisper (v) (*to s.o.*): waʃwiʃ, yiwaʃwiʃ.
whisper together: ʕitwaʃwiʃ, yitwaʃwiʃ (maεa).
whistle (n): ṣuffaara, -aat.
whistle (v): ṣaffar, yiṣaffar.
white: ʕabyaḍ, (f) beeḍa, biiḍ.
white meat (*breast*): sidr / ṣadr.
whitewash (v): bayyaḍ, yibayyaḍ.
who (rel pron): ʕilli.
who, whom (interrog): miin.
who is this (*on phone*)?: miin maεaaya? miin ɦaḍrit-ak / -ik?
who shall I tell him is calling (*on phone*)?: ʕaʕul-lu miin?
who shall I tell her is calling (*on phone*)?: ʕaʕul-laha miin?
whoever: ʕilli.
whole (+ n): kull (+ def. n).
whose (interrog): bitaaε miin; li miin.
whose (rel pron): ʕilli (*used only when antecedent is definite*).
e.g. the man whose name is…: ʕir-raagil illi ʕismu…
why: lee.
this is why, this is the reason: εaʃaan kida.
why, how come: ʕiʃmiεna.
wide: waasiε, -iin.
wide, broad: εariiḍ, εuraaḍ.
wide-spread: muntaʃir, -iin.
wife: zooga, -aat; sitt, -aat.
wife of: (*informal*) miraat (+ n or pron); ʕis-sitt^{e}-btaaεit (+ n or pron) (*formal*): zoogit (+ n or pron).
my wife: ʕil-madaam bitaεt-i; ʕis-sitt^{e}-btaεt-i.
your wife (v. formal): ʕil-madaam, ʕis-sitt (no pron).
wig: baruuka, -aat.
willing (adj): raaḍi, -yiin.
to be willing (v) (*to do s.t.*): riḍi, yirḍa.
win: kisib, yiksab.
win a game, beat (*s.o.*) *in a game*: ɣalab, yiɣlib.
wind (n): hawa; riiɦ, riyaaɦ.
wind (v) (*a watch*): mala, yimla (saaεa).
window: ʃibbaak, ʃababiik.
shop window: vatriina, -aat / vatariin.
little window in a door: ʃurraaεa.
window shop (v): ʕitfarrag, yitfarrag εala-l-vitrinaat.
windshield: barabriiz.
windshield wiper: massaaɦa, -aat.
wine: nibiit.
white/red wine: nibiit ʕabyaḍ / ʕaɦmar.

wing (n): ginaaɦ. ʕigniɦa.
winter: ʕiʃ-ʃita.
winter style, worn or used in winter: ʃitwi, -yyiin.
wipe: masaɦ, yimsaɦ.
wiper: massaɦa, -aat.
wire: silk, siluuk / suluuk / ʕaslaak.
wireless: lasilki.
wisdom: ɦikma, ɦikam.
wise (*sensible, judicious*): ɛaaʕil, -iin; nɑɑʂiɦ, -iin.
wise man, philosopher: ɦakiim, ɦukama.
wish (v): ʕitmanna, yitmanna.
as you (m) *wish*: ɛala keef-ak; zayy^e ma-nta ɛaayiz / ɛaawiz; zayy^e ma yiɛgib-ak.
I wish, if only!: yareet; yarit-ni.
I wish you (m) *every good thing*: ʕatmannaa-lak kull^e xeer.
with (*by means of, combined or mixed with*): bi.
(*accompanied by, in someone's possession, etc.*): maɛa; wayya.
(*kept by someone at home, etc.*): ɛand.
withdraw (*money, troops*) (tr): saɦab, yisɦab.
(intr): ʕinsaɦab, yinsiɦib.
without: min ɣeer; biduun.
witness (n): ʃaahid, ʃuhuud.
eye witness: ʃaahid ɛayaan, ʃuhuud ɛayaan.
witty: nukati, -yya; sariiɛ in-nukta.
woman: sitt, -aat.
women's (*clothes, etc.*): ɦariimi (invar).
wonder: *I wonder, we are wondering*: yɑtɑrɑ (invar).
wonderful: haayil, -iin.
wood: xaʃab. *A piece of wood*: xaʃaba, -aat.
wool: ʂuuf, ʕɑʂwɑɑf.
word: kilma, -aat / kalimaat (cl).
work (n): ʃuɣl, ʕaʃɣaal.
to give work to, to make s.o. or s.t. work: ʃaɣɣal, yiʃaɣɣal.
work (v): ʕiʃtaɣal, yiʃtaɣal.
work permit: tɑʂriiɦ, tɑʂɑriiɦ ɛamal.
worker: ɛaamil, ɛummaal.
working, functioning: ʃaɣɣaal, -iin.
workshop: warʃa, wiraʃ.
world, the:
(*this, as comp. to the other*): ʕid-dinya / ʕid-dunya.
(*with ref. to people, countries, etc.*): ʕil-ɛaalam (f).
World Trade Center: markaz it-tigɑɑrɑ ʕil-ɛaalami.
worms (n): duud (-a, -aat).
worn out: daayib, -iin.
to be worn out: ʕithara, yithiri; daab, yiduub.
worry, be concerned (v) (intr): xaaf, yixaaf.
don't (m) *worry*: ma-txaf-ʃ; matiʕlaʕʃ.
worried (*about*): maʃɣuul, -iin; ʕalʕaan, -iin; xaayif, -iin (ɛala).

worry about (*s.o.*): ʕinʃaɣal, yinʃiɣil ɛala.
worse (comp): ʕawɦaʃ.
worth: *to be worth* (*e.g. a certain amount of money*): yiswa (imperfect only).
to be worth or worthy of: ʕistaɦaʕʕ, yistaɦaʕʕ; ʕistaahil, yistaahil.
it's not worth the trouble: mayistahilʃ it-taɛab; miʃ mistaɦaʕʕ it-taɛab.
it's not worth that price: mayistahilʃ it-taman da.
this is worth a pound: da yistaahil ginee.
it's worthless: maluuʃ ʕiima.
wound (n): garɦ, guruuɦ; taɛwiira, -aat.
wound (v): garaɦ, yigraɦ; ɛawwar, yiɛawwar.
wrap (v): laff, yiliff.
wreck, shatter (v): ɦaṭṭam, yiɦaṭṭam; kassar, yikassar; xarrab, yixarrab.
wrench (n) (*Br.*: *spanner*): muftaaɦ, mafatiiɦ.
butagas bottle wrench: muftaaɦ ʕanbuuba.
monkey wrench: muftaaɦ ingiliizi.
small wrench: muftaaɦ baladi.
vice grip: muftaaɦ kammaaʃa.
wring (v): ɛaṣar, yuɛṣur.
wringer, juicer: ɛaṣṣaara, -aat.
wrinkle: tagɛiida, tagaɛiid.
wrinkled: mitkarmiʃ / mikarmiʃ, -iin.
to get wrinkled: ʕitkarmiʃ, yitkarmiʃ.
wrist: rusɣ, ʕarsaaɣ / ʕarsuɣ; mafṣal ʕiid.
write: katab, yiktib.
writer: kaatib, kuttaab.
writing, inscription: kitaaba, -aat.
written: maktuub, iin.
wrong, incorrect: ɣalaṭ (invar).
wrong, mistaken (personal subj.): ɣalṭaan, -iin.
what's wrong?: ʕee-l-ɦikaaya; fii ʕee.
what's wrong, what's the matter with you (m)?: maal-ak?

X

x-ray (n): ʕaʃiɛɛa, -aat.

Y

yacht: yaxt, yuxuut / yuxuta.
yacht club: naadi-l-yaxt.
yard, courtyard: ɦooʃ, ɦiʃaan.
front/back yard (*of a house*): gineena.
yarn: ɣazl.
year: sana, siniin.
two years: sanateen.
this year: ʕis-sanaadi.
yeast: xamiira.
yellow: ʕaʂfar, (f) ʂafra, ʂufr.
yes: ʕaywa; ʕaa (*informal*).
yes? (*response to a call*): naɛam?;
ʕafandim? (*formal*).
yesterday: ʕimbaariɦ.
day before yesterday: ʕawwil -imbaariɦ.
yet (*still*): lissa.
not yet: lissa.
(*e.g. he hasn't come yet*: lissa ma-gaa-ʃ).
yoga: yuuga / yooga.
yoghurt: zabaadi; laban zabaadi.
(*as a side dish in a restaurant*): salaʈit zabaadi.
you: (*as object, see pronominal suffix chart*).
(*as subject*): ʕinta (m), ʕinti (f), ʕintu (pl).
(*formal*): ɦaɖritak (-ik); siyadtak (-ik).
young: ʂuɣayyar, -iin.
young person (m): ʃabb, ʃabaab / ʃubbaan.
(f): ʃabba, ʃabbaat.
your: *see pronominal suffix chart*.
yours: (m): (m) bitaaɛ-ak, (f) bitaɛt-ak, (pl) bituuɛ-ak.
(f): (m) bitaaɛ-ik, (f) bitaɛt-ik, (pl) bituuɛ-ik.
(pl): (m) bitaɛ-ku, (f) bitaɛit-ku, (pl) bituɛ-ku.
yourself: nafs-ak (-ik, -uku); rooɦ-ak (-ik, -ku) (*as reflexive object*).

Z

zebra: ɦumaar mixaʈʈat, ɦimiir mixaʈʈaʈa; ɦumaar waɦʃi (*wild donkey*).
zero: ʂifr, ʕaʂfaar; ziiru.
Zionism: ʕiʂ-ʂahyuniyya.
Zionist (adj): ʂahyuuni, -yyiin.
Zionist (n): ʂahyuuni, ʂahayna.
zipper: susta, susat.
zodiacal sign: burg, ʕabraag.
zone: manʈiʕa, manaaʈiʕ.
free trade zone: manʈiʕa ɦurra.
zoo: gineenit, ganaayin ɦayawanaat.
the zoo: ginint-il-ɦayawanaat.
zoology: ɛilm il-ɦayawaan.
zucchini, courgettes: koosa / kuusa (-aaya, -aat).

Verbs: Formation of Tenses

Subject pronoun	Past				Imperfect
	Regular	Verbs where huwwa form ends in i.	Verbs where huwwa form ends in a.	Verbs where huwwa form ends in double consonant.	After participles, modals, verbs, and some conjunctions, e.g. ɛaawiz yiktib. He wants to write
ʕana	kataba**t**	miʃ**iit**	ʕistann**eet**	ɦabb**eet**	ʕ**a**ktib
ʕinta	katab**t**	miʃ**iit**	ʕistann**eet**	ɦabb**eet**	**ti**ktib
ʕinti	katab**ti**	miʃ**iiti**	ʕistann**eeti**	ɦabb**eeti**	**ti**ktib**i**
huwwa	katab	miʃ**i**	ʕistann**a**	ɦabb	**yi**ktib
hiyya	katab**it**	miʃ**yit**	ʕistann**it**	ɦabb**it**	**ti**ktib
ʕiɦna	katab**na**	miʃ**iina**	ʕistann**eena**	ɦabb**eena**	**ni**ktib
ʕintu	katab**tu**	miʃ**iitu**	ʕistann**eetu**	ɦabb**eetu**	**ti**ktib**u**
humma	katab**u**	miʃ**yu**	ʕistann**u**	ɦabb**u**	**yi**ktib**u**

1. Preceded by **bi** to form the progressive/habitual:

biyiktib:
- He is writing (now)
- He writes (every day)
- He writes (e.g. an author)
- He has been writing (+ min: since)

2. Preceded by **ɦa** to form the future:

ɦ**a**yiktib:
- He will write
- He is going to write

Hollow verbs where the huwwa form is CaaC:
the vowel in the past comes from the vowel in the imperfect

e.g. to see: ʃaaf, yiʃuuf

ʃuft
ʃuft
ʃufti
ʃaaf
ʃaafit
ʃufna
ʃuftu
ʃaafu

3rd person stays "aa"

exceptions:

to sleep: naam, yinaam
I slept: nimt

to fear: xaaf, yixaaf
I feared: xuft

to stay overnight: baat, yibaat
I stayed overnight: bitt

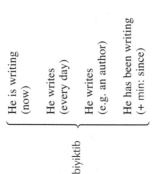

Verbs: Formation of Negatives

Affirmative		Negative	
Imperfect			
He must eat	laazim yaakul	He does not have to eat	**miʃ** laazim yaakul
		He must not eat	laazim **ma**-yakul-ʃ
Progressive Habitual			
He is eating	biyaakul	He isn't eating	**miʃ** biyaakul or **ma**-byakul-ʃ
Past			
He ate	kal	He didn't eat	**ma**-kal-ʃ
Future			
He will eat	ɦayaakul	He won't eat	**miʃ** ɦayaakul
Imperative			
Eat (you m.)	kul	Don't eat	**ma**-takul-ʃ or balaaʃ taakul ʕiwɛa taakul ʕiyyaak taakul
Miscellaneous			
I had	kaan ɛandi kaan maɛaaya	I didn't have	**ma**-kan-ʃ^{e} ɛand-i **ma**-kan-ʃ^{e} mɛaaya
there was	kaan fii	there wasn't	**ma**-kan-ʃ^{e} fii

Pronominal Suffixes

		after 1 consonant	after 2 consonants	after a vowel
me, my	after verb after prep. or noun	-ni -i	-ini -i	-ni -ya
you, your	(m, sing)	-ak	-ak	-k
you, your	(f. sing)	-ik (kiiʃ for neg.)	-ik (-ikiiʃ for neg.)	-ki
him, his, its		-u (optional –hu if followed by li)	-u (-uhu if followed by li)	-h (often muted) (-huuʃ for neg). (-hu + li)
her, its		-ha	-aha	-ha
us, our		-na	-ina	-na
you, your (pl)		-ku (m)	-uku (m)	-ku (m)
them, their		-hum	-uhum	-hum

Lengthen any final vowel before adding another suffix
e.g. ʃuftu … ma-ʃuftuu-ʃ   ɧa-giibu … ɧa-gibhuu-lak

Numbers: Form and Use

		Cardinals (one, two, etc.)				**Ordinals** (first, second, etc.)	
		Long Form		*Short Form*		*M*	*F*
٠	0	ṣifr	+ singular noun				
١	1	waaɦid/waɦda				ʕawwil	ʕuula
٢ / ٢	2	ʕitneen			+ plural noun	taani	ṭanya
٣ / ٣	3	talaata		talat		taalit	talta
٤	4	ʕarbaεa		ʕarbaε		raabiε	rabεa
٥	5	xamsa		xamas		xaamis	xamsa
٦	6	sitta		sitt		saadis/saatit	sadsa/satta
٧	7	sabεa		sabaε		saabiε	sabεa
٨	8	tamanya		taman		taamin	tamna
٩	9	tisεa		tisaε		taasiε	tasεa
١٠	10	εaʃara		εaʃar		εaaʃir	εaʃra

The long form of a numeral is used when counting and with expressions of measurement, money, and food orders, and is followed by a singular noun. The short form is used in all other cases and accompanies a plural noun.

Examples: for 1–10:
the 3rd woman: taalit sitt or ʕis-sitt it-talta
After 10, only one form possible:
e.g.: the 11th woman: ʕis-sitt il-ɦidaaʃar.

Invariable

11	ɦidaaʃar	30	talatiin	200	miteen
12	ʕitnaaʃar	40	ʕarbiɛiin	300	tultumiyya
13	talattaaʃar	41	waaɦid w-arbiɛiin	400	rubɛumiyya
14	ʕarbaɛtaaʃar	50	xamsiin	500	xumsumiyya
15	xamastaaʃar	52	ʕitneen wi xamsiin	600	suttumiyya
16	sittaaʃar	60	sittiin	700	subɛumiyya
17	sabaɛtaaʃar	70	sabɛiin	800	tumnumiyya
18	tamantaaʃar	80	tamaniin	900	tusɛumiyya
19	tisaɛtaaʃar	90	tisɛiin	1000	ʕalf
20	ɛiʃriin	100	miyya (mit + noun)		

(+ singular noun)

Usage of Numerals

1: follows a singular noun, e.g. kitaab waaɦid, one book; kubbaaya waɦda, one glass.

2: there is usually a special dual form of the noun, which stands on its own, formed by adding -een (m) or -teen (f) to the singular form, e.g. kitabeen, two books; kubbayteen, two glasses.

3–10: are followed by a plural noun, except when enumerating money, measurements, and food orders. e.g. talat kutub, three books; taman kubbayaat, eight glasses; but: xamsa-gnee, five pounds: tamanya mitr, eight meters.

11 and over: are always followed by a singular noun, e.g. talaata w-xamsiin kitaab, fifty-three books; ɛiʃriin kubbaaya, twenty glasses.

300–900 followed by a noun: miyya becomes miit + singular noun.

Comparatives

Regular adjectives

	C_1	v	C_2	v	C_3		ʕ	a	C_1	C_2	a	C_3	
big	k	i	b	ii	r	bigger	ʕ	a	k	b	a	r	(+min)

Adjectives ending in *i* or *w*

	C_1	v	C_2	v		ʕ	a	C_1	C_2	a
quiet	h	aa	d	i	quieter	ʕ	a	h	d	a (+min)
sweet	ɦ	i	l	w	sweeter	ʕ	a	ɦ	l	a (+min)

Last two radicals identical

	C_1	v	C_2	v	C_2		ʕ	a	C_1	a	C_2	C_2	
light	x	a	f	ii	f	lighter	ʕ	a	x	a	f	f	(+min)

exception:

new	g	i	d	ii	d	newer	ʕ	a	g	d	a	d	(+min)

Otherwise, if the adjective is over 3 consonants, keep same form and use ʕaktar:

he is busier huwwa maʃɣuul aktar.

Superlatives

comparative form + indefinite noun

Hany is the tallest boy in the school. haani ʕaʈwal walad fil-madrasa.